Neo-Idealistic Aesthetics

Neo-Idealistic Aesthetics: Croce-Gentile-Collingwood

by Merle E. Brown

Denison University

Wayne State University Press, Detroit, 1966

Acknowledgments

It was during a sabbatical leave, in 1961, that I compiled much of the material for this book and conceived the particular relation between Croce and Gentile that has given the book its basic form. To Denison University, which granted that leave, and to the Denison Research Foundation and the American Philosophical Society for their supporting grants, I wish to express my gratitude. While in Naples I received assistance of inestimable value from Professor Alfredo Parente and from the staffs of the Italian Institute for Historical Studies and the Biblioteca Nazionale of Naples. My gratitude also goes to Professor Raymond Hoekstra of Wayne State University for the penetrating questions which he raised concerning the text of my manuscript.

Acknowledgment is made to the *Journal of Aesthetics and Art Criticism* for permission to use my article, "Croce's Early Aesthetics," *JAAC*, XXII (Fall 1963), 29-41, as the second chapter in this book. I also acknowledge the permission granted me by the Oxford University Press to quote from R. G. Collingwood's *The Principles of Art*, and that of the Fondazione Giovanni Gentile Per Gli Studi Filosofici to include translations from Gentile's *La filosofia dell' arte*, and that of Signora Alda Croce to include the translation of a passage from the *Carteggio Croce-Vossler*.

M.E.B.

Contents

Introduction

*I*t is my conviction that neo-idealistic aesthetics develops according to a single, discernible pattern; and it is this pattern which provides the following study of neo-idealistic aesthetics with its essential form. In its early stages the movement can be thought of mainly as the career of a single man, Benedetto Croce. In the 1890's, Croce became dissatisfied with his philological studies and began his search for an aesthetics and a form of literary criticism that would take account of both the vitality and the truthfulness of great art. Although Croce's early years were full of intellectual missteps, it should become clear, in my first chapter, that his thought developed rather directly from a theory of art as passive cognition, as a copying of nature, into a theory of art as a form of both making and knowing, a form in which a feeling is made into an image in such a way that the nature of the feeling can be known as objectified, as imagined. Even as late as his *Breviario* of 1913, however, Croce was having serious difficulty with his idea of art as a dialectical synthesis of a feeling and an image in an intuition. He suggests quite clearly, in these early works, what it is that he is striving for; but he does not attain it. The study of Croce's writings on philosophical method, undertaken in the second chapter, reveals, I think, just why Croce could not grasp the concept of an aesthetic dialectic. As these writings show, he simply could not grasp the concept of any dialectic. He had the words, but not the idea; and again and again what looks to be a full, three-term dialectic collapses into a pseudo-dialectic composed of two terms only. Croce could not shake off a Herbartian theory of logic as the simple process of distinguishing one form of experience from another. The theory was satisfactory so long as Croce was merely a philologist, but when he engaged to be an aesthetician and a philosopher, it proved quite inadequate. Croce must have felt this, and early in his career he was yoking his Herbartian distincts to a Hegelian dialectic of sorts. The best that he could do on his own, however, was an unjustifiable compromise. A new insight was needed, and it eluded him.

A close friend of Croce's, Giovanni Gentile, provided this needed insight. As is shown in the third chapter, Gentile was at work on a theory of the concept as itself a dialectical act of thinking. For the first time neo-idealistic aesthetics had a solid basis, a dialectic simpler and more logical than either Hegel's or Croce's. Croce and Gentile clashed openly over the question of whether this dialectic was a genuine advance beyond Croce's position; and neither visibly modified his initial stance. But Gentile's new concept was evidently a generative force of immense power. A number of younger men took it up and uncrumpled its tight, original form in different areas of thought. In the fourth chapter, my intention is to show that, during the years of 1917 and 1918, Croce himself did this very thing, though tacitly, in the area of aesthetics. In several theoretical essays and in a monograph of practical criticism on Ariosto, Croce unfolds a new aesthetics, the theory of art as cosmic, a theory which is, I believe, fundamentally an extension of the actualism of Gentile. At this very time, the acknowledged disciples of Gentile were making only hesitant and tentative efforts to apply the actualistic logic to art, whereas Croce was carrying it with boldness and authority straight into the heart of artistic activity. Croce did not, it is true, admit to the actualistic connection; his essays were encumbered with ideas out of his past which he would not relinquish. After a short time, moreover, he abandoned the crucial aspects of his theory of art as cosmic, and fell back into notions even less demanding, less accurate, and less interesting than the positions he held before Gentile's discovery of the actualistic dialectic.

Within ten years after Croce's retreat, however, Gentile himself brought forth an aesthetics of comparable novelty and profundity. As I shall show in the fifth chapter, in his critical essays on Leopardi of 1927 and 1928 and in his *La filosofia dell' arte* of 1931, Gentile developed a theory of art as self-translation (*autotradursi*), the act of translating feeling into an objectified world, all performed under the scrutiny of the artist's self-awareness. This theory presents art as part of the elemental act of thinking, in which the mediate self or subject observes and controls its immediate self's expression of itself as its opposite, as an object. The immediate self of this artistic dialectic is pure feeling or pleasure, and this is the principle or essence of all art. Its opposite, the antithesis, is objective, is the expression of the oneness of pure feeling in the multiple world of art. The mediate subject, the synthesis of the dialectic, is the critical awareness by which the artist draws the feeling forth into its expression and evaluates the adequacy of the expression to the feeling. Gentile's theory of art as self-translation is much like Croce's theory of art as cosmic; but its dialectical and active elements are thought through more surely and more convincingly.

Even though it is evident that Gentile's aesthetics is the theoretical peak of the entire movement of neo-idealistic aesthetics, we must resist any temptation to accept it at the expense of Croce's thought. Croce's practical criticism and his theoretical efforts provide a substantial basis for Gentile's rather rarified ideas. To uproot the choice flower from its soil would most certainly cause it to wither. Unfortunately, just such a cleavage between Croce and Gentile occurred in the Italy of the 1930's, when they became bitterly inimical towards each other. The richness of Croce's thought required the clarity of Gentile's; and, similarly, the clarity of Gentile's thought could not shine forth meaningfully except in relation to Croce's thought. But politics ruled the day. If one saw life in Croce, he saw only death in Gentile; if he saw light in Gentile, then he saw only darkness in Croce. Such a situation was disastrous for neo-idealistic aesthetics, and the whole movement ground to a halt because of it. I am convinced that the halt was premature.

Apparently the British philosopher R. G. Collingwood also believed that the thought of Croce and that of Gentile were inseparable. Collingwood was unquestionably the most important non-Italian proponent of neo-idealistic aesthetics. Beginning with the aesthetics in his *Speculum Mentis* (1924), Collingwood sought to bring together the best of Croce and of Gentile. Unfortunately, neither of Collingwood's major combinations of the thought of these two in aesthetics proved successful. His first theory, art as contradiction, is woefully sterile; and our sixth chapter reveals a Collingwood reaching futilely out of a most arid tradition of British aesthetics for nourishment from the great Italians. Furthermore, even though Collingwood's second theory, art as communal, is vital and most suggestive, it is found, in our seventh chapter, to be riddled with ambiguity and inconsistency. By the time of his writing of *The Principles of Art,* published in 1938, Collingwood was a sick man and was himself suffocating in an atmosphere of political bitterness. He did not, we are forced to conclude, make neo-idealistic aesthetics move beyond the point of its halt in Italy. He convinces us that these ideas should have been set in motion again, and that to set them in motion is still possible.

But he does not fulfill the need or begin to draw the possibility into actuality.

As anyone acquainted with this field of thought knows, the idea that neo-idealistic aesthetics develops along the course just outlined is debatable. It is not an obvious fact, and this book is by no means merely expository. Because I believe my idea of its development to be true, I have presented it as precisely and as convincingly as I could. Whether I have succeeded is, of course, open to question. Let me at least affirm that I have tried to avoid tendentiousness. The aesthetics of Gentile is, to be sure, given a much more favorable position in the pattern of neo-idealistic aesthetics, as I conceive of it, than any purely Crocean scholar would grant it. And Crocean aesthetics is given more sympathetic attention than most actualists or post-actualists would concede it. Whatever reactions these efforts at balance may evoke, I would insist that I have not chosen between Croce and Gentile. Together they are profound and penetrating. Why, then, need they be separated or set against each other? By himself Croce is truly confused. How can that be honestly denied? By himself Gentile is aridly logical. And that cannot be easily denied either. Joined, however, they provide so much more than any other aesthetics with which I am acquainted, that it seems irresponsible to continue to consider them separately. As if their tragic enmity had not ceased more than twenty years ago!

If, furthermore, it seems that Collingwood is treated too harshly in this study, I can only say that the pattern of thought culminating in Croce's theory of art as cosmic and in Gentile's theory of art as self-translation has forced such an interpretation of Collingwood's thought upon me. No one could deny that Collingwood's *The Principles of Art* is a dazzling book, or that it is a fighting book, written brilliantly and with emotional intensity. In my opinion, next to nothing written in the English language on aesthetics comes close to it. But there is a value to solid and profound thinking, just as there is an intense pleasure to be had from a brilliant style. Although Collingwood has the style, he gives us all too little of the other. And this is a grave disappointment, especially since no one has followed after him to do what he did not do. He has, nonetheless, provided all who love both art and straight thinking with a ringing challenge.

Finally, it may be appropriate to explain why the idea of development underlying this study is not presented more openly and emphatically than it is. If my main concern were to present an aesthetics of my own, if I were trying to articulate my own philosophy of art, anything so subdued would surely be unjustifiable. But this study is primarily historical. Even though each aesthetician is related to a single, underlying pattern of development, even though I am interpreting his thought in the light of a single idea, it is my obligation to allow him to speak forth his own ideas. If I would hope to clarify his thought with an idea, his thought must be presented with some particularity. A balance, that is, must be struck between his thought as it originated and his thought as it appears in the light of the idea of development of which it is, from my point of view, a part. Because I believe the idea underlying this study to be a discovery elicited from the history of neo-idealistic aesthetics rather than a hypothesis brought to that history from without it, accuracy requires that I do not aggressively stamp each part of the subject-matter with the fully explicated idea ruling my own thought. For the idea became clear and articulated only very gradually, as the movement of thought developed.

Serious criticism of a work of art must elicit the essential quality of the work from the work itself and not simply use the work to illustrate some theory or other. Just so, a historical study of a movement in aesthetics must seek to reveal the underlying pattern of the movement as it truly existed; it must avoid the temptation to abstract the pattern, articulate it fully in itself, and then turn it on the movement from a distance, like a spotlight. Any study, of course, is clearer and simpler if its subject-matter is wrenched to fit an idea separate and distinct from that subject-matter, and if the complications of the subject-matter are obliterated by the bright and blinding light of the idea. A simplicity won at the expense of such complexity is not, in my opinion, worthy of serious consideration. The delicate balance one seeks is this: to see the present activity of thought, the subject-matter under inspection, as pointing toward a future achievement, but not to see it as mere error in the light of that achievement. One strives to balance simplicity with richness, and clarity with the experiential roughness of the material which he would clarify. He would unify, but without distorting or diminishing the rich multiplicity of the object of his study. Such a balance of the one and the many is, it must be admitted, an ideal. In any case, however faulty my achievement may be, that ideal of balance is the aim of this book.

Chapter One

Croce's Early Aesthetics: 1894-1913

*T*he early period of Benedetto Croce's thoughts on literature, art, and criticism is not important solely as illustrating a development from one theory to another; it is also an example of the struggle to move from one kind of thinking to another. In his earliest writings, as I shall show, Croce assumes that art is the simple, passive knowledge of individual impressions; by the time of the *Breviario* of 1913 he conceives of it as a complex synthesis of feelings and images in an intuition.[1] This is not, let it be recognized at once, a change from a theory of art as knowledge to a theory of art as action; it is rather a change from a simple idea of art as knowledge to a very complex concept of art as both knowledge and action. The change is not wholly successful on Croce's part. For, even at the apex of this early period of his thought, Croce conceives of knowledge as a kind of passive and immediate reception, the strength of which depends upon its not distorting that which it receives; and he conceives of action as a kind of making which gives to that which is received a form it did not have before it was acted upon. In other words, whether he conceives of art as knowledge and action in the form of an immediate identity of intuition and expression or in the form of an intuition that synthesizes image and feeling, Croce does not overcome the contradiction implicit in the assertion that art both distorts and does not distort that which it works upon. Looked at in itself, then, this change proves disappointing. Our very point, however, is that it must not be looked at in itself. Croce's theory of art as both passive and active points beyond itself to a maturer theory of art as knowledge and action, to a theory that reconciles the constructive and cognitive aspects of art by means of the concept of artistic self-consciousness. Furthermore, in making the change from art as knowledge to art as knowledge and action, Croce was also struggling to go beyond his originally philological approach to literature and art in order to come to grips with them philosophically.

Although this struggle may not prove interesting to either the pure philologist or the pure philosopher, it should catch the mind and imagination of the student of ideas in the making, the student not so much of thoughts and systems as of the act of thinking itself. It is true that the struggle complicates Croce's early aesthetics immensely; but to ignore it is to take the life and meaning out of his theories themselves and to see even the well-known *Estetica* in a needlessly dwarfed and lifeless form. The choice is between belittling the system—and how one who looks at it as just that is enticed toward a contemptuous dismissal—and comprehending Croce's thinking itself.

In order to grasp the truth of this particular period of Croce's thought we must concentrate as much on its inconsistencies and contradictions as on its steady evolvement. At first Croce thought like a typical literary critic and philologist: he isolated the object of his study, oblivious of its relations to other objects; and he was slow to see connections between one of his own thoughts and another. His was anything but an integrating mind. To some extent, in fact, it remains a characteristic of his writing to isolate one passage from another, leading the reader to think only of that particular passage, possibly in relation to some experience of his own, and not to connect what is being said with what has been or is about to be said. This isolative or separative technique gives Croce's style its initial clarity and simplicity; and it has led some, especally those more interested in philology than philosophy, to declare Croce's occasional and periodical writing superior to his more systematic works. But to call Croce's thought simplifying and isolative is more accurate of his early than of his mature work. He retained the transparent style, but developed coherence and integration of thought. He developed just as any philologist would have to develop, if he wished to become a philosopher without ceasing to be a philologist.

Very early in his career Croce recognized in a general way the severe demands he must make of himself. Although his friends considered theoretical questions mere idle chatter, he knew, and admits as much in his *La critica letteraria* (1894), that the most serious weakness in Italian studies had to do with just such questions. At the very time he was declaring his plan to study German aesthetics, he was open enough to confess the painful difficulties facing him:

The condition of studies in aesthetics in Italy is not propitious. Our students are almost all university students, and they are not likely to go very far in the science of aesthetics. It is because of this that the science has fallen into such neglect. Thus, anyone who would wish to devote himself to these studies is constrained to live in a kind of intellectual solitude; and this solitude not only deprives the spirit of any encouragement and of any legitimate satisfaction but, what is worse, complicates the difficulties by making fruitful discussion impossible. The work of one alone is timid and uncertain; and it has occurred many times to me, for example, in my first steps toward these studies, to look around me distrustfully, seeking my companions.[2]

Such candor and self-awareness should help us to view Croce's early faltering generously, especially if we recognize this period of his thought from *La critica letteraria* of 1894 through

the *Breviario* of 1913 as setting the stage for the more enduring work in aesthetics not only of Croce himself, but also of
such significant aestheticians as Giovanni Gentile and R. G.
Collingwood.[3]

Now the basic direction of Croce's thought during this period—from a narrow concentration on art as a form of passive
knowing to an ampler consideration of it as both knowledge
and action—can be discerned, rough and unsteady as it is, in
Croce's analyses of the ideas of the material of art and of its
content, of artistic activity, and of the nature of literary
criticism.

The Material of Art

Croce's conception of artistic material turns during this
period from a conception of it as something passive and non-
human to one that includes any and all practical human activity. At first Croce has no theoretical interest in the material as
such. He asserts the worth of source studies, but neglects the
basic relationships among the sources, the material of a poem,
and the poem itself. In *La critica letteraria* we are enigmat-
ically put off by the assumption that the material of art is
"nature." "Nature," it is true, is more limited than "reality," the
word Croce uses in reference to the material of art in his "*La
storia ridotta sotto il concetto generale dell'arte*" (1893), an
essay in which he has not yet begun to think independently on
the nature of art. The change in language, however, does not
indicate an increased precision of thought. In his *Tesi fondamentali di un Estetica come scienza dell' espressione e linguistica generale* (1900), his more general concerns force Croce to
be more precise, although he is still quite obscure. The artist,
we are told, works with impressions; and, after some careful
hunting about, we can gather that these impressions are psychic
facts, natural and organic and simply given as "a perpetual and

indistinct flow." Because these impressions have no form at all
until the artist looks at them, his very glance would be a kind
of knowing, the first and only order the impressions would
have. In the first edition of the *Estetica* (1902), of which the
Tesi is an earlier version, he speaks of the material of art in
much the same way. He now calls it "sensations" rather than
"impressions," and is no longer groping after it as some "indistinct flow." He simply says it cannot be grasped and that we
must postulate a concept of it as a "limit." As posited in its
abstractness it is, Croce says, mechanical and passive, an organic fact which the human spirit endures rather than produces. He will also speak of the material as "feelings and impressions" [4] and say they exist in some "obscure region of the
psyche"; but these statements seem mainly to provide a contrast
for feelings and impressions which have been changed from
the material into the content of art and are thus artistically illuminated. Croce does, it is true, defend his obscurity concerning this "psychological fact" which he finds to be the material
of art; and he repudiates the distinctness attributed to it by
certain psychologists:

If the distinction of a triple psychological fact, *representative,*
emotional, and *appetitive,* has sent out such strong roots in psychology, it is because distinctions properly belonging to human
activity have been projected into the unique and indistinct and
indistinguishable psychic fact. The psychic fact is not *representative*
or *volitional,* theoretic or practical; but it is *feeling,* in which both
these facts remain enwrapped and unexplicated, and without the
intervention of any inexplicable human activity. It is useless to de-
claim against the *faculties of the soul* when one sinks back into this
mythology, imagining distinct psychic categories. Only human activity has distinctions, which are not isolated *faculties,* but moments
or grades, genetically connected, of a unique activity.[5]

The material of art—that is, impressions, feelings, sensations,
the psychic fact, or whatnot—is not elaborated upon by Croce
because elaboration, or distinction, is introduced only by hu-

man activity; and the material of art is, by definition, that which has not yet been acted upon. Simple as the theory is, it is defensible, and although Croce drops it very soon, something very much like it is given a prominent place in Collingwood's *The Principles of Art*.

By the time of the publication of the third edition of the *Estetica* (1908), Croce had activated considerably his doctrine of feeling, identifying feeling not with the obscure psychic fact, but with what he calls economic or utilitarian activity, with the satisfying of any and all individual desires. This change, which is worked out in detail in the *Filosofia della pratica* (1909), is incorporated into the third edition of the *Estetica* in the tenth chapter, the only part of the text radically revised for any edition. Croce explains that "feeling" is a word of many meanings, one of which is his old meaning, identical with "impression," the material of art. Another meaning, however, is "economic activity," which Croce describes as a bipolar relationship between pleasure and pain. "Feeling" in this new sense is not thought of as natural and as opposed to value and the spirit; it is a value itself and a form of activity. Although Croce has not changed his theory of the material of art,—for he has not identified the new meaning of "feeling" with artistic material—he has gone as far as he could in that direction without rewriting the entire text. Without saying it he is certainly suggesting the reasonableness of thinking of the material of art as human and active.

This new theory was first proclaimed explicitly in "L'intuizione e il carattere lirico dell' arte," in 1908. Although it is presented in this later essay as having been implicit in the *Estetica*, it would be difficult to imagine anything more clearly absent from the first edition, though admittedly the revision of the third makes the claim plausible. The material of art, according to the new theory, is no longer the concept of a limit, of some obscure, indistinguishable psychic fact, of feeling as the merely passive and natural. It is rather feeling as appetition, tendency, will; it is the practical form of the spirit in its infinite gradations and in its dialectic of pleasure and pain.[6] The material of art is the psychic fact, but distinguished and activated, the very thesis which Croce had declared in his first edition of the *Estetica* to be erroneous, although he omitted that declaration in the third edition. Or to use words even more radically different, the material of the poet is not some unknown, shapeless force which the human spirit endures rather than produces; it is the poet's personality itself, "a soul happy or sad, enthusiastic or distrustful, sentimental or sarcastic, kind or cruel, but a soul." [7] And although Croce says here that the personality in its strictly moral sense is excluded as material for art, in an essay written about the theater in 1905 he includes even moral theses as proper material for genuine works of art:

All works of art which present human actions, battles over ideals, endeavors to attain certain ends, contain, also, theses; and they can be found in the *Iliad* as in the tragedies of Aeschylus, in the poem of Dante as in the dramas of the great Englishman. Neither could they not be there, through the effect of that "personality," which is at the bottom of every true work of art and in which vibrate also moral and utilitarian strings. . . .[8]

Although the idea of the moral personality as the material of all art is not fully incorporated into Croce's aesthetics until much later, the idea of the personality as that material remains from now on. In the *Breviario* (1913) the material is spoken of in much the same terms as it is throughout the volume including the essay on the lyric nature of art, the *Problemi* of 1910: it is emotions, aspirations, a state of mind, feeling as the practical aspect of the spirit which loves and hates, desires and rejects; it is, at its very lowest, tumultuous passion.[9] It will, then, be no surprise if so much more violent a material than those impressions with which Croce began will require a more active form of knowing, if it is to be known at all.

The Content of the Work of Art

The basic change during this early period in Croce's conception of the content of the work of art is that content becomes less and less like the material through being more and more worked upon. To be sure, it is always spoken of as being like the material: it is at first thought of as "nature," then as impressions, next as the psychic fact or feeling, and finally as practical activity. But the artist has always done something to the content and it is this having been worked upon which distinguishes it from the material. What strikes one in Croce's earliest thoughts is how little the artist is said to do. In *La critica letteraria* the content is in one place called "the essential traits of nature" and in another "the interesting." [10] The emphasis throughout is on the great distance of the content from the form, from the activity and expressiveness of the artist, and—of necessity—on its proximity to the material. Analogous to the claim that poetry reproduces the essential traits of nature is the description of literary criticism as the reproduction of the essential traits of the poetry at hand. Everywhere, the underlying assumption is that the closer the content, the worked-upon material, approximates the material itself, the better it would be. We are told openly that criticism is poetry: the patent implication is that poetry, at least great poetry, is nature. When Croce speaks of the content not as nature but as "the interesting," his point is that it has value, but not aesthetic value. It is being considered to be no other than a part of the material, that part of the material which is interesting. It is not *made* interesting, for then its value would be aesthetic; it is interesting as material, and that is why it is chosen to be content. In the *Tesi*, written after Croce had learned from his friend Giovanni Gentile that he should be identifying form and content,[11] Croce does begin to distinguish content from material, though only very slightly. He says, for instance: "The impressions reappear in the expression as water which is put into a filter and reappears, the same and also different, on the other side of the filter." [12] Possibly a chemist would consider the difference more significant than I do, but all I can make out is that the content is that part of the material which is allowed to pass into the poem from outside the poem. In fact, one can find passages in the *Tesi* in which material and content are used as synonymous words. And in one passage it is suggested that the only difference is that the impressions which make up the content of a work are "accompanied" by human activity, whereas those which are material are not.[13] Finally, whatever Croce says he learned from Gentile, he is still distinguishing form and content drastically, claiming that the form of all poems is the same and that the content alone differentiates one from another.[14]

In the 1902 edition of the *Estetica* Croce makes his first serious advance in distinguishing content from material. He finds a quality in the material which one might wish not so much to know about as to be relieved from: that is its quality of being something men must endure rather than produce. The impressions contained in a poem are said to be purified— an echo of the filter—but also their "passivity" is said to be charred away, suggesting something more strenuous than the filtering process.[15] In the third edition, furthermore, the impressions are said to be unified within the work, that is, put into new relationships. And in the 1908 lecture on "L'intuizione pura e il carattere lirico dell' arte," the states of mind which are the new material of art become images when contained within the poem; and as content they are free of time and space, belonging then to the super-world of art, not to the ordinary world. Finally, in the *Breviario* Croce goes so far as to say that, from the point of view of the artistic spirit, the feelings contained within a poem have no existence outside the poem; in the poem they are not, he says, particular feelings at all, but the whole universe observed in a certain way.[16] Such statements are mysterious, to say the least, and one may well ask where the notion of art as a kind of knowledge has gone. For how can a feeling be said to be known if as known it is so very different from what it was before it was known? In answer to this question Croce asserts that from a point of view other than that of the artistic spirit the feelings contained within a poem may be seen outside the poem in a "denatured" state as material. In the poem itself they are freed from time and space and are no longer particular, but still they bear some resemblance to their grubbier nature in the ordinary world. The distance between content and material, however, stretches the whole notion of art as knowledge a good bit; and it may be wondered if art as knowledge is giving way before a contrary notion of art as action or expression. On this point he is far from clear.

Artistic Activity

Croce can, however, be seen struggling with the problem of how art can be both knowledge and action in his analysis of artistic activity itself. He passes during this early period from a notion of art as imitation to the principle of art as an a priori synthesis. If he were passing from a theory of art as knowledge to one of art as action, he would not be in trouble. But he is rather developing from a theory of art as knowledge to a theory of art as both action and knowledge. His agony lies there, but so does his worth; for then he is at least struggling with the full aesthetic experience, contradictory though his views may be. How innocent and happy he seems, in *La critica letteraria*, speaking of art as reproducing nature, and describing the process as "exposition" or "description" or "re-production" or "representation." [17]

As early as the *Tesi*, however, Croce speaks of art as both a knowing and a making, even though he apparently sees no need to explain how the two go together and even though he would relinquish anything in the notion of making which would disturb the knowing. For example, although he discusses the artist's struggle to overcome the passivity of his material and speaks of this as a battle, one is not to take his language seriously. For it has to do not with genuine art, but with artistic failure; and it is, incidentally, very impersonal and only metaphorical: "For there to be *dis-value* activity and passivity must enter into battle without one conquering the other. There must be some expression, but it is *inadequate* to the impression which it undertakes to dominate." [18] On the very next page, moreover, the successful artist is described as the one who "has seen clearly," and nothing about struggle or battle is present even by implication. Although artistic failure appears to be active, artistic success is passively cognitive. Nonetheless, it is true that elsewhere artistic activity is said to be productive of value, even though it is not the voluntary production of things, but only the vision or consciousness of them.[19] The problem appears to exist without being considered.

The same kind of vacillation goes on in the *Estetica* between the artistic process as passive contemplation and that process as vigorously active, although here Croce is more clearly aware of the demands being made upon him. The basic principle of the *Estetica* is the immediate, non-dialectical identification of intuition and expression, of direct, contemplative awareness and a making or a forming; and this principle would seem to be an answer to our basic question of how art can be both cognitive and active. The inadequacy of the answer, the fact that it is really no answer at all, is boldly stated by R. G. Collingwood in his early anti-Crocean stage:

The paradox of art is that it is both intuitive (pure imagination) and expressive (revelatory of truth): two characteristics which contradict one another. Croce resolves the contradiction in his own favourite way, by what I may call *pricking* it, so that the opposition vanishes and the terms collapse into an undifferentiated or immediate identity. But because the opposition thus 'collapses into immediacy,' the outcome is merely immediate, that is, it is just intuition over again. Intuition and expression have not been reconciled. Expression has merely been reduced to intuition; in other words, expression in the true sense has been ignored.[20]

Complications which cannot be considered here are implicit in Collingwood's actualistic definition of intuition as pure imagination and expression as revelatory of truth; and it could be shown that these definitions do not accurately point to Croce's use of the terms. Otherwise, Collingwood's criticism is devastatingly precise. Croce will speak of the concrete form of art, of the essence of artistic activity, as the intuition triumphing over the material, as though genuine expressiveness and making were involved. But he does so weakly, with past participles and in a subordinate phrase: "The *material*, invested and triumphed over by the *form*, gives place to the concrete form. It is the material, it is the content which differentiates one of our intuitions from another. . . ."[21] The spirit is said to intuit sensations only by a kind of making; but this is a making only in the sense that it is not utterly passive and lifeless like artistic material. And once Croce discards his notion of the passivity of artistic material, it would seem that whatever expressiveness his intuition originally had, depending as it did on the difference of the intuited content from the passive material, would disappear. But artistic activity was never significantly expressive.

Here, for example, is another description of the artistic process in the *Estetica:* "Feelings or impressions pass then, through the word, from the obscure region of the psyche to the clarity of the contemplative spirit."[22] There is no formative activity involved here; instead pellets of material are being moved from darkness into the light. Expression has evidently been reduced to intuition. It is true that elsewhere in the *Estetica* the artist is said to liberate himself from the impressions by expressing them, by burning away their passivity and dominating their tumult by means of the form.[23] Further on, however, Croce insists that the poet does not change or create; he simply appropriates things already made[24]—"at least in a certain sense," Croce adds in later editions, as Gentile so cruelly pointed out many years ago. And even though Croce may assert in the eighth edition that the aesthetic act, through the law of unity of the spirit, is also a practical act and, as such, a dialectic of pleasure and pain, this assertion can hardly cancel the fact that he has said art involves no selection because it is independent of the will—which is of course, central to practical activity—and that, for the same reason, the internal poem is distinct from the external poem.[25] With a little negligence, the Croce of this early period can be made to mean almost anything one desires. If his general tendency is observed, however, this meaning is not ambiguous; or if it is ambiguous, the specific ambiguity may be precisely delimited.

The whole range of essays of the *Problemi*, written between 1899 and 1909, and including the important lecture of 1908 on the lyric character of art, offers little clarification on this particular question of the active and the cognitive aspects of the artistic act. We are told that art gathers in the real without alteration or falsification; and that sounds even less active and formative than the intuition-expression of the *Estetica*.[26] Elsewhere, however, the artist is described as translating practical values into theoretic, and states of mind into images; he actually creates, in contrast to the man who uses his fancy playfully, simply moving about the images already created by the imaginative or true artist.[27] Surely this activity is new. How it can be reconciled, however, with the artistic gathering in of the real without alteration or falsification is unexplained.

The *Breviario* only apparently turns these obscure statements into a reasoned explanation of how art can be both a knowing and a doing. Here Croce speaks of artistic activity as an a priori synthesis of an image and a feeling in an intuition. No pretense is made any longer of their being an active, dialectical relationship between intuition and expression; but the dialectic is said to exist within the intuition itself. We are told that our central concern is with the relation between image and feeling. These statements have been given prominence by Professor Gian N. G. Orsini in his recent book on Croce and are there described as providing the very basis of literary criticism itself. According to Orsini, criticism is broken into three parts, one the study of the form or image, another the study of the content, the feeling,—or the emotion as Professor Orsini translates it—and the last the study of their adjustment to each other.[28] Once again, however, Croce— though not Orsini—collapses his dialectic into an immediate unity. He claims that it is a matter of merely verbal opportunity whether one speaks of the form or the content, for it is to be understood that the content is always formed, the form always filled, the feeling configured and the image felt.[29] In effect, this means that there is an identity without a difference, that the image can only arbitrarily be distinguished from the feeling, and that in the synthesis there are not two qualities or elements allowing for a discernible relationship between themselves. To speak of the image, or the feeling, or to speak of the mirroring of the feeling in the image are different ways of saying the same thing. There is no action in any sense of the word "action" that implies mediation; there is no dialectic. Whether one speaks of image, feeling, or mirror, he speaks of something single, static, and pure. Indeed, Croce's enigmatic statement that the feeling in poetry is not a particular feeling or content, but the whole universe observed *sub specie intuitionis*[30] can no longer disturb us on the grounds that it makes feeling, as only one element of the artistic dialectic, the whole universe, a rather indefinite part of a poem. For there is only one element and there is no dialectic. Of course, Croce intends nothing so simple for very long; he is to pass beyond this specious answer soon enough. One may speculate that, at this point, he is following Gentile's advice that form and content must be identified, without understanding that the identity must involve a difference.

Art as Pure and Art as Impure

The inadequacy of Croce's efforts to bring the active and the contemplative aspects of art together stems, I believe, from the fact that he is remaining loyal to philological habits of mind at the very time he aspires toward philosophy. An inability to integrate his major concepts, it must be granted, is plaguing him throughout this early period. More precisely, the problem is that while he strives philosophically to integrate concepts, his inclination as a philologist is to keep them separate. He insists that art is pure, free of all practical and intellectual elements; at the same time he is endlessly connecting art in one way or another with practical and intellectual activity.

Croce's effort to keep art free of all practical activity led him from the very start along strange paths of thought. In the *Tesi* he claims that theory, which includes both artistic and intellectual activity, must precede, and therefore be free of, practical activity on the grounds that to will is to will something. The object must be known imaginatively and intellectually before it can be desired practically. Speaking of art alone he goes so far as to say:

When we have conquered the "internal word," conceived a figure or statue purely and vitally, found a musical motif, the expression is born and is completed. Nothing else is needed. That we next open or will to open our mouth to speak or our throat to sing . . . this is a fact added on, which obeys wholly different laws from the first. . . .[31]

In this early work Croce is categorically separating artistic activity as internal from all physical movement by the artist.[32] The production of physical beauty is a practical act, done willfully. We cannot will or refuse to will our aesthetic vision, but we can will or refuse to will to exteriorize and communicate the exteriorized product to others. To be sure, this sharp separation of art from practice is not left without a basis. Croce argues, for instance, that nothing physical is in itself beautiful:

Michelangelo said to his student Marco del Pino da Siena "that he ought always to make a pyramidal, serpentine figure, multiplied by one, two or three": advice which did not keep Marco da Siena from being a very mediocre painter, as one can see from the many works of his which remain here in Naples. And from sayings of Michelangelo others have drawn a pretext for proclaiming the *undulating* line as the true *line of beauty*. On these laws of beauty, on the *golden section* and on the *serpentine line*, have been composed very bizarre volumes which should be considered as the *Astrology* of Aesthetics! [33]

That such lines are not in themselves beautiful, in Croce's sense of the word, no one would deny. Their lack of beauty, however, is no reason for excluding them from the aesthetic vision; or, if it is, then all psychic facts, all impressions, the interesting content itself, would be equally excluded, on the grounds that they are not in themselves beautiful.

Croce's reasons in the *Estetica* for asserting the purity of art from any practical taint are no more solid than those of the *Tesi*. We are told that there is no technique (which is practical) internal to art, because theory illuminates practice and is not illuminated by it.[34] Why should this be? Just because theory precedes practice? But why say that? Because of the realistic presupposition that there must be some object to be desired before one could possibly desire anything? Not, one may say of a groping idealistic philosopher, very convincing. Croce adds another reason, saying that art is independent of utility and morality, for otherwise one could not speak of an intrinsic value of art.[35] But then one may ask, do utility and morality, which according to Croce are not independent of art, have no intrinsic value? Or possibly it is time to say: who cares about "art" anyway? Is not the intrinsic value of a specific poem or painting what truly concerns us? Be that as it may, Croce has no other significant reasons for his claim that art is free of all practical activity. Later he will add, among other things, that the artist's intentions are separate from his work on the grounds that such intentions are practical; that plagiarism is not of concern in art because it is a matter of morality, and art is free of any moral concerns; and that the characters in a play are not like characters in ordinary life, which is a practical affair, but are like "musical notes." [36] But even though his notion of the impracticality of art is amplified, it is as open to question as ever.

His efforts to keep art free from thought and the intellect seem to be more reasonable, based as they are on the distinction between art as knowledge of the individual, and thought or intellectual activity as knowledge of the universal.[37] The argument in the *Estetica* runs like this: any philosophical concept which finds its way into a work of art is dominated by the individualizing form, thus losing its philosophical nature and becoming purely artistic; whereas every work of philosophy is necessarily also a work of art, its expressive element being only extrinsically related to the thought, as is suggested by the fact that the same thought may be expressed in different ways. The argument is, to be sure, questionable. After all, does a concept remain the same even though expressed in different ways? And if so, how does one establish the sameness except by a third expression which may assert, by way of its expressive elements, a sameness that does not exist? For that matter, does not a poem remain the same even if one thought in it is replaced by another? But here one is not merely requesting good reasons, but is questioning what is the very basis of all Croce's thought, at least in this early period—his distinction between the multiplicity of intuitions and the oneness of the concept. Besides, Croce finds in this poverty of art, in its purity and freedom from all concepts and abstractions, the very strength which allows it to gather in reality without alteration or falsification.[38] In addition, if Croce finds serious thought in a work of art like Schiller's *Mary Stuart,* he willingly calls it good history, though poor poetry.[39] And, finally, the notion of the poet as primitive, as spontaneous and natural and without critical acuteness; the notion that the artist could not be aware of his activity as activity, in its essence and universality, because if he were he would be a philosopher of art; and the belief that the very presence of thinking kills art: these were the commonplaces of romantic criticism and it would have been amazing if Croce had not accepted them, at least in his first efforts at philosophy.[40]

Going against his segregation of art in its purity, however, Croce does begin, with some hesitation, to integrate it with the other forms of activity which he recognizes as real. He does not succeed in reconciling his efforts to segregate and to integrate. At most one can say that he moves from an emphasis upon art as pure toward efforts to integrate it with other activity, a movement parallel to his development from the notion of art as cognitive to that of art as cognitive and active. Now in the thirteenth chapter of the *Estetica* Croce says that art is accompanied with "organic facts" (in the first edition), and with a "utilitarian or hedonistic side and pleasure and pain, which are like the practical resonance of aesthetic value and disvalue, of the beautiful and the ugly" (in the eighth edition). In the *Tesi,* however, Croce had claimed that the very characteristic of beauty is its indivisibility, its lack of parts, whereas the ugly always involves multiplicity. An ugly work may have beautiful parts, but whatever is beautiful cannot be divided into parts.[41] From this point of view, all art, as it is described in the *Estetica,* would be ugly, because it would be "accompanied" by something practical. That is, the art itself would be beautiful, but it would be only a part of a work which would by necessity be called ugly. Such a notion sounds nonsensical, even if it is bearable.

With the purity of art caught up in its individuality, and its individuality essentially its indivisibility, the trouble Croce gets into as early as the *Estetica* becomes steadily worse throughout this period of his thought. It is, for example, difficult to understand how one can talk about the practical judgments and moral tendencies which are "resolved" as "spontaneous lyric motifs" in, and subordinated to, the artistic form of so many poetic works, without talking about a whole made up of parts.[42] If the practical elements of a poem are discernible, in what sense can they be said to be not just unified in the poem, but transformed into something other than parts? With the *Breviario* of 1913, moreover, it is no longer possible to speak of art as pure, as excluding practical and intellectual activity. At the very most one can say that it includes, integrates, and dominates them, as they in their turn include, integrate, and dominate each other and, in their own ways, artistic activity. For in this work Croce says that no one form of activity is real, that only the synthesis of syntheses, the *actus purus,* the Pure Act, is real.[43] A particular artistic act would be real only in so far as it was not pure, but impure. Croce here seems to be proclaiming that the full aesthetic experience can be considered only if one looks not only to its purely artistic aspects, but also to its practical, moral, and philosophical elements.

Croce has, then, quite clearly arrived at the full question

which should concern us; that is, how it is that the knowing and the acting of art can be said to go together. Art is not being called knowledge alone or action alone; it is not being described as knowledge on one page and action on the next with no awareness that the two aspects of art do not go easily together. And the assertion of the integration of the various forms of activity in art does not seem to be a momentary indiscretion, for several pages later Croce speaks of the poet's passion for art as a practical passion, and of his devotion to art as his moral obligation.[44] If one hopes, however, for a precise or concretely illustrated statement as to how artistic, practical, and intellectual activity go together, the *Breviario* must disappoint him. It should be recalled that in the *Breviario* the material of art is said to be practical activity, states of mind, feelings, but that its relationship to the content of art, which is described vaguely as the whole universe seen in a certain way, cannot even be so described. Furthermore, we have found the artistic dialectic of the *Breviario* to be as specious as that of the *Estetica;* for the feeling, image, and intuition are an identity without a difference. Now, concerning the way in which thought, practice, and morality are integrated into art, Croce says no more of a general nature than this: they "are in art as art, either antecedent or consequent; and therefore are there as presupposed (sunk and forgotten there, to adopt a favorite expression of De Sanctis) or as presentiments." [45] And, at this point, Croce claims that it is impossible to speak of the integration of these forms of activity in a more specific or experiential way. When one speaks of an individual poem, he says, one must speak of its poetry only, even though to do so is to exaggerate or even to falsify the distinction between poetry and philosophy and the other forms of activity.[46] One may, to be sure, speak of the philosophy of the poem, but not in relation to its poetry. Such relations are more reality than humankind can bear, it would appear. All in all, then, Croce has moved during this early period from a conception of the artistic experience as pure and simple intuition to a conception of it as a full integration of that intuition with action, knowledge, and morality. But he either speaks of this integration in vague and general terms or says that it is impossible to speak of it as experience. In effect, therefore, even in the *Breviario,* Croce is primarily explaining the question which needs an answer rather than presenting an answer to it.

Literary Criticism

The value of our analysis might at this point be called in question on the grounds that so inconsistent, vacillating, and obscure a thinker as Croce can be of little philosophical worth, and also on the grounds that Croce's thinking about art is "essentialistic," whereas contemporary aesthetics has left all that behind and is now devoted solely to analyzing the language of literary and art criticism. One fact provides a reply to both criticisms: Croce was his own literary critic. As a result, his aesthetics is always interpretive of criticism, and the change and uncertainty in his aesthetics at least parallels changes and difficulties in the practice of criticism itself. Muddled Croce may be, but his thoughts are always relevant to the experience of art and of practical criticism. This immense advantage which he has over most non-Italian aestheticians derives in part from the greatness of the literary criticism of Francesco De Sanctis. After De Sanctis literary criticism was recognized in Italy as so important a form of thought that it would be almost inconceivable for an Italian philosopher of art not to take an active part in it. Probably this situation itself explains better than anything else why twentieth-century Italian aesthetics has been so much more vital and significant than any other aesthetics of the period.

Croce's own theory of literary criticism, it is true, was less complicated and less developed during this early period than were his thoughts on aesthetic activity itself. He was more concerned with the object of his literary criticism, with the nature of what it was that he was criticizing, than with his criticism itself. Just as he was not, at first, very integrative in his thinking, so he was not very self-reflective. In a loose way, however, his notions about literary criticism do develop in a direction parallel to the development of his theory of artistic activity. At first Croce sees the literary critic as facing an art object which is given, a datum, and he is said to do various unrelated or at least unintegrated things with the object. What he does as a critic, furthermore, is much like the material on which he works, the artistry itself; and this idea parallels Croce's early notion that the content of art is almost the same as the material of art. By the end of this early period, however, it is not at all clear that the literary critic is working with data; furthermore, the various aspects of his work are closely integrated; and, finally, his work has become less and less like the artistic object and more and more philosophic.

Just as Croce first conceived of art not as active, but as the passive contemplation of some fact passively given; just so he finds his critic passively contemplating not an active process, but a product. Through much of this early period Croce never fully rejects the notion that the critic must work with an arti-fact, a finished product which somehow or other is above the vicissitudes of time. In *La critica letteraria* the poem is a fixed object passively received and contemplated, and it is the only thing which unifies the various activities called literary criti-cism.[47] The realistic presupposition is evident here: the thing desired precedes the desire; just so the poem to be criticized is completed before the criticism begins. In the *Tesi* Croce's sense of the mysterious and sacred nature of the art object is carried so far that he calls art not just alogical, but impenetra-ble by the intellect.[48] The art object as Croce is here thinking of it is, to be sure, not merely the physical work, obscured by time as it is likely to be; it is that physical object as seen by the artist in the moment of production.[49] That is what the critic must contemplate, and Croce has faith that with the help of erudition this object can be approached. Although it is not merely the physical object which is being spoken of, as late as 1908 Croce is describing it as something merely finite. He asserts this, for example, in reference to Tansillo's sonnet, "Poichè spiegato ho l'ali al bel desio," which Tansillo thought of as expressing his amorous aspirations, but which Bruno interpreted as expressive of philosophic aspiration. Croce resolves the problem of whether the new interpretation by Bruno means that the original poem has taken on new meaning or that a second poem has been created:

One is accustomed to saying that the work of art brings with itself inexhaustible, infinite interpretations. But, in effect, the single work of art is always something finite; that which is inexhaustible and infinite is the human spirit, which comes to rest in no work of art and creates always new images.[50]

The poem is finished in form and in meaning, although endless interpretations may be brought to it. There was a time, moreover, when Croce found the art object to be not only finite, but enough like a physical object for him to say that if it were not for the practical activity of "exteriorization" the object would perish.[51] In later editions of the *Estetica*, however, Croce replaces that gloomy idea by saying that nothing which is born dies. And in the 1908 Heidelberg lecture on art as lyrical, Croce finds the poem to be an eternal object, free of time and space, ready for re-creation in its "ideality-reality" from any point of time or space.[52] Such idolatry of the finite object is gone from the *Breviario*, fortunately. The poem endures, but as the individual universalized, surviving like any action of the past, as a part of history rather than above it.

Croce's description of what the critic does with the art object goes through three distinct phases during the early period
of his thought. In *La critica letteraria* the critic is said to approach the art object from several different directions, none of
which is preferable to the others, and with no connection
among them except the object, which all of them are humbly
approaching.[53] Aesthetics, which determines the general categories of beauty, is excluded from criticism, which considers
not general categories, but the work of art in its individuality.
In fact, at this stage all criticism is as free of philosophy as the
work of art itself is. But this similarity between criticism and
art is more than an analogy, for the stage of criticism which
follows upon the passive contemplation of the sacred object
is no other than another work of art.[54] The critic describes
what he has read; he reveals the special situation, the motif,
the individual note which the poet had discovered and developed.[55] Contrary to the belief of the greatest of all expository critics, De Sanctis, Croce claims that evaluation or judgment is quite distinct from this expository, critical poem. Evaluation, we are told, is one's subjective reaction, which is the value
we accord to the work and which has nothing to do with our
knowledge of the work. The third stage, as separate from the
first two as they are from each other, is historical; one considers the causes and the effects of the work. None of these
stages of criticism, it appears, involves our classifying a poem
and putting it in its proper genre. That sort of thing is as
separate from criticism as aesthetics is.[56]

The second phase in the development of Croce's theory of
literary criticism involves the re-ordering and the integration
of the three stages of criticism described as separate and of
equal value in *La critica letteraria*. What had been the third
stage becomes the first and is now called erudition: it includes
all the historical labors which serve works of art, but for
extraneous purposes (biography, civil, religious, political his-

tory, and other such things), and all historical erudition directed to the preparation of the aesthetic re-creation itself.[57] The second stage, the reproduction and enjoyment of the work of art, depends upon the first stage but goes beyond it; and its climax is an exclamation of approval or disapproval. The third stage, which is looked upon in the *Estetica* as the only true form of literary criticism or history, depends upon the second stage and the first stage, but goes beyond them both. It is the expository stage and, as in *La critica letteraria,* it is another work of art created upon the first work of art. The true critic, however, is not just an artist; he is an historical artist. That is, he has received from aesthetics the criteria by means of which he goes beyond the reproduction of the poem and determines what parts of it are poetic, and what parts are ugly and just what kind of activity the ugly parts are.[58] Now in both the *Tesi* and the *Estetica* the poem remains logically ineffable; it cannot be defined, it cannot be classified, it can only be intuited. The critic's concern remains with the individual and the finite, and his own work is individual and finite, even though he makes use of some universal definitions of a logical nature. His goal now is single, it is to get back to the original "feeling" of the artist, to the *macchia,* the lyric wave, the individual accent from which the poem took its shape.[59]

In his third phase, as it is represented in a 1909 essay of the *Problemi* and in the *Breviario,* Croce has gone beyond his integration of erudition, taste, and exposition and has integrated them all with logic and aesthetics. He has moved to an integration of criticism and philosophy much as he moved from a concept of art as free of practice and intellect to the notion of it as fully integrated into the *actus purus.* Criticism is no longer the artistic re-creation of the original poem; it is as different from "pure poetry" as it could be, as different as philosophy is from poetry. It is, in fact, described as an individual judgment, the synthesis of intuition and concept, the proposition, for instance, that this particular poem *a* is aesthetic, or is aesthetic in some parts and practical in other parts. The new theory of literary criticism is much richer and more complex than either of the earlier two; it parallels the enrichment of Croce's ideas about artistic material and content, the artistic act itself, and the relationship between art and other forms of activity. Like the earlier theories, it involves severe difficulties.

For example, are we to infer that the poem which becomes a part of the critical judgment is identical with the poem before it is judged? If not, then can it be said that we actually have knowledge of the original poem when we carry out our judgment? This problem, it should be noted, parallels the question of how a poem can be called intuitive knowledge of a feeling when the feeling within the poem is so drastically different from the feeling as a part of practical activity. One solution would be to say that the poem from its inception involves judgment. But the Croce even of the *Breviario* could not accept this. He is still arguing for the purity of poetry, and even when admitting that poetry may include intellectual elements, he insists that the relationship between the included ideas and the poem itself cannot be discussed.

A more treacherous solution runs like this: a poem is only its poetic aspects; its practical, moral and intellectual implications are burned away in the very re-creation performed by the man of taste, so that when the poem comes to be judged, lo, it has been reduced to its essence, it has already been judged. That is, the existent poem is no concern of ours. We exaggerate, we falsify, man cannot avoid it, Croce says in the *Breviario*. When we come to predicate the concept of aesthetic activity upon the existent poem, when we come to say that *a* is *A*, what we find ourselves saying instead is that *A* is *A*; and we are making not what Croce calls an individual judgment, but what he calls a definitory judgment. Our dilemma seems to be: either criticism is a definitory judgment, no dialectic at all, a logical tautology, the monotonic "Poetry is Poetry"; or else it is a judgment which fails to give knowledge. Croce sought to move from a theory of criticism as immediate, intuitive knowledge to a theory of criticism as a mediate, dialectical knowing which includes the immediate intuition within it. What he appears to have attained, depending upon how one looks at it, is either an active criticism which gives no knowledge at all or a cognitive criticism in which not an individual is known as an individual, but a universal is known to be itself.

Through studying Croce's early aesthetics as his struggle to move from philology to philosophy, not just as a change from one theory to another, we have, I think, come to understand the meaning of his errors and confusion. His thought during this early period points beyond itself to an as yet unrealized theory of art as both action and knowledge and to a theory of literary criticism as a different form of action and knowledge. Croce set out with unanalyzed assumptions that art and criticism were both passive forms of immediate knowledge. By the end of the period which we have studied, he has attained a very clear recognition of what it is that he lacks. Although his efforts to provide answers are quite inadequate, his questions are the right ones. They are the foundation itself of all the most impressive aesthetics developed by neo-idealists, the mature aesthetics of Croce himself, the actualistic aesthetics of Giovanni Gentile and his disciples, and the aesthetics of their most original non-Italian follower, R. G. Collingwood.

Chapter Two

Croce's Philosophical Method: Thought as Distinction

*I*t is imperative that we now probe beneath the development of Croce's early aesthetics in order to consider his ideas concerning the kind of thinking by means of which his aesthetics developed as it did. For beneath the errors in his aesthetics lies a fundamental flaw in his theory of philosophical method. His aesthetics changed, it will be remembered, from the conception of art as passive intuition to the theory of art as both knowledge and action. Even though his change involved impressive improvements, it proved to be inadequate even in its most advanced form. For although Croce envisaged art, in the *Breviario* of 1913, as both simple and complex, we found that he was still grappling with art as pure intuition, different from its earlier counterpart only in the haze of unexplorable relationships which it was allowed to have with other forms of activity. What was intended to be an artistic dialectic of image and feeling synthesized in an intuition was seen to collapse into a static kind of emotional observation. And although Croce asserts, in a general way, that art is related to practical and intellectual activity, he says that a study of these relationships as they inhere in actual works of art transcends man's capacity. Literary criticism, as Croce saw it, developed in a parallel fashion from an historical form of poetry based upon poetry to the more complex logical judgment of poetry. But here too we found the peak of Croce's thought disappointing, the complex critical judgment as he defines it radically ambiguous. The judgment is either an active dialectic of intuition and concept, an individual judgment which fails to achieve any knowledge at all; or it is a definitory judgment, the tautological assertion that the particular concept of poetry is indeed the particular concept of poetry. The primary objective of our present analysis of Croce's ideas on his own act of thinking is to uncover what kept the movement in his aesthetics from fulfilling its promise.

As in our study of Croce's early aesthetics, we shall continue to avoid the conventional formulas of Crocean criticism and try to break down any of Croce's own phrases which appear to be hardening into formulas. Words, we believe, have meanings only as used; they can be understood only as part of a context which is more than verbal. Even within a specific context, words as multi-pronged as "art," "poetry," "intuition," "expression," "dialectic," and "judgment" are rarely obvious in their meaning; they must be analyzed and interpreted before they can be understood. For it is simply too easy for a writer to say that he means a certain thing by a particular word and then to proceed immediately to use the word with a very different meaning. Such a recognition of the flux and the slipperiness of speech, even in its written forms, is not merely an act of distrust and skepticism; it is, much more, a recognition of the richness of language, of the active nature of speech, and, finally, of all understanding as basically an act of translation. Nothing is understood immediately, even if all sorts of immediate misunderstandings are possible. One must, to be sure, hear the word; but he must then translate it according to its use and context, if he would hope ever to understand more than his own distortions of what others are saying.

The words with which Croce explains his method of thinking during this early period of his development do not themselves represent significant changes. Thought, he persistently maintains, is essentially distinction; it is by means of distinction that one elaborates whatever concepts he considers. But a study of his three basic works written during this period on the nature of thought reveals a movement almost as complex as that of his early aesthetics. If we proceed, in our analysis, from Croce's *Lineamenti di una Logica come scienza del concetto puro* of 1905 through the "Ciò che è vivo e ciò che è morto della filosofia di Hegel" of 1906 to the *Logica come scienza del concetto puro* of 1909, we shall find that thought is always spoken of as distinction, but that distinction itself shifts in meaning from a kind of sharp-edged separation to a subordinate part of a somewhat vague form of integration.

Thought, in the earliest work, is defined, in what Croce calls the manner of Herbart, as the distinction between one form of experience and another. Of course, things are not as simple as this definition might suggest. Herbart, in his theory of thought as distinction, was reacting against the Hegelian concept of thought as a dialectical synthesis; and he retained in his own theory much of that which he opposed. Similarly, in the *Lineamenti*, the forms of experience which Croce analyzes as "distincts" are fixed in an inalterable series which seems ripe for Hegelian syntheses. The possibility for such syntheses is present everywhere, and much of Croce's language suggests that he is on the verge of bringing the various forms together in some such way. The order of the forms of experience is a necessary one, and one form implies another which grows out of it; thus the distinctions among them are very different from the merely analytical distinctions of science and philology. The order of the theoretical forms, which are three in number, imaginative, logical, and historical, calls for a dialectical synthesis: but Croce resists the temptation, designates the forms "distincts," and merely analyzes them and their relationships by means of distinction. The Hegelian background is present and Croce resists it, even in the face of much of his own language.

In the essay on Hegel which follows hard upon the *Lineamenti*, and in the later *Logica*, Croce shows much more readiness to accept the Hegelian concept of thought as an a priori synthesis or dialectic than he was in the *Lineamenti*. Because Croce interprets Hegelian opposites to be no more than contradictories, however, he finds it necessary to replace the dialectic of opposites with what he calls a dialectic of distincts. This revision involves him in what may rightly be called a compromise between Herbartian distinction and Hegelian dialectic. The act of thought, or logic, is no longer distinguished as the second distinct in a series of three. Instead, Croce defines it as a synthesis of two distincts, the imaginative intuition and the definitory judgment, or what was the act of thought itself in the earlier *Lineamenti*. The act of thought in the *Logica* is much closer to the third distinct form of the *Lineamenti*, the historical judgment, than it is to the second, the pure act of distinction, of that earlier work. Whereas the tentative historical judgment of the *Lineamenti*, however, merely made use of elements in the two distincts preceding it in the series, Croce's maturer concept of the historical judgment is said to synthesize its two presuppositions, the intuition and the definitory judgment. In effect, then, distinction and the distincts come to have two quite different meanings in the *Logica*. As parts of the historical judgment, the distincts are no longer distinct in the earlier, Herbartian sense: they are part of a dialectical act of thought (an a priori synthesis) even though they are said to remain, in some sense, distinct. At the same time, the first of the two distincts synthesized, the imaginative intuition, remains distinct from the historical judgment in the earlier, Herbartian sense of distinction. A poetic intuition is distinct in the sense that it can be properly experienced only in itself, as independent of everything conceptual. One cannot think about a poem and refer to it by means of concepts unless he has first experienced it as distinct, as pure intuition. Nonetheless, this same intuition is also a different kind of distinct form. It is the subject of an historical judgment, a dialectical synthesis the predicate of which is a definitory judgment (*e.g.*, "Poetry is pure intuition"). In this way Croce would retain the best of his earlier theory of thought as distinction, while he acquires what he considers to be the best of the Hegelian theory of thought as a dialectical synthesis. In my opinion, this compromise cannot be justified intellectually; and the very difficulties which we found present in Croce's theories of poetry and literary criticism are present here in their most elemental form.

The compromise between thought as distinction and thought as dialectic hides a contradiction. In the Hegelian tradition, thought and reality are dialectically identical; and every individual action is ultimately at one with the full concept (the dialectical act of thought). As a consequence of this, no individual action is identical with any part of the full concept; it must be more complex than any part of that concept. The full concept alone is concrete; thus, to understand any individual action fully, one must think it out as the realization of the full concept. Any thinking through of an action that stops short of that identification must leave the action abstract, as something less than concrete and less than real in the Hegelian sense. Croce is quite aware of this. At the same time, he insists that imaginative activity, as a distinct form of activity which is only part of the full concept, is itself concrete; and he continues to assert that an individual action which realizes that distinct form is itself concrete. A poem is concrete even though it excludes everything essentially conceptual and practical; but no form of activity is concrete unless it includes, along with its own dominant form, all the other basic forms, unless it is a realization not only of the poetic form, but also of the conceptual, practical, and moral forms of activity. According to one theory, no individual action is concrete unless it is identical with the full concept itself; according to the other, at least certain individual actions are concrete if they are identical with only a part of the full concept.

The practical consequence of accepting both theories is, in my opinion, disastrous. Because he identifies the distinct form of art with an individual work of art, he introduces into the distinct form greater and greater complexities when he defines it, for he is thinking of that form as identical with an individual artistic action, which he elsewhere identifies with the full, universal concept. In explaining an individual work of art, furthermore, he simplifies it excessively, reducing it to the purity of the distinct form of art, a purity which it has as art but is not limited to because it is a fully existent action. He complicates the distinct form of art excessively, and he over-simplifies the individual artistic action: such is the unavoidable consequence of his acceptance of the two incompatible theories.

This tangle in Croce's thought may well be the result of his most impressive strength, of his concentration upon the practical job of literary criticism and philology, the very absence of which makes most aesthetics such an arid study. Every good critic becomes accustomed to an intensive concentration upon an individual poem and attempts to re-create it as fully as possible, ignoring no element in it and making no reductive abstractions from it. When he comes to speak of the poem, he strives to integrate his every statement with his whole statement—if he is as good as he should be—in order that his words may always point to the fully realized poem. Critics who go on to seek out the nature not only of individual poems, but of poetry itself tend to treat the concept of poetry or art in the same way they treat an individual poem. They look upon it as an individual, concrete activity. If they look long enough, this particular concept is bound to take on all the complexity of the full concept, of the dialectical act of thinking itself; and all the reality they are capable of thinking gets heaped into a particular concept which, in fact, is only a part of the universal concept. Having eaten of the apple of such philosophical speculation, they then return to individual poems and look at them as the full embodiment of the particular concept of poetry. If they retain the concept of poetry as overloaded, as the whole heap of reality itself, then the poem appears to be chaotic. If, instead, in this effort to apply their philosophical discoveries to a poem, they try to reduce the concept of poetry to a manageable size, then the poem which they are considering undergoes a similar reduction, and it turns out to be pure poetry. To identify a poem with poetry, then, tends to make the individual poem either chaotic or abstract. This, in fact, is where we were at the end of the preceding chapter. As Croce saw it, literary criticism was either a complex, dialectical action which could say nothing truly informative about a poem or it was an assertion which reduced the poem to poetry and said that this poem, reduced to poetry, was poetry. The poem was either so complex that one could say nothing adequate to it, or it was so simple that what one said was hardly worth saying. This confusion about criticism is like Croce's confusion about art: it is a mass of vague relationships, no less than the *actus purus* itself, or it is no more than an act of emotional observation. Art must no doubt be both simple and complex. Croce's problem throughout his early period was that he could see it as simple and he could see it as complex, but he could not integrate the two characteristics meaningfully and precisely. Behind this difficulty lies his persistent and futile effort to define the act of thought itself as both distinction and dialectic.

Lineamenti di una Logica come scienza del concetto puro

In his earliest study of philosophical method, the *Lineamenti* of 1905, Croce's whole bent is toward defining thought as the purest kind of distinction.[1] This analysis of thought as separative, however, takes place against a Hegelian background; and at times the background becomes so prominent that one might consider it the foreground. For example, in one introductory statement Croce describes the concept as though it were organic and synthetic:

The intrinsic requirement of the true concept is the connectedness of all reality in an organism of concepts; and the parts of an organism cannot stand one beside the other, one indifferent to the other, as in mechanical aggregates. The order of the pure concepts cannot thus be that of supraordination, subordination and coordination, but must rather be that of implication and of progress. That it is thus can be seen in philosophy (of which logic must mirror the tendency, giving its theory), in which it is impossible to think the concepts in truth and completely if not through genetic connections and developments. The concept of imagination is distinct from that of logical thought, but logical thought is also imagination; theoretic activity is distinct from practice, but practice is also theoretic activity: the spirit grows upon itself, but not indeed as a heap of stones to which other stones are added. Here appears the profound truth of the concept of conserving and going beyond (*aufheben*), which Hegel discovered as the rhythm of concepts and their order.[2]

Taken at its face value, a statement like this denies flatly that Croce is setting about an analysis of thought as distinction; but it must not be taken in that way. He retains the order of the concepts referred to in the quotation. Imagination comes first and then logical thought. And he even adds a third theoretical concept, history, as though he is vaguely toying with the notion that the first two need a third to synthesize them and make them real. He will stoutly insist that these concepts are "deducible" one from another and are "organically connected." [3] But his analysis of the relationships among these concepts is most emphatically anti-Hegelian; they are in no sense "opposed" to each other, nor are they ultimately synthesized; they are distincts and they are related by distinction.

Throughout the *Lineamenti* Croce's Herbartian theory of thought as a separative form of distinction dominates over the Hegelian organic unity of thought:

A logical judgment is a unity in diversity, in so far as, rising from the variety of the representations, it attains the one. But especially necessary, it seems to us, is the identification of the logical judgment and definition, which would not admit into the logical judgment any distinction of a subject and a predicate, precisely because it does not contain heterogeneous elements which could function, the one as subject and the other as predicate. Where it seems that it contains them, the distinction is only apparent, the force of the judgment being, as we have noted, not in the inclusion of a concept (subject) in another more general (predicate), of a species in a genus, but in thinking out the specific difference, which is the unique and simple act of thought. [4]

The logical judgment may arise from the imagination, from the representations; but in order to be pure or homogeneous it must remain entirely free of them. There is no synthesis or integration of the two, for that would result in heterogeneity. It is true that Croce does not carry out his plan to make this study of logic a study of pure "form," of that form "which is synonymous with the universal." [5] For he elaborates not only on the idea of the material of the concept as that which individuates logical facts, distinguishing one thought from another; but also, without noting that he is doing something quite different, on the specific materials of the concept, like imaginative activity, logical thought, and the historical judgment. The Hegelian series of three activities, which would merely be illustrative material if Croce were being true to the pure "form," has for him a strangely compelling necessity. Given this one limitation, however, he is relatively consistent

in turning the parts of his "conceptual organism" into the very
thing he said he was opposed to, into "mechanical aggregates"
standing distinct and separate from each other.

The relations of Croce's concept are much more like those of
a heap of stones than he willingly admits. He gives much space
to the distinction between imagination and logical thought;
and one who knew Croce's later, more Hegelian works might
expect him to integrate tightly these illustrations of the parts
of the pure concept (They are illustrations, let it be noted,
because they are not formal parts of the concept, but instances
of its material). But here Croce is not integrating so much as
he is separating. Part *a* is free of part *b*, and part *b* is also part
a although *a* is related to *b* only extrinsically and accidentally.
Or, to say it in "logic illustrated," with "expressive form" and
"verbal form" serving as synonyms for the imagination:

If the concept cannot do without the expressive form, the expressive
form does not have for its necessary condition a logical form or a
concept. The verbal form remains always, in respect to the concept,
but only in respect to the concept, something accidental and extrinsic.[6]

This "accidental and extrinsic" relationship hardly seems like
one of the "genetic connections" which were said to make up
the "organism" of the pure concept; but that is what it is supposed to be. Croce tells us that he emphasizes the extrinsic
nature of the relationship between imagination and thought
because the same thought may be expressed in different ways.
If an individual expressive form were necessary and intrinsic
to a logical form, then the logical form could not be expressed
otherwise. Experience, Croce thinks, contradicts this. But
such a principle increases our mystification as to what is "organic" about the relationship between logical thinking and
the expressive form which is presumably always added to it.
It looks here as though Croce's very theory of the series of

distincts, or what he calls "the nexus of grades," comes into being because he conceives thought, confusedly, as one of several types of existent activity. Although Croce says that after *a* must come *a* plus *b*, with the "plus" meaning "extrinsically and accidentally related," it is difficult to think of the "must" as a logical necessity. If Croce is mixing up logic and existence, if he is thinking of an existent thinker and is trying to pile up all the ingredients of an event in which the thinker thinks his thoughts, only then can one understand why Croce adds expression extrinsically to logical thought as though it were a necessary implication. It is reasonable to say that, existentially, one cannot think without expressing his thought in some kind of language; but this need not mean that language is part of the concept of thought, although it might seem to imply this if one is confusing the concept with an individual experience of thinking the concept.

Nor is it clear why these two distincts, imagination and logic, must be thought out in the particular order Croce insists upon. The order is certainly not dialectical as Croce thinks of it, even though something vaguely dialectical in the background may be the ultimate rationale for his acceptance of the order. He does, it is true, suggest something "organic" about the relationship; for he asserts that one can think of universal thought as arising only with the presupposition of something which contains the need of the universal, but is not itself universal:

There is something in the intuitions themselves which spurs it [the spirit] to go beyond them. . . . Representations are various, individual, changeable; and in their variety, individuality, and changeableness, is the perpetual desire for the constant, the one, for the universal.[7]

Fortunately, this intimation of animism, with intuitions in need of the concept, and then the concept, because of its need for intuitions, conceiving the historical or individual judgment as a union of intuitions and the concept, genetic as it may sound, is not pursued in the *Lineamenti*. All that Croce adds to the animistic metaphor is that the concept arises as the non-individual, as that which is diverse from the individual.[8] In sum, then, imagination and logic are related in this way: *a* is alone and desires *b*; *b* arises as non-*a* extrinsically and accidentally related to *a*. This relationship can, I think, best be described not as an "organic connection," but rather as a separative distinction.

Finally, in the passage quoted to indicate that Croce's notion of thought in the *Lineamenti* is mainly that of a separative differentiation, it should be noted that the concept is not truly a unification of diversity. The variety of the representations from which it is said to arise is quite excluded from logic on the grounds that logic is purely universal, is homogeneous, not heterogeneous.[9] So pure a concept, so distinct a concept, could hardly be related to imaginative intuitions except in an accidental way.

Before turning from the first relationship in the series of distincts, or "nexus of grades," to the second, that is, from the relation between imagination and logic to the relation between logic and history, we should emphasize again that Croce rarely concentrates upon the pure "form" of the concept, even though it was his plan to do so. His objective is to explain the concept as distinction; but he does not do this by analyzing the concept in itself. One does not learn of his concept of distinction by attending to the pure concept of logic as distinct from the particular concept of the imagination or as distinct from the concept of the historical judgment. Instead one must attend primarily to his distinction between imagination and the logical concept and to his distinction between the logical concept and the historical judgment. That is the only way to discover what his concept of distinction truly is. As the second distinct in the series of three, the logical concept is used mainly to illustrate the content of the concept. The pure form of the concept is to be discovered only by abstracting the pure relationship of distinction holding between the illustrative forms, or particular concepts, of experience. The second distinct, the form of the concept, is, to be sure, identical with the relationship between itself and the imaginative form of experience; and it is identical with the relationship between itself and the historical form of experience. Instead of elaborating upon the distinct logical concept, however, Croce chooses to elucidate the logical concept by concentrating primarily upon the relationship between that concept and the other distinct forms of experience. The fact that he does not himself explain the relationship between the second distinct and his act of distinguishing the distincts from each other makes the *Lineamenti* confusing, at least initially. If, however, it is kept in mind that by analyzing the distinctions between the forms of experience Croce means to be analyzing the second distinct of the series, the logical concept, most of the confusion evaporates. If, on the contrary, one attends only to what Croce says explicitly about the second distinct, he simply will not learn very much, even about that. The only serious alternative is to watch the point at which Croce's genuine thought occurs, that is, the distinctions which he makes among the distincts.

If we turn now to the second relationship in the nexus of grades, to the distinction between logic and history, it should be even clearer than before that Croce's original idea of thought as distinction is separative rather than integrative. Logic, in this early work, is most abstract; it is homogeneous; it predicates a universal upon a universal (asserting, for example, that the concept is distinction). History, on the other hand, is heterogeneous; it predicates a universal upon an individual intuition (predicating "existence" upon a single man: "Napoleon existed as real, not merely as a myth"). Now a

Croce with Hegelian aspirations would at this point seem ready to make a genuine synthesis of the individual and the universal, of intuition and concept, in an individualizing or historical judgment. But, in fact, he is careful to avoid any such thing. The intuition and the concept are, we are told, the "presuppositions" of the historical judgment; but within that judgment itself their relationship is curiously distant and vague. To begin with, the intuition and the concept are said not to be "resolvable" into each other on the grounds that such a resolution would destroy the relationship between them. More important, Croce insists, according to an idea which he presented as early as 1893, that history is basically a form of art and that its character is primarily intuitive. "Distinction," the concept, would appear to be only extrinsically related to history, just as art was to logic. In fact, it enters into history indirectly, by means of the idea of existence. The historian is said to write poetry, but of a distinct kind. He writes the poetry and at the same time shows just what kind of existence his subject-matter has. He determines whether the snow on a mountain in a poem exists as real snow or whether it exists merely as somebody's wish or fancy. The pure poet would not make this distinction, the historian or historical poet does; thus it is that not only the intuition, but also the concept, as distinction, are the presuppositions of history. Because the idea of existence does not come from logic, history and logic are not so close as we might, momentarily, have expected. This idea of existence arises not from the concept, but from the concept as it reflects upon other forms of activity. How this reflective act slips in between homogeneous logic and heterogeneous history we are not told. But it is clearly as important to history as the idea of distinction is; for according to Croce "existence" is the primary predicate of all history, and no historical judgment is without it.

Undoubtedly, Croce's relationship between logic and history

is more reasonable than that between imagination and logic. There is no serious reason why logic must follow imagination; for imagination is in no way intrinsic to logical activity. Without the concept, without distinction, however, history would be inconceivable. The order, then, between logic and history is a necessary one; logic is properly established as a presupposition of history. It is true, however, that logic is only vaguely and distantly incorporated within history. It is present as part of an idea arbitrarily attached to it, the idea of existence. And that idea is a part of history only as the result of an undefined and unanalyzed idea of reflection, of the reflection of the concept upon forms of activity distinct from it.

Given the complications issuing from this second illustration of Croce's theory of thought, one can define it with some assurance as a separative, externalizing form of distinction. The grades of the concept depend upon one another only in a vague and arbitrary way. Subsequent grades do not incorporate the grades which precede them, although they may incorporate aspects of them. Each grade "presupposes" the grades prior to it; that is, what is presupposed is "put outside of and before" that which does the presupposing and is thus external to it. Finally, the separative nature of the idea of distinction in the *Lineamenti* is corroborated by most of the vaguer tendencies of the text, the tendencies of different ideas to be akin but only indefinably so. For example, at one point philosophy is described as preceding logic and being the object of its study;[10] at another point, it is described as coming after logic and, as the "doctrine of the categories," of which logic is one, including logic within it. If one puts the two statements together, Croce is saying that philosophy includes that which is outside it, logic, and that logic mirrors the bent of philosophy and is its theory. Croce is unaware of the paradox, however, and is using the word "philosophy" quite ambiguously in this early work. But such inconsistency is not surprising if one keeps in mind that in the *Lineamenti* Croce is emphasizing the separateness, the externality of the relationship between one particular concept and another, and at the same time attempting to adapt himself to a kind of Hegelian logic which is almost entirely a logic of internal relationships. Calogero has said that Croce's philosophy during this early period was really a "superior form of positivism." If positivism is superior when confused with something alien to it, then his description fits the *Lineamenti* perfectly.

"Ciò che è vivo e ciò che è morto della filosofia di Hegel"

Croce's interest in Hegel flowers brilliantly in his "Ciò che è vivo e ciò che è morto della filosofia di Hegel" of 1906, and Raffaelo Franchini has recently said of the volume which includes it, the *Saggio sullo Hegel* of 1913, that it is still one of Croce's most vital works.[11] There is certainly far more logical sophistication and far more integrative thought in it than there was in the *Lineamenti*. Nonetheless, it is, basically, Croce's defence of the position of the *Lineamenti* against the Hegelian dialectic of opposites.

What Croce does, in effect, is to defend his belief in distinction as the "unique and simple act of thought" by interpreting the Hegelian synthesis of opposites as no more than a "synthesis" of contradictories. He supports his theory of distinction primarily on the grounds that by it alone can one retain the autonomy of the particular concept of art, which he thinks of indiscriminately as an existent activity or a "form of experience." He then attempts to incorporate the "synthesis" of contradictories (the Hegelian synthesis as he understands it) into his nexus of distincts in such a way that each distinct is a conquest of its contradictory. This essentially sums up Croce's expanded theory of distinction as it stands at this stage, the theory which both Carlo Antoni and Raffaello Franchini have in recent years described as Croce's greatest contribution to philosophy.[12] In analyzing this advance in Croce's thought, I must ignore his often brilliant analyses of certain other strengths and weaknesses in the Hegelian system, to concentrate only upon his explanation of Hegel's dialectic of opposites and upon his replacement of the dialectic with his own theory of distinction.

In his essay on Hegel, Croce distinguishes his nexus of distincts from the dialectic of opposites in the following way. Distincts a and b are two concrete concepts, with "concrete" meaning that the concept is a full and adequate description of the form of an existent activity. Now concept a, a poetic intuition, is concrete in and by itself, whereas b, a logical thought, would be arbitrary and abstract without the first, but is in fact "in nexus with" the first and is thus real and concrete like it. In contrast to the distincts, opposites A and B, outside their synthesis C, are not really concepts at all, but only abstractions, and C is the only real and concrete concept.[13] In the nexus of distincts, as we saw in the *Lineamenti, a* is "gone beyond" in $b;$ it is suppressed as independent and conserved as dependent. Thus, in passing from imagination to logic, from a to b, the spirit goes beyond the imagination but also retains it, as the "expressive form" of logic. In the Hegelian dialectic of opposites, however, A and B, we are told, are not really suppressed and conserved, except in a metaphorical sense; because neither of them ever truly existed, neither is a genuine distinct.[14]

Now in Croce's description of the opposites and of the distincts, something crucial to the whole Hegelian tradition is lost; that is, the struggle in which multiplicity is unified. All that Croce actually sees in the dialectic of opposites is the unity, the "synthesis" which alone is real and concrete; and all that he succeeds in giving us with the nexus of distincts is multiplicity. The distincts are not unified because even if one can push beyond the accidental and extrinsic relationship of *a* as a part of *b,* the concrete *a* which is a presupposition of "*a* plus *b*" remains outside that connection and is distinct from it in a most separative and external fashion. And the opposites are not multiple because Croce thinks of them as no more than contradictories. *B* is merely not-*A.* And the synthesis, *C,* will at best be a re-assertion of *A.* If not-Being is no more than the contradictory of Being, then the synthesis is no more than a monotonal Becoming which is really just another Being.

Contrary to Croce's understanding, it is essential in the dialectic of opposites that the antithesis be recognized as more than a contradictory. If the antithesis is no more than the not-thesis, then the synthesis will be no more than the thesis and no growth or development can occur. A serious Hegelian does not exclude contradiction, but goes beyond it. For example, if the thesis is unity, the antithesis is, to begin with, not-unity. Croce would go no further, but for the dialectic to move it is necessary to recognize not-unity to be multiplicity, which is not the contradictory of unity, but is what I am calling its opposite. To reason out the synthesis of unity and multiplicity is not so simple or so sterile as reasoning out the synthesis of unity and not-unity, which would no doubt be simply unity all over, with something of the "life-urge" added to it. Whatever his words, Croce's antithesis is the not-thesis and nothing else. Death as the antithesis of life is not-life, ugliness as the antithesis of beauty is not-beauty, and so forth. The best evidence to support my claim lies in the fact that Croce never succeeded in describing one of his particular concepts of theoretical activity as a dialectic of opposites, even though he claims to have incorporated the dialectic of opposites into his nexus of distincts. For example, artistic activity is said to be the conquest of beauty over ugliness; if one seeks a difference between beauty as thesis and beauty as synthesis, however, he will seek in vain. Furthermore, "ugliness" is never in itself more than not-beauty. The clear evidence for this lies in Croce's failure to infer any qualities from "ugliness" and his effort to make up for that failure by inserting arbitrarily into his pseudo-dialectic the distinct concept of utilitarian activity as the opposite of beauty. Ugliness was too weakly conceived to put up a struggle, so that something stronger had to be substituted; the substitution is not, however, deduced, and there is no reason at all why Croce did not employ "intellectual activity" instead of "utilitarian activity," since it would have been as "not-beautiful" as the other. Croce's reduction of opposites to contradictories wrecks the Hegelian dialectic, and his incorporation of this wreck into his own nexus of distincts reveals that he thinks of each distinct, each form of experience, as something completed and thus stilled and static, and then extrinsically or externally related to the other distincts.

At this point it should be asked what Croce was gaining by his reduction of the dialectic of opposites and his expansion of the nexus of distincts. With a as concrete and by itself, what he gains is the autonomy of art from b, from logic. If one is identifying the particular concept of art with the individual activity of a poem, his conviction that an individual poem does have its own worth could easily lead him to assert that art must be allowed to have its own worth, independent of logic. One's theory of distinction may make it impossible for him to unify the multiple so that he is left with multiple distinct concepts; but it does leave autonomous one particular concept, aesthetic activity, which he has mistakenly identified with an existent activity. As the actualists will say later on, at this stage Croce's empirically-oriented philological activity is causing him to mistake a part of the whole concept for an individual action and to forget the universal concept itself.

Logica come scienza del concetto puro

With the publication of his *Logica come scienza del concetto puro* in 1909 Croce makes the major integrative advance, during this early period, in his conception of philosophical method, the advance which lies behind his efforts in the *Breviario* of 1913 to present artistic activity as both a knowing and a making, as both simple and complex. Throughout the *Logica* Croce's efforts are directed toward going beyond the idea of thought as a separative form of distinction in order to attain a conception of thought as the unification of multiplicity. Franchini recognizes how radical the change is from the *Lineamenti* to the *Logica* in his claim that "by 1909 Croce had possessed in depth the Hegelian distinction between Intellect (*Verstand*) and Reason (*Vernunft*) and thus of the true philosophical method." [15] And Antoni, who recognized the lack of movement and integration in the *Lineamenti,* claims that Croce's identification of the definitory judgment (which is the same as the Logic of the *Lineamenti*) with the existential or historical judgment in the *Logica* of 1909 is "the crucial point in the development of his thought." [16] Croce himself felt the importance of the change. Although the *Logica* is presented as the second edition of the *Lineamenti,* it is advertised as a second edition entirely re-made, and in the preface Croce tells us that it is a second edition not so much of his book, as of his thought.

Although it is obvious that Croce is now striving for Hegelian syntheses, if we read the *Logica* with the *Lineamenti* and the essay on Hegel in mind, we shall find that Croce no sooner asserts a synthesis than he falls back upon distinction and the distincts. This repeated withdrawal from the full implications of the dialectical synthesis forces him to begin all over again time after time as the *Logica* unfolds. It causes the book to be disjointed, with new sections being written as though nothing preceded them. This failure to achieve integration of his thought lies behind Croce's inability to conceive of art in the *Breviario* as an active dialectic.

Nonetheless, the *Logica* is more integrative than anything we have seen thus far. To begin with, Croce no longer separates logic from philosophy as he did in the *Lineamenti:* they are the same. Philosophy, moreover, is not to be separated from particular studies in philosophy. There simply is no concept set off from all other human activity. As Croce now puts it: "The exposition of the characteristics of the concept, thought correctly, is resolved in the compendious exposition of the whole philosophy of the spirit." [17] Furthermore, the concept is no longer separated from the intuitions from which it arises, as it was in the *Lineamenti:*

What is most important, in any case, to keep in mind is that logical activity or thought rises upon the variegated spectacle of the representations, intuitions, or, as some say, sensations; and by means of these, at every moment, the cognitive spirit absorbs within itself the course of the real.[18]

The concept does not merely arise from the intuitions; that it did in the *Lineamenti*. It actually takes those intuitions into itself, it is heterogeneous, or as Croce will say here, it is not abstract, but concrete:

If the concept is universal and transcendent in respect to the single representation, taken in its abstract singularity, it is on the other hand immanent in all the representations, and thus also in the single one. The concept is universal in respect to the representations and is not exhausted in any of them; but, since the world of knowledge is a world of representations, if the concept were not in the representations themselves it would not be any place: it would be in another world, a condition which cannot be thought and thus is not. Its transcendence is also immanence.[19]

The concept here would appear to be both one and many: one as transcendent, as unifying all representations, and many as immanent, as distinguishing one from another. In a later passage, when speaking of the concept as an a priori synthesis, Croce will add that reality is not outside thought, and neither is thought outside reality, nor is one extraneous to the other:

The representations are docile to thought, and thought covers the representations even less than the thin and rare veil covered the beauty of Alcina: the compenetration of the two elements is perfect, and they constitute a unity. The false belief in an exteriority and extraneousness between reality and thought cannot arise except when the pure concept and the a priori synthesis are replaced by either abstract concepts with analytical judgments annexed . . . or empirical concepts with merely synthetic judgments annexed.[20]

Reality, he will say elsewhere, is thought.[21] Furthermore, he identifies logic or philosophy with history, admitting that his separation of them in the *Lineamenti* was an error resulting from his prejudice that philosophy must be "a form free from the shackles of history, and constituting in respect to history a precedent and independent moment of the spirit."[22] This abstractive prejudice he believes he has conquered with the assistance of his "carissimo amico" Giovanni Gentile. Thus, there is much evidence in the *Logica* that Croce now conceives of thought as a dialectical unity of multiplicity, as a synthesis of formal unity and material multiplicity.

In effect, however, Croce does not take this unity of the simplicity and the complexity of thought very seriously. When it comes time to introduce his various distincts, his particular concepts, as concrete, he writes as though he has never in his life even imagined the concept of concepts, the universal concept, as concrete, as a synthesis of unity and multiplicity. He begins reasonably enough, showing a genuine concern for the fact that the concept must somehow involve both unity and multiplicity:

With every subdivision necessarily excluded from the *form* of the concept, the multiciplicity of the concepts cannot refer to anything else than the variety of the *object* which is thought within the logical form of the concept. The concept of goodness is not that of beauty; or, better, both are logically the same thing, both being the logical form; but the aspect of reality which the first designates is not the same aspect of reality as that of the second.[23]

If Croce is saying here what he has said elsewhere, that thought and reality are identical, and that the concept is concrete (if it contains within it the course of reality), then he seems on the verge of capturing a concept of logical thought as a dialectical synthesis of a form which is one and active and of a content which is the very idea of objective multiplicity itself. Since Croce did not grasp this concept, however, we can only speculate as to what that achievement might have been. It might well have been the very concept of the dialectic with which Gentile will seek to remedy the ailments in the *Logica*. The logical form itself, as the individual judgment, would then be the act of thinking by means of which the intuition and the pure concept are synthesized. In accord with Croce's essay on the lyric nature of the intuition, the intuition would itself be utter oneness, everything indistinguishably fused within the dominant feeling. The concept would be pure distinction: the oneness of the intuition, of the vital flash, would of necessity be split asunder in the very act of its expression; that is, it would be broken down into objectified parts distinguishable from one another. The subjective intuition, then, would break down, in expression, into an objective, analyzable set of statements. This subjective thesis and objective antithesis would be synthesized by the act of thinking itself, an act in which the subjective oneness of the intuition and the objective multiplicity of the distinctions would be unified as an identity of opposites. The form of the concept as an act of thinking would thus be a dialectic of opposites; in itself it would be one, a harmony of oneness and multiplicity; but its antithetical element, its objective element, would be essentially the idea of multiplicity; and this multiplicity would be contained within the form of the concept.

If Croce had pursued this path, he would have been forced to relinquish his notion of the distincts as externally related to each other, for the intuitive thesis and the distinctive antithesis would be internally identified as opposites within the act of thinking. The elements of such a dialectic would not be contradictories; they would be genuine opposites, different but also identical. Furthermore, even though an individual action could be real and concrete only in so far as it was identical with the full act of thinking itself, it might vary from another individual action according to which of the three elements of the dialectic was its dominant element. A genuine poem would be an act of thinking in which an intuition as expressed was an identity of opposites. But unlike all other actions except artistic ones, the poem would have as its dominant element the thesis of the dialectic, the intuitive element. A philosophical treatise would, on the other hand, be an act of thinking in which the synthesis itself dominated over both the intuitive and the distinctive elements. Different actions, then, could be distinguished according to which of the three elements in the dialectic dominated them; and thus the elements of the Gentilean dialectic of opposites would function much as Croce's "distincts" functioned. At least they come closer to Croce's distincts than they do to the Hegelian contradictories, as Croce envisaged them. Croce, however, did not take this step toward a theory of the concept as a synthesis of purely internal relationships.

At this very point, where he seems on the verge of grasping a genuine dialectic (pages 52-53 of the third edition of the *Logica,* pages 47-48 of the fourth edition, and pages 48-49 of the seventh), Croce makes, in my opinion, a crucial misstep.

He errs just as we would have expected had we recalled that ever since Gentile convinced him in 1899 that form and content are identical, he has thought of them as an identity without a difference, and had we remembered his reduction of the Hegelian dialectic to nothing more than the completed conquest of one contradictory over another. For him, the form and the content of the concept are simply identical; they are just one and nothing but one. The object as the idea of multiplicity, as that which might have been contained within the logical form, as the only way in which the course of the real can be conceived of as being at one with the concept: this inclusion of the object as part of the concept has vanished before it has been more than hinted at. Instead of tracking down the unity of the logical form in its subjective and active aspects, instead of thinking of the concept as the form of thinking, as he seemed about to do, Croce approaches the form as he should have approached the content, as nothing more than an object. What else could he do, if he must have an identity without a difference between form and content? He must lose everything distinctive about both. All the variety of the object must stand outside the concept whose content must be as much one as its form is, if form and content are to be identical in the Crocean fashion. What is retained after this exclusion of so much variety is an objective concept whose unity is assumed and whose multiplicity is arbitrarily introduced. And the only grounds for this arbitrary intrusion are the grounds that unity alone is empty, that one desires an organic unity, that, in fact, one needs here the very theory of distinct grades which was presented as a theory of extrinsic and external relations in the *Lineamenti*. Croce asserts that without its distinct parts, the concept would be a mere simplicity beyond the representations, and thus would be ineffable because without even the possibility of articulation. He can assert this only by forgetting that he has defined the concept in an earlier passage as concrete, as at one with every representation although limited to none. That is, he justifies the introduction at this point of his distinct concepts as the essential parts of the pure concept for reasons which simply do not hold in so far as the concreteness of the concept has already been established.

In this same passage of the *Logica*, moreover, Croce loses not only a dialectical synthesis of unity and multiplicity, but both unity and multiplicity themselves. He says: "A whole is whole only because and in so far as it has parts, rather, is parts; an organism is such because it has, and is, organs and functions." [24] Hereafter he will not speak of the whole concept, but only of its parts; from his point of view, it does not matter because the whole is immediately identical with its parts, and one has the same kind of indiscriminate identification here that exists in the *Breviario* between the image and the feeling of the artistic intuition. Furthermore, on these very pages Croce explains that the particular or distinct concepts could not be of infinite number because if they were they would be the same as representations. They are, he asserts, four in number: the Beautiful, the True, the Useful, and the Good. Now if he were not ignoring the unity of the concept, he would recognize that representations as thought, as penetrated by the concrete concept, would not be an infinite number of different items. They would rather be infinite representations all conceptually unified, all thus resembling one another and thus all at one in the dialectical act of thinking. But Croce ignores unity just as he ignores multiplicity; he has replaced them both with "Quadruplicity." From this point on, he cannot surprise us when he speaks of individual poems as though they were the concept of "poetic activity," the Beautiful in all its distinctness. For Beauty and the other three particular concepts have swallowed up everything else, and it is no longer possible to talk about the many individuals or about the one except as reduced to one of those particular concepts.

In later years Croce was evidently disturbed at his having missed something on these few pages, for in the later editions of the *Logica* the statement "the multiplicity of the concepts cannot refer to anything else than the variety of the *object*,"—an idea crucial to any development of the concept as dialectical—has been changed to "the multiplicity of the concepts cannot refer to anything else than the variety of the *objects*." [25] By shifting to the plural of "object" he obscures the notion that, given the identity of reality with thought, the object of thought must be included, as the principle of multiplicity, within the action of thinking. This obscured notion, which is in harmony with the concept as concrete and with the identity of reality and thought, is inconsistent with Croce's immediate rather than dialectical identification of the form and the content of the concept. It is inconsistent with the notion that all that variety of objects stands outside of and distinct from the activity of thought. Finally, it is inconsistent with Croce's reduction of the concept to a static nexus of four distinct concepts. The change from "object" to "objects" veils the deep rift between Croce's new but half-hearted Hegelianism and his old theory of distinction.

Upon the heels of this failure follow several others of importance. In the light of what we have just seen, what appears to be the successful transformation of the historical judgment in the *Lineamenti* into the philosophical judgment of the *Logica* collapses into a series of errors. It may be recalled that in the *Lineamenti* the historical judgment was heterogeneous; it was the somewhat mysterious predication of the universal concept upon an individual representation. It depended upon its two presuppositions, the representation and the concept, the one individual, the other universal, both radically distinct from each other. Unfortunately, the philosophical judgment, the individual judgment, of the *Logica* does not turn out to be the successful transformation of this vague historical judgment of the *Lineamenti*. The new judgment is the predication of a definitory judgment (e.g. Aesthetic activity is intuitive) upon an intuition (e.g. a single poem). Croce calls the judgment the a priori logical synthesis, the integration of an individual and a universal. And, in some ways, it looks like a significant improvement over the *Lineamenti's* distinctness of all the parts of the concept from one another. The intuition is no longer merely an extrinsic addition to philosophy, its "expressive form"; it is rather an intrinsic part of the philosophic act of thought itself, being the subject of the individual judgment. Furthermore, the pure concept or the definitory judgment is no longer left abstract and transcendent; it is a part of the individual judgment, a partner equal to the artistic intuition of which it is the predicate. Finally, the individual judgment would seem to be a genuinely dialectical synthesis of opposites, of an intuition and a concept, and it appears to be something more than its parts or their mere sum. The new judgment resembles closely the aesthetic judgment of the literary critic, as that is presented by Croce in the *Breviario*.

Lamentably, an analysis of the philosophical judgment proves it to be no more of a dialectical synthesis of opposites than was the critical judgment of the *Breviario*. It is, at bottom, simply one more identity without a difference. One problem is that, with all the integration going on earlier in the text, the definitory judgment, the assertion that a concept is a concept, is envisaged as an individual judgment even before it enters into the synthesis of the individual judgment. It is so, to begin with, because the concept is concrete, and thus is necessarily connected with individual representations. But it is individual for another, more specific reason. Croce asserts that the definitory judgment is always the answer to an individual, historically limited question.[26] As a definitory judgment, A is A, it is the predicate of a proposition the subject of which, *a*, is the individual question, Is *a* A or not-A?[27] One cannot avoid recognizing that Croce is here thinking of a particular concept, the definitory judgment, as an existent activity, as a man making such a judgment, and he is adding to it whatever it needs to be existent. Thus, the antithetical element of the individual judgment, the definitory judgment, is the same as the individual judgment itself and the dialectic breaks down. For example, before the definitory judgment "Aesthetic activity is intuition" is ever used as the predicate of the individual judgment "*The Four Quartets is* aesthetic activity," it has already been individualized as the predicate of my historically limited question, asked here and now, "What does Croce mean by his concept of aesthetic activity?" Of course, such an individualization of the definitory judgment cannot be said to cancel out those other statements about it as truly definitory; it is simply inconsistent with them. When Croce differentiates, he has a genuine predicate for the individual judgment; when he integrates, he lacks one.

In a like fashion, he does and does not have an individual intuition which may serve as the subject of the individual judgment. If Croce's concept were truly concrete, as such statements as this imply, "The concept is not applied to the intuition because it does not exist even for an instant outside the intuition":[28] then if the concept is truly universal and thus immanent in every intuition, the intuition would always be the subject of an individual judgment. But elsewhere Croce distinguishes between the truly individual intuition and the "intuition" which is the subject of an individual judgment. He will say, for instance: "The concept contains the intuition, but the intuition transfigured; and it is a synthesis, not now of itself and its opposite, but of itself and a distinct from itself, indistinguishable from it except by abstraction."[29] When transfigured, when thought, is the intuition still immediately individual, or must one say that it is now as much an individual judgment as its predicate, the definitory judgment, is? And if it is basically different from a true intuition, which is distinct from logic, how can the true intuition even be said to be known by means of the individual judgment? In any case, when he puts his distinctions and his integrations together, Croce is not achieving a higher synthesis than he did in the *Lineamenti*. Things go more closely together, but they are badly blurred.

At bottom, even while he strives for Hegelian syntheses Croce continues to work with pictures. He sees an intuition as a world; then he sees that, in answer to its mysterious being, a sun called a concept arises and sheds its light upon the intuition. That, basically, is the situation of the individual judgment of the *Logica*. Is the form of the intuition as illuminated by the concept the same as it was before? Clearly no. Before, it was distinct from philosophy; now it is an indistinguishable part of it. So the distinct intuition is unknowable. If, furthermore, the sun-concept with which one wishes to illuminate one intuition-world has already arisen to illuminate another intuition, if it is already an individual judgment before being called upon for the new judgment, why it should be appropriate or adequate to the new situation is not clear. Why should the new intuition have, for the answer to the question it raises, the answer to the question of another intuition? All in all, picturing concepts, imagining them as existent activities, is quite incompatible with dialectical thinking.

As a matter of fact, Croce's efforts to integrate his thoughts without giving up his separative theory of distinction complicate the connection between imagination and thought even more than we have thus far suggested. From the *Lineamenti* Croce brings to the *Logica* the intuition, the imaginative activity, as the "expressive form" of the philosophic judgment.

This raises the question of how the intuition as expressive form of the judgment is related to the intuition which is the subject of the judgment. Although it is difficult, Croce tries to keep both forms of intuition as part of the philosophical judgment. He distinguishes the intuition as expressive form from the subject of the judgment by saying that the expressive form is a new representation, one conditioned by the concept.[30] Unfortunately, he says elsewhere the same about the intuition which is the subject of an individual judgment.[31] Finally, it may be remembered that the intuition is present in the philosophical judgment in a third way, as the question to which the definitory judgment provides an answer.[32] Croce is here merely existentializing his distinct concepts and letting his mind run back and forth between them. Essentially, he is repeating himself without connecting the repetitions, so that there is neither development nor genuine identification. More than anything else, there is serious confusion.

The other difficulties of the *Logica* are either slight derivatives from those which we have considered, or merely minor lapses of thought. For example, at one point Croce describes the unique concept as a dialectic of opposites which are not only inseparable, but not even distinguishable.[33] We know, of course, by now that the concept is not really a dialectic of opposites at all: it is really a jumble of subjects and predicates. At one moment, the subject and the predicate seem to be the same, so that the judgment is merely tautological. At another, the subject and the predicate seem so different, so distinct, that one cannot think of them as rationally related and is reduced to imagining them vaguely. By calling the concept a dialectic of opposites, Croce must mean simply that it is a "dialectic" of contradictories: if one asserts that A is A, then he implicitly rejects the assertion that A is not-A, and the assertion rejected is the contradictory of the assertion asserted. This does not sound much like a dialectic of opposites, but it must be what Croce was thinking of. Otherwise, he surely would have distinguished the concept as a dialectic of opposites from the concept as an a priori logical synthesis of the individual and the definitory judgments. For the latter are said to be indistinguishable within their synthesis, just as the opposites are said to be within their synthesis. Since Croce ignores what appears to be a problem, it seems wisest to decide that there is no problem. Although he spoke of a dialectic of opposites, he was not thinking either of a dialectic or of opposites.

Furthermore, Croce does not adequately explain why the person who has made an individual judgment must go on, if he wishes to communicate the judgment, to use all sorts of empirical abstractions. His example is of a person who first judges that the *Transfiguration* is an artistic work and then goes on to characterize it empirically as a holy picture.[34] The first judgment is existential and, we are told, must be the basis of the second. The question which arises is, what is the connection between the "expressive form" of the existential judgment, which should provide the critic with plenty of words, and the empirical abstractions to be employed in the act of communication? Croce has been fairly clear in explaining the distinction between expression in art and the practical exteriorization of the work; but it is not obvious that the same difference holds between the "expressive form" as used in philosophical judgments and their exteriorization. After all, would not the expressive form be enough of a dress for the communication of one's thought in public?

Such matters become more confusing the more one thinks about them, unless it be kept in mind that Croce is not unifying many of his ideas primarily because he thinks of them as separate activities, as types of existent activities. At one point, it is true, Croce warns himself against doing this very thing.[35] But it is easier to warn oneself than to heed the warning,—

especially when the very heart of one's book is a contradiction surviving only because one does take concepts for types of existent activity.

For all that we have said, the *Logica* is more Hegelian than either the *Lineamenti* or the 1906 essay on Hegel. Croce has come much closer here to the idea of thought as the unification of multiplicity. But at crucial points his thought falters and he misses both unity and multiplicity. In their place he sets up four distinct concepts as types of existent activity and then weaves relations within each and among them. These relations either appear to be fundamentally the same—so that Croce is saying that really no distinct is concrete, that only the concept of concepts, the *actus purus,* is real; or they seem to be quite different from one another—so that Croce is assuring us that the distincts are real, and that an analysis of an existent action as the realization of a distinct may exhaust its reality. The *Logica* makes for relatively easy reading mainly because it lacks the strenuous connections characteristic of seriously logical thinking. If one seeks for such connections, he finds abysses and cave-ins.

On the basis of this analysis, Croce's failure to develop an artistic dialectic in the *Breviario* does not stem necessarily from the non-dialectical nature of art. Nor does it come from any intrinsic flaw in the terms which Croce uses: image, feeling, and intuition. It comes ultimately from the fact that Croce did not understand the nature of dialectical thinking. He could not grasp the concept of thought as the unification of multiplicity because he refused to give up his theory of distinction, a theory which is obstructive because it rests upon the notion that distinct concepts are "forms" of existent activity undistinguished from individual, existent acts. Working with such stonily substantial distincts, Croce cannot make his way to an idea of the unity of the concept; and without an idea of unity, he cannot relate artistic activity to other forms of activity, except in a vague way. Having missed the unity of a dialectic, he reduces unity to the parts of a whole. Thereafter he never again thinks about unity,—although he may claim to do so—because he has come to identify unity with the parts. If he speak of parts, he apparently tells himself he is speaking of the unified whole. Parts, it seems clear enough, cannot be very precisely related unless one can conceive of the unity to which they belong. The most Croce will give us in lieu of a concept of unity is an imagined circle divided into four parts, Beauty, Truth, Utility and Goodness; and we are to call the unthinkable image the *actus purus*. Finally, if at times Croce's own literary criticism proves overly generic, it is not because he lacks an interest in the individual so much as that he has reasoned himself out of even looking at an individual action except through the very "generic" apertures of his distinct concepts.

Problems which cling to Croce's effort to conceive of art as both simple and complex, as both knowledge and action, indicate his need for clearer and more actively dialectical thinking. From what we have seen thus far, he will need help from others.

Chapter Three

Croce and Actual Idealism

*W*ithin two or three years after the publication of
Croce's *Logica* in 1909, Giovanni Gentile initiated
a philosophical movement whose immediate objective was to overcome the weaknesses of that book. Gramsci
was right in saying that Actual Idealism, as the movement
came to be known, was born from the matrix of Croce's philosophy;[1] and those who condemned the movement as nothing
but philosophy about philosophy were not simply ill-tempered.
Gentile himself claimed:

Every act of thought is the exclusion of another act of thought (not
of all the other possible ones, but of that one thought immediately
preceding it). *Omnis determinatio est negatio.* And thus merely
observing an error and freeing myself from it, I know a truth, and,
that is to say, I think. In this vital knot which links the truth (concrete) to error (abstract) lies the source of thought and the fundamental law of logic.[2]

He meant his philosophy to be a remedy for Croce's inadequate
notion of the concept, and for Croce's inability to unify theory
and practice, historiography and history, and philosophy and
science. Nor should the immediate popularity of Gentile's work
obscure the fact that he was improving substantially upon
Croce's thought; nor the excesses of some of his more aridly

logical adherents hide the riches for neo-idealistic aesthetics which Gentile himself was able to draw out of ideas at first having to do almost wholly with philosophical method. Croce himself, for that matter, made important changes in his own philosophy as a result of Gentile's arguments, even though long after, in 1950, he would say that the only thing he learned from Actual Idealism was what not to think.[3]

For any one looking across World War II from this side in time, the controversy between Croce and Gentile and other Actual Idealists may indeed appear to be dominated by personal and political animosity. From the year 1925, when Croce wrote an anti-Fascist manifesto for intellectuals in reaction to Gentile's Fascist manifesto for intellectuals, feelings of ferocity were the most obvious result of the controversy. Intellectual bludgeons rather than insights became the common weapons. An actualist could insinuate that Croce was a proto-Fascist without knowing it. A foremost actualist, Guido De Ruggiero, repudiated his position, joined Croce in spirit, and began writing at times for *La critica,* for "moral reasons";[4] and Adolpho Omodeo, one of the great historians of the time, appears to have gone through a similar change of heart. Within a few years after the publication of his actualistic *Speculum Mentis* in 1925, R. G. Collingwood, who was a friend of De Ruggiero's, made what appears to be a similar break; and in his later *Autobiography* (1939), he points to Gentile without naming him by saying that once there was a very able philosopher who became a Fascist and that was the end of him as a philosopher. All would agree today, I think, that Gentile's allegiance to Mussolini led to a tragic perversion of his philosophy. It is, however, possible and reasonable to agree with H. S. Harris that Gentile's philosophical position did not lead directly or necessarily to his political and propagandistic activity as a Fascist; and we may recognize, as Harris does, the immense importance of several books which Gentile wrote years after he was severely and even irreparably compromised in politics. Plato's greatness survived his flirtations with Sparta and his efforts to assist Dionysius the Great of Syracuse. Intellectual greatness does not excuse political corruption, but it has redemptive power. In any case, during the fifteen years or so after the publication of the *Logica* and before Fascism had become totalitarian, the controversy between Croce and the actualists proved both thoughtful and fruitful.

At the crucial point of the *Logica* where Croce went astray, Gentile made the right choice. It will be recalled that Croce defined the pure concept as having its form and content immediately at one and as being one, as excluding multiplicity. Instead of developing a concept which included the object as its source of multiplicity within it, he slipped into the non-idealistic notion that the object of the concept exists outside it so that without some kind of special distinctions the concept in itself would be void. To escape the dilemma of creating a spotlight of knowledge which is supposed to illuminate the outer darkness but cannot because it is dark itself, Croce arbitrarily introduced four distinct concepts into the pure concept, each of which is a concrete form itself and also material for the one which follows it. As it turns out, having missed the very idea of a subject and an object, a form and a content, as meaningfully different, Croce is unable to establish an active, internal relationship in either of the theoretical concepts, the imaginative or the philosophical. In aesthetics image and feeling may be talked about interchangeably and there is apparently no third alternative. In philosophy a three-term dialectic is missing because the predicate turns out to be a judgment, like that of which it is supposed to be a part; and at times Croce comes close to finding that the subject of the judgment, the intuition, is a judgment too, an intuition conceived, so that the philosophical judgment, like the aesthetic intuition, is a single, static moment describable in different, but basically synonymous terms. In other words, the definitory judgment "Art is feeling imagined," is itself part of an individual judgment before it is predicated of an intuition, because it is the answer to the question "What is art?" and that question is a historically limited and individual event; and a poem, to the extent that it is available to thought as a possible subject of an individual judgment, is an intuition conceptualized or an individual judgment. As a result of these difficulties, there is not enough difference between the parts of the individual judgment for it to be a genuine dialectic.

This failure of Croce's to activate his theoretical concepts is, in my opinion, the reason for his distinction between theory and practice. In his analysis of practical action in the *Filosofia della pratica* Croce recognizes that an actor begins with many desires and one choice and that a genuine struggle of conquest must occur so that the choice may issue in an action. The completed action, the product, is seen to be the result of a process much of which it excludes; that is, the defeated desires are outside the product. Clearly there is no knowledge involved here, especially knowledge in the receptive, realistic sense; one does not take in or receive the given whole; one rejects all but one desire, even though all the desires may be pressing. The strenuous effort required for the rejection is implicitly a deliberate choice not to know, not to receive. So long as knowledge is the passive appropriation of something given, it must remain distinct from action. Because Croce never admitted, however, to the passivity of his conception of theory, he never possessed a solid reason for distinguishing between theory and practice. But because he sensed the actual nature of his position without reasoning it out, he remained loyal to this distinction until the end of his career. This confusion, though not the distinction itself, came from Croce's crucial misstep in the

Logica, as did so many other of his difficulties. He began the *Logica* moving toward a Hegelian dialectic, but lost his way. It was to be Gentile who recovered the direction.

The Origin of Actual Idealism

In a series of lectures given at the Biblioteca Filosofica of Palermo in 1911 and 1912, some of which were then published in the summer of 1913 in his *La reforma della dialettica hegeliana,* Gentile gave Actual Idealism its first form. The concrete concept is here presented as a genuine dialectic of opposites, as that which Gentile finds absent from Hegel's logic and which is clearly missing from Croce's. Gentile's concept is the subject positing its object and knowing itself as positing its object. Nothing is existent, conceivable, or imaginable outside the concept. It is a full dialectical synthesis, ultimate reality itself, the self-conscious or mediate subject, knowing itself as asserting its opposite. The immediate subject, the thesis of the synthesis, and its object, the antithesis, are opposites in this sense: the one posits, the other is posited, the one asserts, the other is asserted. As contradictories they may be said to be action and not-action, thinking and not-thinking: but as opposites, they are action and that which is overcome or surpassed in the action, thinking and that which is thought. The subject and the object are recognized as not only opposite, but also identical by the synthesizing subject, the a priori synthesis, the self-conscious, concrete act of thinking. In every act of thinking the mediate subject recognizes the thought object as the thought of itself as immediate subject. The entire dialectical act is epitomized by Roger Holmes in this way: the thinking subject asks, am I the thinking subject or not? The very question is its own answer as both affirmative and negative. The question as put is the putting of the question and yet it differs from it: they are an identity of opposites.

Now it might be said that if the mediating subject, that which is ultimately concrete and real, recognizes the immediate subject as positing its own opposite but identical thought, then this dialectic collapses into a pseudo-dialectic of two terms only, of the mediating subject and that which it posits or knows. What is known would then be indiscriminately called the immediate subject or the object. Both the immediate subject and the object, that is, would be thought of as the opposite of the mediating subject; they would be the posited, each abstract, and thus real only as posited by the actual thinking itself. Conceived in such a way, they are no more clearly different than are Hegel's Being and Not-Being. Roger Holmes has apparently interpreted Gentile's dialectic in this way in his *The Idealism of Giovanni Gentile,* for he analyzes it as completed in the two terms, the object or *pensiero pensato* and the subject or *pensiero pensante.* The object is abstract and is governed by the laws of traditional logic, the principle of identity and that of the excluded middle. The subject is concrete, governed by the law of the dialectic, the principle that A is not-A. Holmes believes that this two-term dialectic is truly a principle of tolerance. Each subject, each thinker, is thinking his truth, his *pensiero pensante,* as against some one else's error which is his own *pensiero pensato.* All objectified systems, as he sees it, are then of equal worth except as being asserted, except as a subject thinks them, one as his own truth and another as his error. Thus, Holmes says, from Gentile's point of view, materialism is an error, but for the materialist it is *"my* truth." And he chastises Gentile for calling positions other than his own "unthinkable" and "absurd." [5]

Holmes' one grave procedural error in his otherwise brilliant book is that he ignores Gentile's own historical development and simply asserts that Gentile is all of a piece and may be best understood through the study of his one work, the *Sistema di logica,* the first volume of which was published in

1917 and the second in 1923. One of Gentile's basic principles, the one Holmes ignores here, is that philosophy is dialectically identical with the history of philosophy, the principle which led Croce, by his own admission, to identify the definitory and the individual judgments in his *Logica* as he had not done in the *Lineamenti*. This Hegelian principle is the earliest important concept worked out by Gentile and the main one which precedes his discovery of the act of thinking as the ultimately real dialectic of opposites.[6] It grew not so much out of Gentile's purely philosophical thinking as out of his numerous historical writings on philosophy, writings which include two studies on the philosophy of Marx, as well as his *Dal Genovesi al Galuppi: ricerche storiche,* and his *Le origini della filosofia contemporanea.* With some assistance from his later discoveries, I may describe Gentile's identification of philosophy and the history of philosophy in the following manner. One's own philosophy is his own act of thinking: it is its own norm, because it has no model outside itself; it is universal because nothing outside it can be thought; it is necessary because one cannot be thinking other than he is; and it has value because one cannot but be certain that his present thinking is true: these are all essential elements in Gentile's concept of the act of thinking as the ultimately real. Now the object of one's thinking, that which one is asserting as the thought about which he is thinking, this one's own present thinking transcends; and this object will be the most complicated, accurate, and self-conscious error one can conceive; for if one knew of any thought superior to the object of thought which one's own thinking is transcending, by that very knowing of it one would be transcending it. Because it is a series of thoughts,—which were once forms of thinking—that lies within the object of one's thinking, in thinking through the object of one's thought fully, one is actually thinking through a history of philosophy. One's own thinking, one's own philosophy, is a history of philosophy; it unfolds all the thinking that one is in the act of transcending, and nothing is being left out of one's history of philosophy, because if one thinks of anything as left out, by that very thought it is included. To be sure, one may think any part of his thought in such a way as to find in his later thinking that he has been shamefully inadequate, so that his history of philosophy must change and improve as his own philosophy improves. Essentially, however, the whole history of philosophy is the object of one's philosophical thinking.

Now, if one is self-conscious enough to realize that his own thought is true only as actual, only as dialectical thinking and not as thought, he could hardly ignore the inference that the thought which he is striving to transcend must be thought through as an act of dialectical thinking. In other words, one's thinking, the fully real thinking, posits as its object a subject positing its object. One thinks the thoughts of others as those others were once thinking their thoughts and translates them according to one's own thinking. Stating the three-term dialectic in a more common way, one may say that in order to understand the thought of another, one must re-enact his thinking, translating it into one's own thinking. In Gentile's thinking, such a system of thought as thinking is clearly justified as superior to any other. Gentile's use of "absurd" and "unthinkable" may be blameworthy as arrogant, but it does not violate his theory of the concept as the act of thinking thought as thinking.

One's act of thinking is always the exclusion of one other act of thought: just as one is, in his thinking, summing up the history of philosophy, so the immediate predecessor to one's thinking, the thinking which one is denying, was as thinking a summing up of the history of philosophy. Even though one's philosophy then is the history of philosophy, one's thinking transcends only one other act of thought directly, that is, the one closest to it in solving the problems which it considers essential. According to Actual Idealism, and contrary to Holmes' interpretation of it, the better the object which one is transcending, the better one's thinking would be. Thus we are told:

That concept which a historian has of philosophy can be called true only if it is adequate to the historical moment to which he belongs. That of Lange, for example, is evidently false, if one holds his neo-Kantianism superior in nothing, rather as speculatively inferior to pre-Fichtian Kantianism. Every subjectivity deriving from a criterion of judgment inferior to part of the points of view already conquered by reason in history is false, is incapable, therefore, of giving the reasons for all the systems which have thus far appeared. Every subjectivity whatever, aesthetically and philosophically, is false if it leaps outside the modern consciousness at any point in its judgments of ancient systems. . . . Philosophy has criticized and can criticize every system in reality, only by means of the system immediately successive. The philosophic consciousness of the historian must mirror the history of philosophical consciousness in such a way that the re-construction itself must contain, within its historical movement the progressive criticism of the systems.[7]

As a historian of philosophy and thus as a philosopher, Gentile is conceiving of all philosophy as a movement toward the clarification of the relationship between the one and the many, between identity and difference, between the first principle of things and things.[8] In his effort to clarify this fundamental relationship, Gentile has established his dialectic of opposites as the successor to Croce's nexus of distincts. There is evidence, furthermore, that in thinking out his own philosophy Gentile is thinking through not just Croce's thought, but rather Croce's thinking out of his thoughts. He thinks out Croce's thinking at the crossroads, his neglecting the subject, and conceiving of the concept as a mere object partitioned four times, according to its four distinct sub-concepts; and he recognizes that to make four and only four such distinctions will arbitrarily stifle thought rather than encourage it. For the object within the dialectic of opposites is the source of multiplicity itself; the source not of four distinctions, but of all the articulation of both one's thought and one's action. To reduce the distinctions to four, he finds, is to idolize four particular ideas which are basically no different from any other ideas. These four ideas differ, fundamentally, only from the three moments of the dialectical act of thinking: the thesis or immediate subject, the synthesis or mediate subject, and the antithesis or object, the last of which is not multiple, but rather the idea of multiplicity, the opposite of the immediate subject, which is the principle of oneness. With his dialectic of opposites, then, Gentile unifies the one and the many. The act of thinking, which is both active and cognitive, is a synthesis of simplicity and complexity, the very kind of synthesis which Croce himself was in search of during his formative years. Since Gentile worked closely and amicably with Croce during most of those years, it should be no surprise that Gentile's novel theory of the dialectical concept is so intimately related to its Crocean counterpart, the nexus of distincts.

From the evidence available it seems clear that Gentile reformed the Hegelian dialectic in an effort to go beyond Croce's laceration of it by means of his sharp-edged theory of distinction. In an essay written as early as 1907, Gentile criticizes Croce's analysis of what is living and what is dead in Hegel's philosophy.[9] Although he lacks his own dialectic of opposites, he works skillfully with Hegel's, showing that the nexus of distincts and the dialectic of opposites cannot survive together as Croce claimed they could,—though Gentile's efforts to show that the dialectic of opposites must of logical necessity absorb the nexus of distincts and that the nexus is in truth the dialectic with one of the three terms left only implicit are not very convincing.

Nonetheless, it is likely that Croce contributed to Gentile's creation of actualism mainly by leading him to interpret

Hegel's dialectic as no more than a kind of completed Becoming, a Become, the thesis and antithesis of which are not opposites, but contradictories. In fact, Gentile comes close to accepting Croce's analysis of Hegel's dialectic; but instead of accepting the dialectic thus interpreted as a minor part of a nexus of distincts, he rejects it utterly in favor of a reformed dialectic, a genuine synthesis of opposites. He reverses the whole order of the dialectic; instead of beginning with abstract Being as Hegel did, he begins with the concrete act of thinking. Hegel, he finds, failed to establish Becoming as a synthesis, because he could not establish an effective difference between Being and Nothing. The first was immediate indeterminateness, "the pure void," and the second was the absence of determination and of content, or the same thing all over again. Hegel describes them as identified with each other so as to give rise to Becoming; but he admits that the difference between them is ineffable, a matter of opinion; and he excludes opinion, as a form of subjectivity, from the dialectic at this point. Without a difference between Being and Nothing, the identification cannot take place; thus the dialectic vanishes, leaving nothing but a static identity without a difference. From this initial error Gentile finds that several others follow, the most important of which is Hegel's claim that Being truly changes, a claim on which hangs the strength of his extremely elaborate deduction of the categories. In opposition to this, Gentile defines the only change in Being to be its Becoming:

In the actuality of the idea, which is Becoming or the concept (thinking), there is no undetermined which is not such in an absolute way, there is no immediate which would not be absolutely immediate, no Being, in sum, which would not be absolute Being. There is no more or less determined, but rather the undetermined and the determined. The real (the act of thinking) as determined, which has gone beyond and contains within itself the undetermined: the Becoming, in sum, of Being. Actual Idealism sees the change of Being, and hence Being different and multiple outside the actuality of thought, in the *pensato* abstractly considered, in the Platonic manner.[10]

Looked upon as mere facts, looked upon empirically, acts of thought, concepts, and the categories themselves are infinite in number; but taken in their concreteness, as the thought of thinking, all their multiplicity is resolved into unity. It is with this apparently so simple dialectic, in place of Hegel's so intricate one, that Gentile would transcend Croce's nexus of distincts.

The Public Debate Between Croce and Gentile

In a series of three articles, two by Croce and one by Gentile, published in the semi-popular journal *La Voce* in 1913 and 1914, the controversy issuing from Gentile's discovery was opened to a wide public. It is far from fashionable in America for serious thinkers to attack each other openly, and almost inconceivable that they should do so in a popular journal. It would seem that such direct encounters could lead to nothing but heated and unenlightening debate. Croce and Gentile, however, prove that this need not be. Their articles are heated —the best evidence of which, I suppose, lies in the gentle sprinklings of "miei cari amici," "caro Benedetto," and "mio caro Giovanni," which serve to settle the dust on the field of battle. And in the first two articles, which are by far the strongest, each goes so far as to organize his arguments around the amusing idea that the other is a mystic. But behind the debater's tricks, the mock amazement, the efforts to prove the other simply absurd, the perceptiveness of both thinkers is amazing; and it convinces one that neither could have been nearly so sharp without the aggressiveness of the other. Much of the criticism which I have made thus far of Croce's aesthetics and philosophy can be found, at least in an implicit form, in Gentile's article. And the confusion which results from taking Gentile's dialectic to be composed of two terms rather than three lies at the heart of Croce's first article.

Croce's basic claim in his first article,—a claim which is, to be sure, surrounded by a good bit of emotion and wit—is that the actualists deny all distinction and then surreptitiously introduce a distinction between thought as act and thought as fact. One is tempted to dispose of Croce's argument facilely. After all, he is on the defensive and, one might assume, could not possibly understand Gentile; for, if he could, surely he would already have given up his own confused position. Croce is quite right, one might argue, to say that the actualists reject not just certain distinctions, but all distinctions, if by "distinction" Croce means that Herbartian kind of distinction which lies at the basis of his own "nexus of distincts." Such a notion of distinction obliterates unity and multiplicity, and catches only the mirage of a dialectic; in actuality, it establishes nothing but four particular, static, and abstract concepts for the whole of reality itself. And when Croce claims, one might conclude, that the actualists use his "distinction" to distinguish between act and fact, what he is really revealing is his incapacity to grasp a genuine dialectic of opposites.

In fact, however, Croce is pointing out the most serious ambiguity in Gentile's early dialectic, that is, his frequent failure to distinguish it from that two-term pseudo-dialectic which Roger Holmes claimed it always was. At times Gentile has spoken of the object of the dialectic as nature, as the irrevocable past, as sheer error, as the thought which one can no longer think. At other times, to be sure, without distinguishing what he is saying from what he has said elsewhere, Gentile speaks of the object of the dialectic not as nature but as the idea of nature; not as the irrevocable past but as the revocable past; not as unthinkable error, but as the *felix culpa*, the very best erroneous thought conceivable, the thought which one's own thinking re-enacts and transcends as an essential part of its own truth. Behind this confusion lies Gentile's negligence about distinguishing between the pseudo-dialectic of the *pensiero pensante* with the *pensiero pensato* as its object, and the three-term dialectic, with the mediate subject thinking its immediate self as positing its opposite. He neglects this difference even though his dialectic was at first related closely to his theory of the circle composed of philosophy and the history of philosophy, a theory which requires that the dialectic be based upon three terms. Given his interpretation of Gentile's dialectic as having only two terms, Croce is quite right to point out that he himself has something in his own system superior to Gentile's object:

For my part, I had been industrious to deduce nature in the abstract sense as a product of the practical form of the spirit, which mutilates and fixes for its own ends the result of thought and creates an apparent mechanical world or natural world, unthinkable precisely because abstraction as such is unthinkable (except as the consciousness or theory of abstraction itself). And I deduced nature in the concrete sense as the practical form of the spirit itself, in its immediacy of life, of passion, of economic will. . . . The fact, the thought, the past have nothing to do with the . . . mechanical or the natural. If the latter is impossible, the former is eternally re-thinkable: the "irrevocable days" of Ermengarda and the "tempo felice" of Francesca, brought as examples, are yet imagined and re-thought in the poems. . . . It is said that the past does not return; but it does not return precisely because it is all in the present, and cannot return, or so it is pretended, only as abstracted from the present and otherwise mutilated and rendered unreal.[11]

If, that is, the Gentilean dialectic is thought of as composed not of three terms but only of two, so that the immediate subject and its opposite, the object, are reduced to a mere identity which is then considered the object of the synthesizing subject; then it is impossible to distinguish the abstract, unthinkable "mechanical world or natural world" from a concrete object which is vital and active itself, whatever one may call it. And it is impossible to distinguish an impenetrable past from that past which is always present, that very past which Gentile the philosopher thinks as part of his history of philosophy. If the confusion between the pseudo-dialectic and the genuine dialectic is characteristic of early actualism, then Croce is again correct in saying:

> You claim that error, outside the corrective process which qualifies it as such, is truth, and evil, outside the remorse which feels it as evil and frees the spirit from it, is morality . . . and since you must yet differentiate in some way this truth from that which is called truth and this morality from that which is called morality, you have recourse, as I have indicated, to the criterion of past and present, fact and act, and you posit error as past truth and evil as past morality (or truth).
> But in one's past he distinguishes thought from non-thought, good from bad actions. Error and evil exist and do not exist: they exist as positive acts, although deprived of truth and good; they do not exist as privations aware of being privations and yet satisfied with themselves, because the privation just observed, the error and evil enter into the process of transcendence (*superamento*).[12]

With the distinction between the erroneous dialectic and the full dialectic in mind, however, it is quite easy to distinguish error which was once true thought from error as the privation of thought, and to distinguish evil which was good from evil as the privation of goodness. The error, the object of thinking, which is the immediate and indistinguishable identification of the immediate subject and the object, this error is sheer, unthinkable error, the past as irrevocable, the thought which one cannot penetrate. The pseudo-dialectic which posits this unthinkable error, however, can be thought of within the three-term dialectic as itself an error which once was true. That is, Gentile's three-term dialectic is itself the thinking out of Croce's pseudo-dialectic and is its transcendence. In thinking out

Croce's pseudo-dialectic, one finds that Croce is not considering his object as itself a thinking which he can in his own thinking transcend; he is rather repudiating the object as a product whose process cannot be repeated, and is chopping it up and using it for his own purposes; in other words, he is treating the object as if it were a corpse. In fact, one finds this pseudo-dialectic, with its deadening effect, in Croce's analysis of Hegel; he dissects Hegel's thought and puts what is "alive" on one side and what is "dead" on the other. Furthermore, the "history of aesthetics" appended to Croce's *Estetica* is much the same; it is a series of objects carved up so that they all point in his own direction. Croce himself later agreed with a critic who called his history of aesthetics a graveyard. The very idea of unthinkable error, then, proves to be an error which one thinks through as an error once true but now transcended by one's own thought. The pseudo-dialectic as thinking is, like all thinking, a three-term dialectic, but by thinking it through one discovers that it reduces the immediate subject to its opposite. It does what we saw Croce doing again and again, starting out to posit a dialectic of opposites, but concluding in an identity without a difference.

All Gentile's thought, it should now be clear, was the fully dialectical transcendence of the abortive pseudo-dialectic; that is another way of saying that Gentile's thinking was born out of the matrix of Croce's philosophy. Nonetheless, although all this may be abundantly clear from our vantage point, in the arena itself it was not always clear even to Gentile, and most certainly not to many of his followers. Croce could not have chosen a more vital point to criticize if he were seeking to further the transcendence of his own position.

Gentile's immediate reply to Croce's article, however, is a model illustration of what I have said that he should be doing, that is, thinking the thoughts of another as that person was once thinking them and translating them according to one's own thinking. There is, of course, no overt admission from Gentile that he is here avoiding the confusion which is the basic object of Croce's criticism. That would surely be bad debating. In fact, the first long section of Gentile's article seems bent on showing nothing more thoughtful than that Croce and not Gentile is truly the mystic. In other words, it looks as though this is a flyting match, a name-calling contest. Giving vent to his spleen in a clever way is not, however, Gentile's primary objective. He strives to think out the history of Croce's thinking and to transcend it by means of the principle that "all reality must issue from the subject as subject and the subject must conceive of itself in a manner equal to this its function." [13]

After glibly showing that Croce is at least an incipient mystic because of his very distinction between theory and practice— an amusing stunt since Croce had called Gentile a mystic because he rejected all distinctions—Gentile settles down to the serious job of showing Croce what he is ignoring about the nature of his own philosophy. His notion of philosophical knowing, to begin with, the knowing which is defined as the definitory judgment in the *Lineamenti* and as the individual judgment in the *Logica*, is not the only philosophical knowing in Croce's system; in fact, it is not so much knowing as it is the object known. Croce's true form of knowing, which Croce unself-consciously ignores, is the knowing by which he constructs the distinct concepts of knowledge and of practical action. The first form of knowledge, which Croce has posited as a judgment, presupposes practical activity; and between that practical activity and itself it also presupposes the imagination, which tames practical activity so that it can be known philosophically. Croce's genuine knowing, however, the thinking by means of which he constructs the entire system, presupposes nothing; it posits as its object the inferior or passive knowledge and the non-thinking action which Croce tries futilely to filter into the inferior knowledge so that it can somehow be represented there. Croce's true knowing is itself an error which Gentile is transcending because, in my language, it conceives of itself as a two-term pseudo-dialectic, even though it is, in fact, like all thinking, made up of three terms. Croce thinks of the subject thinking as though it were an "object" which can never really know its own object, practical activity. As a matter of fact, however, by means of his actual thinking Croce does come to know that element of his object which he calls "practical activity"; and this genuine knowing is in contradiction with the knowledge which he seeks to know as the other element of his object. His thinking is defective, then, in failing to think of itself as thinking; his failure is a failure of self-consciousness.

Gentile's other telling criticism of Croce has to do with his idea of individuality in aesthetics. From Gentile's point of view, the individuality characteristic of art must have reference to artistic activity itself, to the immediate subject giving form to feeling; it is fundamentally different from the many elements by means of which the artist objectifies or expresses his feeling, from any of the characters, for example, which are made use of in a play. Because the immediate subject of the full dialectic is ultimately at one with the mediate subject, the universal acting or thinking, Gentile identifies individuality and universality in art dialectically. Croce, on the other hand, had kept universality out of art, at least until the *Breviario,* and defined the individuality characteristic of art not as having to do with its activity or form, but as that which characterizes its object or its material. Croce's individual, in other words, is Aristotelian; it is a being which is not the whole and is not in relation to itself and thus free, but is limited and deprived of its intrinsic value: whereas Gentile's individual is Kantian; it is the universal as that which is in relation to itself. Curiously enough, in his theory of practical activity, Croce recognized that the particular individual, one self among other selves, was limited in just the way Gentile says the individual of Croce's aesthetics is; but with his non-integrating mind, Croce failed to make the transfer from his theory of praxis to his aesthetics. In effect, then, Croce has treated the individuality of art as an object, just as he has treated philosophical knowledge as an object. His own thinking was active enough; but whatever he was thinking about, whether it was philosophical thought or aesthetic intuition, he thought about as an object. He did not, that is, conceive of it as a subject positing its object, but instead reduced it to a subject which has already posited its object, so that the subject and object are basically objects with no difference between them, are, in other words, an object.

This Crocean position which Gentile criticises is not radically different from Roger Holmes's conception of Gentile's own position. The temptation to which Croce succumbed and which threatens Gentile's philosophy constantly is the reduction of the three-term dialectic to two terms only. The fact that we lack single words to distinguish the thesis from the synthesis, and must call them both the "subject" or the "Ego" or the "I" or "thinking" in contrast to the "object" or the "non-Ego" or the "non-I" or "thought" contributes to this confusion. Gentile undoubtedly lacked a flair for words, a sensitivity to language comparable to Croce's. If the ideal had become real and, after the publication of Gentile's article in *La Voce*, Croce had admitted to the transcendence of Gentile's thinking over his own, much of the confusion and excessive simplification which has plagued Actual Idealism might well have been avoided.

Croce's second article, in reply to Gentile's, might have been taken as a sign of his weakening, if the confident tone could have been discounted. For Croce has little of importance to say. Most of the article simply asserts that he believes in all the right things. He does, it is true, raise a thoughtful question. He asks how Gentile can, within his system, explain the generation of errors, of the errors which are unthinkable. Gentile's answer, it would seem, should have been ready at hand. He might have said: the error in your philosophy, "caro Benedetto," is that your thought is oriented toward the antithetical moment of the full dialectic, toward the object; you conceive of thinking as thought and the artistically individual act as an individual fact. Habits from your youthful positivism have not been transcended. Another kind of error, Gentile might have added, arises from an excessive concern for the immediate subject; and a third from a concentration upon the mediate subject to the neglect of the thesis and the antithesis. Gentile's own tendency was, to be sure, toward the third kind of error, the very kind of thing which could give rise to Croce's question as to how error arises. For Gentile often writes as though every activity, every act of thinking, must be as full and complete a dialectic as every other. He tends, that is, to neglect the difference between a thinking weighted toward the object and a thinking weighted toward the subject, and between those and a thinking like his own weighted toward the whole and away from its parts. This is the very tendency which could lead to Holmes's misinterpretation of Gentile's dialectic; it is a tendency which Gentile was very slow to overcome. Croce apparently sensed this weakness. But, aside from this astute perception, his article is itself quite weak; he seems to be spinning out words rather than thoughts.

At this point in the controversy, the crucial difference between Croce's method of thought and Gentile's is explicit for the first time; and, since our primary interest is in the originative moments of thinking, it seems proper to pause here in order to sum up this difference as simply as possible. For purposes of clarity I shall break Gentile's single, originative act of thinking into two acts, the one critical and historical, the other constructive and philosophical. Actually, the two acts are one and the second is simply a more articulate form of the first; but the first may be thought of as Gentile's criticism of Croce's thought and the second as his construction of his own. The immediate subject of the first act of thinking is Gentile's identification of himself with the spirit of Croce's logical method. The objective moment of this first act is Croce's articulated system, his "nexus of distincts," his distinction between theory and practice. Now the third moment of this dialectical act, the mediate subject, is Gentile's thinking through of the limitations of Croce's thought. His fundamental criticism is that Croce's articulated system, his theory of philosophical thought and the other distinct forms of activity, contradicts Croce's actual philosophical thinking, and, furthermore, that Croce is unaware of the contradiction. Croce's actual thinking is both practical and theoretical: he makes a system of distincts; and the system, as a product, lacks nothing essential to any product of practical activity. Furthermore, to the extent that he is self-conscious, Croce knows the system he is making in the very act of making it. His thinking, in other words, transcends the objective system, is the actual awareness of the diverse ligatures which unify and differentiate the elements of the objectified system. Croce's knowledge, however, is defective, for he ignores the self-conscious awareness which is an essential part of his act of thought. As a result, his theory of knowledge is also defective: the thought, the concept, within which intuitions are subsumed, is not the mediate, subjective thinking through of the intuitions as explicated by means of abstractions; instead it is itself an abstraction, an objective proposition into which intuitions have somehow or other been inserted. The thought itself contradicts Croce's own act of thinking through the thought; and the intuition as thought contradicts the intuition about which one would think.

Implicit in Gentile's act of denying Croce's method is the affirmation of his own method. In fact, Gentile's negation is an affirmation; the two acts of thinking are actually one, and the negation could not arise except for the affirmation. Let us, however, simplify by describing the affirmative act of thinking as arising out of the negative. The immediate subject of the affirmative dialectical act would be not Gentile's identification with the spirit of Croce's method, but his sense of the need to articulate a concept of thought which transcends the contradictions in Croce's thought. The objective moment, the antithesis, of the affirmative dialectic would be not Croce's nexus of distincts, but Gentile's dialectic of opposites. The mediate subject, the synthesis of Gentile's dialectical act of thinking, would be the self-conscious act of thinking itself, the thinking through of the objective moment so that it is adequate to the need of the immediately subjective moment.

As historian, Gentile has re-enacted Croce's thinking and revealed its limitations; as philosopher, he has thought out the concept of the act of thinking on the basis of which his criticism of Croce rests. Croce's reaction to the originality of Gentile's thought is not, as we have seen, merely a misunderstanding of its novelty; instead it is, basically, Croce's clarification of the ambiguities in what Gentile has done. Gentile appears to blur the difference between the immediate and mediate subjects of his dialectic. He does not always distinguish between objective thought as the antithetical moment of the dialectic of thinking and objective thought as abstracted from that dialectic of thinking. Furthermore, he does not distinguish between acts of thinking dominated by one of the moments of the dialectic rather than by another. As a result of this failure, Gentile cannot easily account for the origin of error; for all thinking appears to be actual and true and thus equally valuable. At this point, then, Gentile is right, but obscure; Croce is wrong, but clear.

After Croce's second article, the third of this series published in *La Voce*, a wise and detached observer might well have said that the open and direct controversy should be halted, and that the thoughts of each man should be allowed to work away within the other without the flaunting of personalities. In fact, that is what a close friend of Croce's, Karl Vossler, wrote to him after reading the first two articles. Vossler assures Croce that he is still sympathetic with his position and opposed to mysticism, and that Gentile's "pensiero in atto" reminds him of Bergson's "slancio vitale:"

> If something like this is being announced in the thought of Gentile, if, that is, it is truly mysticism, I fear that later discussions between you and him can have no other end than that of argumentation *ad hominem*, which moreover are already foretold, especially in your first attack. There would be, in sum, the danger of personal displeasures which could bring a certain coolness into your good and long friendship. This would grieve me. In discussions there is a certain point where personal certainty creeps into the logical truth, and there it is wise to halt, because the "certain" is a respectable category, different from the "true," whether one considers it as a religious fact (as I would wish to) or as a practical fact (as you would wish, if I am not mistaken). Mixed "truths," not distinct from "certainties" nor fused into them, become "invidious" and hateful. In so far as I may know Gentile, it seems to me that the identity of thought with life, both practical and theoretical, is for him something certain, hence undiscussable. With this faith all his life is informed. If not, how could he, so exact and prudent in science, be able to shoot on ahead, so careless and heroically imprudent in practical affairs? In this lies his human greatness and, maybe also, the logical weakness of his philosophy. But if you continue to touch this point, for him vital and lethal, certain woes may occur from which both of you will have pain, and philosophy no advantage.[14]

Vossler began this letter, be it said, by expressing his pleasure at the noble and elevated tone of the polemic. The brilliant kindliness with which he shifts all the dangers of personal weakness away from Croce,—although, to be sure, he claims to see "argumentation *ad hominem*" in the bud only in Croce's article and not in Gentile's—might distract one from the hard truth of what is being said. Even a great thinker, he is suggesting, is not *that* free. Stop while you still can.

They could not, as all know, stop. The argument continued

in reviews and in notes and as an undercurrent in many of the books written thereafter by both men. For years the "coolness" was no more than that; there was bitterness but immense respect; and only when their breach became unequivocally political did the antagonism become invidious and hateful. Both men unquestionably suffered deeply from their failure to stop when Vossler advised it. But Vossler erred in thinking that philosophy could not profit from a combat which was painful in a personal way. Neither man, so far as I know, admitted to having learned anything from the other as a result of the controversy, although both could find that much earlier they had learned from each other. In my opinion, however, quite apart from what they would say, the most important things the two men learned once the controversy became an open one were learned the one from the other. They could not learn directly; while each is rejecting what are often very minor criticisms from the other, he may be found to be accepting without acknowledgement the very word that allows him to overcome a crippling weakness. No thinker, however Olympian he may be, can help taking threats to his deepest convictions most personally. But if he is a great thinker, he will learn and develop and transcend himself in spite of the pain. Whatever their denials, both Croce and Gentile continued to feed upon each other.

Omodeo's Actualistic Historiography

Even as early as the end of 1913 it was too late for Croce and Gentile to stop the controversy which they had stirred up. It was already of such widespread interest that Giuseppe Prezzolini could write:

With 1914, then, *La Voce*, still directed by Giuseppe Prezzolini, plans to take up again the tradition of Italian idealism which has always inspired many of its collaborators, but as a practical and daily exercise of arms, penetrating into the national life, embracing every order of facts, taking its occasion from the most dispersed happenings in order to lead back to the unique light. The example of what we intend to do is so near that it is useless to extend ourselves with more words. *La Voce*, like every other review, will be that which its collaborators make it. And those who mean to continue working with us are requested to write us.[15]

But quite without any such popular appeal, a number of superior students of Gentile's at the Biblioteca Filosofica of Palermo were engaged in translating the various aspects of Croce's philosophy into Actual Idealism.

Although much that these students did merely repeated Gentile's thought, several of them worked out a most significant criticism and translation of Croce's theory of the pseudo-concept. If our analysis of Croce thus far has made him appear less sturdy than his power and popularity warrant, it may be primarily because we have slighted this particular notion. All generalizations, abstractions, and empirical hypotheses—whatever is not concrete and universal—are in Croce's system not concepts but pseudo-concepts. Pseudo-concepts are not theoretical, but practical: they do not give knowledge; for the most part they merely serve to classify what historians have already come to know. Those who work with pseudo-concepts—all thinkers who do not qualify as artists, philosophers and historians—classify things known by others for purposes of preservation. Putting scientists and philologists in so ignominious a position was part of Croce's whole attack upon positivism, and at first it was justified as countering an opposite excess. But whatever its immediate justification, it was emotional indulgence. Croce makes philosophy and history seem as significant as he does primarily by contrasting them constantly with mere philology and mere science, and his very shaky concept is made to seem solid because of its elevation above all pseudo-concepts. The entire contrast depends, it may already be clear, upon Croce's distinction between theory and practice. With the rejection of this distinction by the actualists, the sharp separation of science from philosophy and philology from history fell too.

The actualists themselves interpreted science and philology, like everything else, in the light of their three-term dialectic. They argued that Croce, with his reduction of these two forms of study to the classification of pseudo-concepts, was concentrating upon only one of the dialectical moments, the objective. In effect, they were saying, he is cutting the thesis and synthesis right out of science and claiming that it is nothing but the antithesis. Although nothing so extreme could be said against Croce's analysis of practical activity itself, his analysis of the pseudo-concepts comes perilously close to such a contemptuous diminution. Croce, it is true, does back away from his position by saying that his analysis refers only to the "sciences," not to the scientists themselves, who are, as human beings, philosophers and historians as well as scientists. Their primary activity, however, and their proper objective remain the same: classification of material so that it may be preserved in anticipation of the day when it may be subjected to genuine thinking. Adolpho Omodeo, in the field of historical research, and Guido De Ruggiero, for the natural sciences, wrote decisive revindications of such studies as forms of genuine thinking.

Omodeo's "Res gestae e historia rerum" [16] was composed as transcending Croce's "Storia, cronaca e false storie." [17] Croce's conception of genuine history was worked out at the expense of mere chronology and philological erudition. Real history for Croce is contemporary, which means that the historian begins with a practical problem, a contemporary one, and that he works with documents which are contemporary. What the genuine historian then does is to re-create the practical events of the past by means of his imagination and to judge them according to his concrete concept, partitioned as it is into the four particular concepts of Beauty, Truth, Utility, and Goodness. He can, Croce claims, know actions of the past because they are man-made: what man makes, he can know; nothing more, nothing less. Between the maker or the doer and the knower there is, to be sure, a gap. Croce fills it with the chronicler and erudite collector of facts. The living history comes first; then comes the dead record, what the chronicler dustily does; finally, the true historian comes to re-vivify the past, so that what was once active, but then a dead husk, comes alive as the truly known.

The actualist Omodeo, like all his fellows, approaches every problem with the dialectic of opposites to the forefront. The dialectic is reality itself. Every person and every thing, every act and every thought, every temporal and spatial distinction, are real and meaningful only as part of this dialectic. For the actualist, to call history contemporary is to say that every action is at one with the pure act, which is an eternally present activity and which spins all distinctions out of itself, out of its objective moment, even the distinctions between past, present, and future.[18] There is no gap comparable to Croce's between a past action and the historian's present knowing of it. The past action is contemporary because it achieves presence; it is part of the pure act. This means that the single man, as distinct from other men, is not just one object among many. He is also the immediate subject asserting his limited self and the whole world of multiplicity in which he bargains and tussles. And he is also the mediate subject, conscious of itself not only as the immediate one asserting itself, but also as the opposite many, among which the one limited self in contrast to other selves may be counted. The particular action of a certain group of conspirators is in reality part of the act, both immediate and mediate, both conscious and self-conscious, both an action and a knowing. The historian who writes about the particular action of this group of conspirators is, in reality, also part of the dialectical act within which he understands the ultimate oneness of himself and the conspirators, and also the endless differences which separate him in time, space, and nature from them. The primary point to notice here is that because of the ultimate oneness within which all distinctions occur, Omodeo does not have a gap to account for between past action and present knowing. As part of the dialectical act, the past action is both assertion and awareness, it is acting and knowing; it in itself is essentially like the action which we call historiography, the activity in which one man imagines the act of another and judges it, or imagines his own past activity and judges it.

It would be simply crude to misjudge Omodeo and think of him as saying that since all men are mystically at one, the good historian simply feels himself at one with the object of his "study" in the pure act and then writes away, ecstatically. The objective moment is extremely important in historiography: the historian can understand his personage and thus be at one with him only through the most scrupulous analysis of all that distinguishes that personage from himself; that is, all the differences in time and place, differences which the historian can understand only if he studies not just a particular period in the past, but also the period in which he himself lives and also the periods of other historians who have made his personage the object of their study. The actualistic historian, then, will need all the help of chroniclers and philologists that the Crocean historian needs. But he will not, like his Crocean counterpart, think of these useful collectors as merely useful, and as working with nothing but dry husks. It is true that the efforts of such collectors are heavily weighted toward the objective moment of activity; but, nonetheless, chroniclers are themselves ultimately at one with the actor whose deeds they record and with the historian who makes use of their dating of events. The subjective drive and the self-conscious awareness of the chronicler may well be weaker than those of the historian who is making use of his distinctions; but all the essential elements of historiography are present in chronicling and philology, for they are both knowledge and action, the complete dialectical synthesis. As Omodeo says:

The philologist most infatuated with a false objectivism, the philologist for whom the sources themselves are history, and not the spirit which revives the sources, how could he permit himself to correct a text, or reconstruct a mutilated epigraph, or deny the historicity of Romulus or of any one of the seven kings of Rome, if he were not certain of carrying within himself the criterion of truth, if in that act of his he were not affirming the absoluteness, the universality of his own thought? [19]

The most minute historical analysis is, he tells us, a part of the full dialectical synthesis:

The analysis of a document is an analysis only in respect to a spiritual moment no longer actual, in respect to the document as a document; but, as a spiritual activity, this is a synthesis. It is that document resolved, that document which rises up truly to the level of a document, which, even if we reject it as valueless, teaches us something; it is our reconstruction, the re-evaluation of that document in our experience.[20]

Just as important, the steady implication of Omodeo's article—an article written at a time when he was preparing to write significant works in religious and political history—is that the great historian must, as part of his very historiography itself, be first-rate at philology, must be constantly evaluating and re-evaluating his sources and his documents. Croce's separation of history from philology not only depressed the prestige of philology, but also weakened the quality of highly synthesizing and self-conscious historiography by suggesting that it somehow began only after the more menial tasks were completed. Omodeo's integration of historical philology with genuine historiography, an integration which most Italian historians have come to accept, proved to be an improvement over Croce's theory of historiography. Mario Fubini, for example, has argued, in an exchange with Croce, that the mere analysis of the various implications of a complex word in a poem is properly a part of the full synthetic act of literary criticism or history. Croce conceded the truth of this; in fact, he claimed that he had always said that very thing. But he came to see himself as saying that kind of thing primarily, I should say, because of the arguments of actualists, opposed as they were to the Crocean distinction of theory and practice.

De Ruggiero's Theory of Science

As early as 1913 De Ruggiero did precisely the same thing for the natural sciences as Omodeo did for historical research. In a much more elaborate way than that of Omodeo, he showed that no science can be understood from an analysis of its objective moment alone. His basic argument against Croce is that the moments of science are identical with the moments of consciousness itself. Croce, of course, would grant that consciousness is imaginative, conceptual, and historical as well as abstractive and classificatory. But he would argue that the natural sciences are only abstractive and classificatory. It may indeed be difficult to believe from our perspective that Croce could have claimed such things. But he had arrived at them in battle against naturalism and against the positivism which he had himself indulged in as a youth. In context his claim makes sense, excessive as it was. Possibly he limited his studies to textbooks which merely classified the results of the creative and exploratory activity at the heart of every serious science, whether natural or social.[21] He was, after all, a literary critic and might well have been cut off from the serious talk of scientists whose minds would have been lively enough to impress him with the vigor and the originality of their studies.

Unlike Croce, De Ruggiero took seriously the scientific way of thinking. Here is the full scientific process, as De Ruggiero describes it in actualistic terms:

The positing of the subject as otherness, as development, is the positing of the relationship of subject-object, not as the unity of a pre-existent dualism, but as a reciprocal connection. The moment of objectivity is that of pure ideality, of negation, and as such it is non-being. Reality has to do with the being which contains within itself the non-being, and, that is, it has to do with becoming as knowing, as the development of science. In the concreteness of knowing, the subject posits itself denying itself; and this negation is the object. But it is nothing except for the affirmation and hence it is transcended in so far as it is posited. Subject and object do not exist except through this reciprocal conversion; taken in themselves, they have nothing but a transcendental value, as the abstract moments of knowing, whose concreteness is their synthesis.[22]

Croce would distinguish science as excluding both subjective or imaginative activity and logic, the definitory and individual judgments; he envisaged science as abstract ideas collected in a neat form so that they may prove useful for theoretical activity. De Ruggiero, on the contrary, defines science as the dialectical relationship between imagination, thought, and thinking. The first, immediately subjective moment of science is imaginative; it is like play, the asking of questions, just supposing. Properly understood, the second moment of science is not the inert object, the table of classification; it is rather the subject positing its object, mere supposing negating itself through analysis and experiment. The synthesizing moment, the mediate subject, becoming as knowing, is the constant development from questions to answers which then in turn give rise to new questions. In his lengthy and at times obscure monograph, this seems to be approximately what De Ruggiero claims. At the very least, he comes much closer to what serious scientists say they are doing than anything Croce has suggested; and he does not imply that one ought to banish the biologists from the universities on the grounds that they are merely pricking pins through butterflies and then arranging them in a pretty display. In sum, what De Ruggiero claims is that science actualizes all moments of the dialectic just as philosophy does.

From our point of view, we may say that Croce misunderstood both historical research and science because he saw every form of thinking different from his own, every kind of thought which he felt he was above, even though he might indulge in it in lax moments, as wholly objectified. His own act of thought was always composed of two terms rather than three, and he thought of that about which he was thinking as detached and complete and thus statically analyzable by his own thinking. And, of course, he did not think of his own thinking as a dialectical process at one with that which he was investigating. The whole bent of his mind, even after he had developed an interest in Hegel and in the concrete concept, remained separative, and worked against his desire to integrate and unify the various forms of activity in a single philosophy. His system appears to be destined not to hold together from the very start. The actualists, on the contrary, were all bound to make everything hang together. One of them, in fact, Maggiore by name, set out to show that madmen are not so very different from ordinary people who make errors in thought. Croce, who at this time was being accused from many sides of fundamental errors, found the idea quite amusing. Gentile defended Maggiore's argument as a truly human one, as showing that madmen are still human and differing from erring mortals only in degree, not, as Croce would have preferred, in kind.

Flaws in Early Actualism

Like any movement which wins popularity, Actual Idealism developed certain excesses, upon which most of its critics concentrated their attention. Even though the critics were prone to seek out some ignorant perversion of Gentile's thought rather than the thought itself, the general tone of criticism was intelligent for fifteen years or so. Only later did it become fashionable to fire away with such Crocean epithets as "philosophical diarrhea," "philosophical cretinism" and "intellectual narcissism." The most obvious and probably the most frequent excess to be found among Gentile's followers, though rarely in Gentile's own writing, was the stamping of an individual action with the formula for the dialectic of opposites as a substitution for actually thinking through the action as a new realization of the dialectic. This use of formulas in place of thought, resembling as it does Croce's habit of branding various events with one of his particular concepts, led Croce to name actualism "philosophical cretinism." He describes Vito Fazio-Allmayer's habit of calling every action philosophical in the following way. Having experienced the dialectic as a philosopher, Fazio-Allmayer wishes to call all dialectical experiences philosophical:

Many years ago now, on the occasion of a great cholera epidemic in southern Italy, I met in a small village a boy who, from hearing so much talk of cholera, had come ingenuously to call all pain "cholera"; and he said, for example, of a prick which he had on his finger, "I have a cholera on the finger." [23]

Omodeo, as a matter of fact, makes much the same kind of criticism as an actualist of De Ruggiero's *La filosofia del cristianesimo*, which was published in 1920:

There is too much De Ruggiero, too much actual idealism, and too little of the scent and the color of Christian thought. De Ruggiero's idealism remains a little too much formula, and is not sufficiently resolved into the historical category which re-lives the past, tranquilly, in its "reason for being" and in its reasons for not being more.[24]

Eugenio Garin has argued that such a tendency was inevitable because Gentile had juxtaposed, without mediation, absolute Unity and infinite multiplicity;[25] but that is based upon a misunderstanding of the dialectic.

Another excess into which actualism was carried may be found in its most pronounced form in Gentile himself; that is, negligence about distinguishing rhetoric from philosophical thinking. His theory that action and knowledge are at one in the dialectic is soundly thought out; but he seems to suggest that there is no difference between philosophy in the strict sense and haranguing a group of citizens to try to be a little more patriotic. Properly conceived, rhetoric is polarized toward the objective side of the dialectic; the one individual has distinguished himself from all the others, the less fortunate people, and he is trying to coerce them by words to be more like him. In philosophic thought the particular man strives to rise above himself as one among many and to be fully conscious of the pure act of thinking itself. Rhetoric assumes a certain completeness of what one has to say; the essence of philosophy is that it is an endless struggle to achieve greater clarity, precision, and comprehension of the nature of thinking than has yet been achieved. Philosophy is ceaseless self-transcendence; rhetoric succeeds as transcendence over others. By failing to keep the two kinds of thinking distinct, Gentile gave far too much importance to his own rhetoric and to that of others. Such a perversion is much closer to being inevitable than the "cretinism" is, for Gentile felt that the oldest malady of Italy was its habit of separating thought from everyday life. He believed that since the Renaissance the individual in Italy had opposed himself, in a strictly aesthetic development, to both history and nature, and that only with a culture in which the problems of the intelligence and those of life are no longer distinguished could Italy be reborn.[26] But nothing even in this belief would have led necessarily to Gentile's calling Mussolini a great philosopher.

Such excesses, however, blindnesses of the little man who must hide within every thinker, no matter how serious and strenuous he may be, are easily criticized and have little to do with the kind of thinking which makes Gentile and other Actual Idealists of interest. The necessary criticism of actualism, the criticism which alone could keep it from becoming nothing but "un bizantineggiare su parole vuote prive di vita," as Garin said it did in fact become,[27] was that it must develop the nature of each moment of the dialectic more fully. If this criticism could have been made in a precise enough form, the excesses which we have just described could have been avoided or at least made less damaging. If the objective moment of the dialectic, for example, had been given more weight as the principle of multiplicity itself, it might have bridged the gap between the absolute one and infinite multiplicity, so that events would not have been reduced to mere instances of the pure dialectic. And if more attention had been given to the distinction between the antithetical object of the dialectic and the mediate subject, the confusion between rhetoric and philosophy could have been lessened.

Santino Caramella offered a plausible reform of the subjective moments of Gentile's dialectic, with one of the earliest strategies to reconcile Croce and Gentile. He argued that because it is impossible to deduce any distinctions which can stand solidly within the objective moment of the dialectic, we should make our distinctions within the "formal" part, and that these distinctions should be, to be sure, just those four which Croce had already made:

The historical course of post-Kantian idealism has shown the ship-wreck of every attempt to deduce, beyond the form in itself and the formality of the content, the content itself in its concreteness. I see "qualcosa" but not the "quale" of the "qualcosa." The infinite va-riety of the object and the cause of the single concrete experience as precisely that, are not deducible in any way: having wanted to try this has been the great need of the post-Kantians, but also their failure. In order for the deduction to be possible, experience would have to be finite, and instead it is infinite. Whence beyond the formal theory of the spirit there remains the individuality of the content, and its cause; there remains, that is, speaking frankly, the *mystery*. Not that the light will not penetrate this mystery too; the individuality of the content explains itself with its history, its cause is clarified by its end: but history and the end mean *then*, not *before* or *now*. . . . Every force which carries the spirit nearer the mystery is fruitful. Such is the circular phenomenology of Croce.[28]

Until Caramella's article, so far as I have made out, the run-ning argument has been that Croce's four distincts should be taken as divisions of the antithetical moment of the dialectic, and that he had reduced the infinite distinctions of the object to a meager four. Caramella is claiming that the infinite and contingent multiplicity of the object should remain, but that a quadruple edge should be put on the form, on the form into which the endlessly variable material then flows. Contrary to Caramella's denials, however, this creates a dualism between the purely formal becoming, the "eternal ideal history" of the four distincts in the pure form, and the movement of concrete history, a dualism similar to that of Croce's as De Ruggiero had interpreted it several years before.[29] If Caramella had been right in his analysis of the dialectic as composed of only two terms, if it were a formal becoming into which rolled the ma-terial in need of a form, then the dialectic would have been so crude that the splitting up of its form would have been neces-sary. But as a three-term dialectic, it offers possibilities for the development of its three moments so that no arbitrary and ex-traneous distinctions need be introduced.

There was space for Caramella's criticism, however, because the actualists were neglecting, more than anything else, the "pure form," that is, the immediate subject, in its relations with the object and the mediate subject. Gentile's most brilliant work before *La filosofia dell' arte* of 1931, his two-volume *Sistema di logica come teoria del conoscere,* led to, and actually deserved, severer criticism of the same kind. While Croce reviewed the second volume playfully, like a deft courtroom lawyer, claiming that Gentile was in truth a mystic, or else he was panlogistic or a phenomenologist,[30] Armando Carlini wrote a series of three articles which lay bare the most serious weakness of actualism. If one discounts Carlini's "personalism," his criticism comes down to this: since about 1912 there have been two basic motives behind Gentile's thinking, one Hegelian, idealistic and rational, the other romantic and emphasizing the immediate intuition of the interior life; Gentile has been concentrating almost wholly on the first and neglecting the second. Spaventa, according to Carlini, had worked out a "Metaphysic of the Mind" through his analysis of the act of thinking as unable to grasp itself, and thus as always grasping an object, a "pensato," which was mere nature, that which is wholly different from itself. Croce, he finds, went beyond Spaventa by making the object of thinking history and psychology. He could not, any better than Spaventa, think out a thinking which could grasp itself; but at least the object of Croce's thinking was not utterly alien to it, it was at least human. Gentile, by 1912, had gone beyond both Spaventa and Croce with his concept of thinking as the act of thinking oneself "and thus as self-creation—of the self (one notes) as subject, not as object. It also concerns the self as object, but in so far as the objectivity is a moment of the subjectivity." [31] Carlini thinks, however, that instead of developing the "coincidence of that act of thinking with the personality or spiritual individuality which is realized freely in it," Gentile has been backsliding and that the object of his act of thinking has become more like Spaventa's and less like Croce's. He has, that is, concentrated so much on the object as object, on the abstract Logos, on those elements of the object which are furthest from the immediate subject, that even his subject, which grasps itself in the object, is proving to be more like a mere object, more like nature, than like the living personality. Although one cannot be blind to the passages in the *Sistema* in which Gentile speaks of the mediate subject knowing itself as positing or asserting its opposite but identical object, Carlini is correct in the general direction of his argument. In the *Sistema* Gentile drastically slights the immediate subject and thus tends to reduce the thesis to the antithesis and to speak of the dialectic as though it had only two terms, as though the mediate subject were not thinking itself as asserting its opposite, but were thinking merely its own opposite, the object. It should be recalled that it is on the basis of his analysis of the *Sistema* that Roger Holmes defines Gentile's dialectic as having only two terms, the *pensiero pensante* and the *pensiero pensato*. Nor is Gentile's effort to rebut Carlini at all convincing.[32] His statements can, with a little wrenching, be made to imply that he has lost his hold of the third term, the immediate subject, of the dialectic:

There are no examples, neither doctrines, with which others can edify us, if these examples are not our examples, if these doctrines are not the free construction of our spirit in its infinite solitude. When others are not non-I . . . they are completely identified with the I, who in this company finds no limit of any kind to its own expansion in the infinite world, which is its own. Every great example of the creative spirit is the transcendence of multiplicity, the creation of universal consensuses through the mediation of the forms of spirituality, which resolve within themselves the universe of things and of persons in the unity of immortal, unmultipliable forms.[33]

Gentile is giving far too much emphasis to the completed dialectic, to the achieved unity, and is virtually ignoring the process and development of the dialectic, in which the mediate subject transcends by means of objectification the immediate subject, although remaining at one with it. Ten years before, Gentile was not thinking in an "infinite solitude"; he was at one with that most diverse Croce, whose thinking he was re-thinking and transcending. The fully active dialectic of opposites, it hardly needs to be said, is not easy to hold on to. The very feebleness of Gentile's reply to Carlini's articles—he says nothing new and reveals little thought—suggests that he has been caught off guard. But within a few years, certainly by 1927, he is repairing the damage of the neglect by the actualists of the thesis of the dialectic, of its immediately subjective moment.[34]

Early Actualistic Aesthetics

As late as 1920 Luigi Tonelli, who was certainly not very sympathetic with Croce, begrudgingly admitted that Croce's thought in aesthetics was as yet unsurpassed.[35] The actualists may have surpassed Croce in their concept of the dialectic of opposites, and in their studies of logic, historiography, and the theory of the natural sciences; but in what had always been Croce's stronghold, aesthetics, they scarcely began to translate and to transcend Croce until the late twenties. Croce himself, for that matter, made far more important changes in aesthetics before 1920 as a result of actualistic arguments on the unity of thinking as the pure act than any of the actualists themselves did. For by battering away at the weaknesses of Croce's logic, the actualists were helping him at the very source of all his trouble, of the trouble not just in his logic, but also in his aesthetics. He needed no help in reading aesthetically; he did, however, need help in understanding the nature of thinking so that his thought about art could be more coherent. This help, I hope it is now clear, the actualists gave him.

In a handful of articles, it is true, certain actualists make some categorical assertions about art, and one may be tempted to read into them what becomes explicit thought only in Gentile's *La filosofia dell' arte* of 1931. In general, however, these assertions are not enfleshed, they are asserted in a skeletal way in order to fill out the revolutionary scheme of actualism. The actualists are rather heavily asserting the complexity of art in opposition to Croce's assertion of its simplicity. Very early in the development of actualism, for example, Vito Fazio-Allmayer identifies art fully with philosophy. Says he, the aesthetic intuition is self-consciousness:

The work of art is the creation and transcendence of the I itself, it is not the immediate life of the spirit, but, like all life, mediation. Leopardi, who was bewildered before the eternal enemy "che ascosa a comun danno impera," mediates his vision of nature in the concept of transcendence, of the eternal contradiction between the I and the non-I. The Leopardi who sings this vision of his transcends it, and because of this transcendence he may cry to his heart, "ormai disprezza te, la natura, il tristo fato. . . ." This Leopardi who sings is the act of thought in which that I which has "il tristo fato" against itself is transcended, is posited there as subject opposite nature; but it is not the true subject of this moment, it is not the I who sings. The I who sings contains within itself along with nature that other I which is limited by it; and it observes them, one against the other, serene in its divine act. Thus art is act, is self-consciousness. With this, one attains the identity of art and of philosophy.[36]

This argument seems much too easy. Yes, one wants to be able to assert that artistry is self-conscious, but must it be no different at all from philosophy? We may grant that the immediate I, or subject, must somehow or other be transcended even in a poem. But what, one needs to know, is that immediate I? Certainly it is not the persona of the poet confronting nature within his poem; that is not the immediate I, but part of the object, one of the many elements by means of which the poet expresses himself, as much a part of the object as the nature against which it stands.

Elsewhere we may find Guido De Ruggiero, who of course agrees that art is philosophy, describing the artistic dialectic as a genuine struggle, as quite different from the serene observations of Fazio-Allmayer's mediate subject:

> The artist's effort to equal nature turns out to be an effort to equal himself, in his most intimate ideality. Whence the distinction between art and nature which is presented in the genesis of the work of art tends to a higher and more reflective unification. This act is not the spirit trying to conform to a model, but rather the spirit realizing itself more profoundly. . . . The realization of this work lies in the conquering of the spontaneity of life and nature by means of reflection.[37]

In contrast to Fazio-Allmayer, who saw art as the philosophic awareness of certain oppositions within the dialectical object, De Ruggiero here speaks of it as the strenuous movement from subject to object, from nature and spontaneity to reflection. Although he accounts for the immediate subject, he appears to collapse the mediate subject into the object. His dialectic is active enough, but seems to lack the self-consciousness which one would expect from art which is identical with philosophy.

Gentile alone during this early period of actualism writes suggestively enough about art to make one think that if he put his mind to it he could pass beyond the formulas:

> What is the subject of a judgment without the predicate? Sense, says Vico, as Kant and Rosmini will also say; that is, sensation: not an object but the subjectivity itself of the subject which does not yet reflect upon itself, and does not possess itself, does not think itself. But at the same time it is thought, because this is the living contradiction of art as it is the vital contradiction of the subject of every judgment: a something unthinkable which is thought. Here is the profound significance of the a priori synthesis in which thought consists. It needs a subject which would be the contrary of the

predicate, that is, unthinkability itself; but in the act which needs it and seizes it, its unthinkability is denied, and the act thinks it identifying it with the predicate with which it equates it. And thus art always has something ineffable to say, a "non so che divino," which is poetic enthusiasm and furor, indominatible, ungraspable by thought; in sum, nature. All the same, this nature is not realized if not as displaying itself to thought, and thinking itself, since the poet who sings listens to his song moved, and in hearing his own voice judges it. Art exists in criticism, as nature, always, in thought. The artist can be without the criticism of others, he cannot be without his own, shadow to the body of his art.[38]

Nothing before *La filosofia dell' arte* is fuller than this. All three terms are at work; the principle of art, the immediate subject, is clearly distinguished and meaningfully related to the full dialectic and thus could be related to an existent poem. The notion of the poet as listening, emotionally moved, to his own song and judging it is, to my knowledge, the first suggestion of Gentile's magnificent conception of poetic speech as the dialectical identification of the word being spoken and the word being heard. At the most, however, the idea is a hint. It must wait ten years for its full development, for Gentile had other, more pressing obligations.

In his 1921 article in *L'Arduo* De Ruggiero picks up an idea expressed the year before by Gentile concerning not the impossibility of translating poetry as Croce had always asserted, but the inevitability of such translation.[39] Just as the poet criticizes his poetry as he writes, so we criticize it as we read and thus in a sense translate it into our own language. There is no aesthetic experience, then, free of thought and judgment. Even when one gives himself up to Dante's poetry and reads it as purely as possible, he is, according to De Ruggiero, making comments on it with his eyes, with his way of reading, and with his way of understanding. The best poetic reading then is not an utter identification of the reader with the poet, but a spiritual collaboration between them.[40]

Finally, De Ruggiero argues that when one comes to write about Dante, he should not distinguish him from, say, Thomas Aquinas as a poet from a philosopher, but rather as one person from another, as Dante from Aquinas in his unmistakable individuality. For, we are told, the value of the artist does not reside in the force which he exerts to express himself in a more transparent way, but in the force which he exerts

to make himself more truly man. What must be most energetically denied is the mere *literary* development of what is called art. An expression which had its end and limit in that would generate the "letterato" and not the artist. Art becomes more truly art in so far as it more profoundly denies all the particularity and the initial distinction of its being, and, forgetting itself, descends more deeply into the common root of spiritual activity.[41]

However noble this may sound, it seems to imply that reality is composed of nothing but the one dialectical act and infinite multiplicity, the very error of which Garin accused actualism.

Still very strong in his aesthetics, Croce was ready to handle such nonsense. In all the volumes which De Ruggiero has written, Croce tells us, he has never concerned himself with any poet or artist,[42] an omission which might explain his ignorance:

For De Ruggiero the true and real categories are not art, philosophy, science and such, but persons, and, without incommoding Dante and Thomas Aquinas, those of our daily acquaintance, Peppino, Giovannino, Gaetanino, Michelino, and so forth. It is serious, but it is thus. Reality is to be individuals physically and empirically distinct. I have believed until now that not those names were in truth real, but rather the acts and series of acts which the unique spirit accomplishes and which are only empirically and naturalistically grouped under those names.[43]

Of course, Croce is joking, as he does so often in *La critica*. But there is enough wrong with actualistic aesthetics at this stage of its toddling for it to be the subject of humor. One's democratic affection for the delivery boy Michelino should not rouse him at this point against Croce.

Besides, Croce's serious reaction in aesthetics to Actual Idealism does not occur in the informal parts of *La critica* or, for that matter, in any direct comments which he makes about his amicable enemies. By 1917 a new Croce is to be found in both his essays of practical criticism and those of a theoretical nature, one who has taken the actualistic logic very seriously and has formulated a new conception of art superior to anything that the actualists were themselves thinking about at that time. One fights and jokes, most of the time, for personal dignity, comfort, and entertainment. But one thinks for the truth.

Chapter Four

Croce's Mature Aesthetics: Art as Cosmic

*T*he controversy between Croce and the Actual Idealists had very little to do with aesthetics directly. When art was in question the actualists were rather absurd and Croce was full of laughter. Croce and Gentile opposed each other primarily over the nature of thought, with Croce arguing for the nexus of distincts and Gentile for a dialectic of opposites. Of secondary questions aesthetics was the least important, with logic, historiographical research, and the natural sciences drawing far more attention from both sides of the controversy. But when Croce and Gentile left the arena and withdrew within themselves to think about aesthetics, then one might almost say that instead of opposing each other, each became the other. Or, at the very least, it may be said that the most important changes that take place in their philosophies as a result of the controversy occur in their aesthetics.

Before Gentile could do much with aesthetics he had to recognize the sensuousness and immediacy of art. The complexity of art, its philosophical implications and active and dialectical elements he was quick to admit; but its simplicity, its elements of feeling and intuition, were slighted in his early actualistic writing.[1] As we shall see in the next chapter, however, his *La filosofia dell' arte* and other writings of the late twenties and early thirties give prominence to these elements of simplicity, to the very aspects of the dialectic which Armando Carlini could claim, as late as 1924, that Gentile was almost wholly neglecting. Croce, on the other hand, was so dedicated to the simplicity of art that even when he tried to complicate it with a dialectic in his *Breviario* of 1913, that dialectical form of art collapsed almost at once into a form of immediate, emotional awareness. Just as Gentile's problem was to introduce simplicity into art without losing his sense of its complexity, so Croce's was to work out a concept of art as complex without capitulating and making it indistinguishable from philosophy. Croce achieved this synthesis of the simplicity and the complexity of art much earlier than Gentile did, and his achievement is compactly grouped in three theoretical essays written in 1917 and 1918 and now to be found in his *Nuovi saggi di estetica,*[2] and in several essays of practical criticism, the most important of which is his monograph on Ariosto of 1917. Croce's achieved synthesis, however, was extremely fragile; and, as we shall see, it soon broke apart and remained in fragments thereafter.

Art as Cosmic

In our analysis of Croce's new conception of art, of what has come to be known as his third aesthetics, and of its breakdown, we must continue translating not just words, but thoughts; that is, we must continue incorporating Croce's thought into our thinking rather than obliterating our thinking in his thought. In order to do this without rendering his thought lifeless, without making it a corpse which we then dissect, it is necessary that we think out his process of thinking his thoughts. That is, our thinking must be a full, three-term dialectic.

Our task is complicated immensely by the fact that Croce,

master stylist that he was, did not write as he thought. As editor and main contributor for *La critica*, Croce cultivated his early tendency to write sentences each of which seemed complete and transparently clear in and by itself. He seemed to carry the Goethean aphorism that poetry is "the cry of its occasion" to the extremity of making each sentence the cry of its occasion! Now if one confuses Croce's process of thinking with his process of writing, if, that is, one plays the common language analyst with Croce, one will soon be driven to ignorant contempt or embarrassed despair, as the few comments on Croce in *Aesthetics and Language,* edited by William Elton, bear out all too clearly.[3] Croce writes always with an immediate audience in mind and he has a number of polemical points which he wishes to keep in the foreground. Even though thinking much like an actualist, Croce will arrange his thoughts so that he appears to be opposing actualism; and, although he is making a drastic change in his aesthetics, he is committed to the position that he is doing no more than deepening his own thought. Unless one discounts his journalistic tactics, his thought will inevitably appear contradictory and full of arguments proving nothing. In truth, however, beneath the journalism he is thinking out a conception of art as both simple and complex, as both a knowing and a making.

According to Croce's new aesthetics, an artistic action, like every practical action, is the domination by one feeling of all other feelings in the world of the man who performs the action. In practical action, however, the one feeling, the genuine intention, dominates the others by rejecting and repudiating them; whereas in artistic action, the one feeling dominates the others by including them within itself, by drawing them all together in a single complex image the unity of which depends upon it, the dominant feeling. Practical activity is exclusive; artistic activity is inclusive. Thus it is that in these essays of 1917 and 1918 Croce can speak of art as cosmic, as having a certain "totality" which is absent from practical action. The dominant feeling of a poem works differently, furthermore, from the dominant feeling of any practical action, because every artist worthy of the name is controlled by another feeling, by what Croce calls the "love of cosmic harmony." [4] This feeling fuses with the particular, dominating feeling of the occasion and drives the poet to unify all his feelings and images dialectically in such a way that he finally achieves aesthetic form, an embodiment of aesthetic activity, a perfected harmony of image and feeling. Poetry, according to this new conception, begins with an immediate feeling which is then unfolded dialectically into a mediated complex of image and feeling. Croce has burned away all the remnants of poetry as imitation or copying, and the poem is in no sense a re-doing of something outside the poem. Thus it may truly be called an a priori synthesis, for its elements exist only as synthesized and the synthesis exists only as composed of its elements. The dominant feeling is the feeling fully realized in the poem, and the dominated feelings and images of the poem exist only in the world of the poem.

Even though the poem is in no sense imitative, it is a kind of knowing, a knowing which is at the same time a making, a doing, or a creation. For the immediate feeling with which poetry begins is different from the feeling of practical action; it is inseparable from the poet's love of harmony, a love which makes the immediate feeling with which poetry begins a kind of problem,[5] which makes it a question of what the entire world, the cosmos, would be like if dominated by that immediate feeling. Thus the inclusive process of art may be thought of, in contrast to the exclusive process of practice, as the solution of a problem, as the answer to a question, rather than the mere domination of one feeling over all other feelings. Because of this, Croce can still speak of art as the auroral form of knowing, even though he has abandoned the notion of poetry as receptive and imitative. He at least can conceive of art as both a making and a knowing. The artist begins with a question, what would my world look like if unified by this particular feeling? Or, what does this feeling which I have look like, what is it when fully objectified and imagined? The answer to his question is the making of the poem. And internal to that making is the criterion by which he knows whether his feeling is being fully imagined. His particular love of harmony drives him to realize the universal concept of aesthetic harmony; and, by means of that, he knows whether he is leaving certain parts of his world out and whether he is faking other parts with unfelt images rather than including only what he truly feels.

Artistic Individuality and Universality

Now it may be fair to describe this new concept of art as nothing more than a development and a deepening of Croce's earlier aesthetics; for it is true that the new concept answers the very needs which Croce's previous efforts failed to satisfy. It meets his need to account for both the unity and multiplicity of the poem; it allows him to relate the constructive and cognitive aspects of poetry in a meaningful and precise way; and it enables him to conceive of literary criticism as dialectical. At the same time, one cannot deny that the concept of cosmic art is so radically new that little remains in it of his previous aesthetics except the words. To begin with, Croce's earlier notion of the individuality of art does not survive in the new concept. In his early *Estetica*—he now refers to it as his "ormai giovanile trattato di *Estetica*" [6]—he had contrasted art as knowledge of the individual with philosophy, which is knowledge of the universal. According to that early position, the object of philosophy was unlimited, transcending history, and the object known in art was limited, was one individual rather than another. If art was knowledge of individuals, then the more fully "individualized" the characters of a poem were, the greater the poem could be said to be. Shakespeare could be recognized as greater than Ariosto and Spenser because his Cleopatra and his Desdemona are fully rounded individuals whereas Alcina and Una are only types. And Cleopatra's and Desdemona's individuality would be their uniqueness, their not-universality, their being so very different from other individuals; and Alcina's and Una's lack of individuality would be their similarity to other feminine characters. This particular conception of the individuality of art could not survive in Croce's mature aesthetics for a number of reasons. It made a certain kind of material more appropriate for art than other kinds. It gave prominence to the empirical or abstract individual and was thus in conflict with Croce's analysis of that individual in the *Filosofia della pratica* as nothing more than a pseudo-concept. And, most important, it violated the obvious fact that great artistic characters like Cleopatra and Falstaff and Hamlet are so amazingly typical that their individuality does not appear to be in opposition to typicality or to universality at all.

The individuality of cosmic art, as Croce conceives of it, is quite a different thing from his earlier notion of the individuality of art. It is the artist's way of apprehending his world, his unique way of seeing, of shaping and fusing all the feelings and images which make up his imaginative vision. It is an essential characteristic, that is, of the dominant feeling of a poem, of what begins as immediate, as a flash, a *macchia,* and then becomes mediate, the unifying attitude, the central harmonizing sentiment, of the entire poem. It becomes, in sum, that which makes the poem indivisible or, in other words, a genuine individual. Whether a character in a poem is rounded and is thus fully "individualized" is no longer in itself of artistic importance; what matters is whether the character is in harmony with the entire poem, whether it manifests not itself, but the individuality of the poetic cosmos.[7]

A similar change occurs in Croce's notion of artistic universality. Even though he emphasized the individuality of art in opposition to the universality of philosophy, he did have some notion of its universality even before developing his conception of art as cosmic. Aesthetic activity he very early recognized as universal in the sense that it was an element in all human experience; that every event contained in some way or other an intuition, an expression of a feeling in an image. The intuition might not be dominant, it might simply be the material of a judgment or part of the context of an action; but, as a form of activity, Croce thought of it as omnipresent. As a result of this notion of aesthetic activity as a universal form of activity, Croce could argue that a work of art is at least potentially available to all human beings, since all are acquainted with its essential form. Furthermore, this notion in no way cancels out the individuality of art, for every intuition could have its own unique content, even though the intuitive form was accepted as universal. In addition, such a notion of universality involves no magic or mystery. One need not be probing for archetypes, for night journeys of the soul beneath the odd and idiosyncratic experience of little William, say, of Wordsworth's *The Prelude* in order to understand the widespread appeal of the poem. The poem appeals just because its dominant form, its imagined feeling or felt image, is an element common to all experience. With all these advantages, however, such a notion of artistic universality is of little worth because it does not make a poem any more clearly "universal" than the experience of eating spinach would be. Eating spinach is a form of practical activity, a form which is an element of all human experience. Thus, it is potentially available to all human beings. My point is that, according to this conception of universality, intuition is universal just as practical activity is; but there is nothing distinguishing the universality of the experience of reading a poem or of writing it, for that matter, from the universality of the oddest act of indulgence. The notion simply is not doing its job.

With his theory of art as cosmic, Croce remedies this situation. The universality of art, like its individuality, lies in the artist's apprehension of his world, in the fact that, no matter what his individual way of feeling his world is, it is a universe, it is one, it holds together, and is thus a realization of his love of harmony. His dominant feeling might, for instance, be a sense of intense and irreconcilable opposition. If he unfolds this feeling artistically, if, that is, he creates an imagined world unified around this sense of opposition,—as Croce, in one of his most impressive studies during this time, argues that Shakespeare did—then he will have achieved artistic universality as Croce now conceives of it. The inclusiveness of the artist's apprehension gives his work its universality. It is infinite in the sense that it is self-limiting, not in the sense that it includes an innumerable quantity of feelings and images. Whatever the artist imagines as he creates his work of art, he includes within that work, doing so harmoniously because he is realizing his own love of harmony as aesthetic harmony itself. If the artist is a true artist, if he is actualizing the universal form of artistic coherence, then he is leaving nothing outside the limit of his cosmos.[8]

More important to Croce at this time is the fact that his new conception of universality is meaningfully at one with his new conception of individuality. The artist's all-inclusive apprehension, his self-limiting act of creation, is essentially his individual feeling which began as immediate and then went through a process of mediation, as he explored its ramifications by making a world of images charged with that feeling.

Art achieves this special union of individuality and universality because the artist's immediate feeling, the feeling to which he gives himself, is fused with his love of harmony, whereas in ordinary life the feeling we take seriously we wed to our love of exclusiveness, so that we deliberately leave outside our action every feeling except the one which we intend to realize. Our action is neither individual nor universal in the sense in which the artist's action is. Our world of practical activity is a world of divisibles and of particulars; and even though conceiving of it as such a world may have its universality and even its individuality, living in it does not.

Art and Morality

Closely related to the dialectical identification of individuality and universality in his conception of art as cosmic is Croce's new analysis of the relationship between art and morality. They are, quite baldly, identical, as they distinctly were not in Croce's earliest writings. At first, it may be remembered, Croce thought of art as the most primitive form of human experience, as passive contemplation free of will and decision and thus as quite separate from all action, immoral, moral, or amoral. The artist was said to see in such a way as to give form to what he sees. Since his gazing required no choices from him, it had nothing to do with morality. By the time of the *Breviario*, however, Croce has shifted his position considerably. Poetry has become more strenuous and involves effort. One cannot will to make a poem, but once one has begun to make a poem he is morally obligated to finish the job; he is morally obligated, that is, to be steadily amoral, not to introduce his own moral principles, not to judge his characters morally any more than he would judge them historically. To be moral is to decide against self-centered action and for action which takes the interests of all into consideration. The poet is obligated to ignore the distinction between the self and the whole; his job is to express his feelings in an image.

With his conception of art as cosmic Croce goes beyond the notion of the poet's having a moral obligation to be amoral and asserts that his obligation is to be moral, on the grounds that poetry, by its very nature, is moral. The one feeling which all artists, as artists, share is the love of harmony; only through this can they realize aesthetic form. In effect, this means that the artist is committed not to take one interest within his world so seriously that he slights or ignores another; he must balance opposite feelings, passions, and desires against each other. The poet as poet never pushes one feeling or interest excessively; he puts each in its proper place and gives it its proper value within the cosmos of his making. Even though his dominant feeling might be one of hate, as a poet he could not but be moral.[9] His hatred would be balanced by some form of love, possibly as a feeling of deprivation or anguish tingeing all aggressively hateful acts included within the poem. According to his sense of aesthetic harmony, the poet, then, is constantly judging whether his imagined feelings are in or out of balance. This very sense of balance and proportion is the heart of Croce's new morality and has replaced the old notion of morality as a choice for the interests of all and against the interests of one's self. Although the shift in his conception of morality may be slight, that in his conception of the relationship between art and morality is drastic.[10]

Literary Criticism

On the basis of his new conception of art as the dialectical unfolding of an individual and immediate feeling into a universal and cosmic harmony, into a moral balancing of opposites in perfect proportion, Croce undertook at this time a reform of literary history and criticism. He asserts the need for reform not as against his own earlier theories of literary criticism, but as against sociological criticism of the nineteenth century. This assertion, however, is part of his journalistic rhetoric; the important reform is in Croce's own position and depends upon his transcendence of the notion of art as individual to the new theory of art as the union of individuality and universality. Criticism is no longer the writing of poems about poems, nor is it simply the historical judgment of a particular poem for the purpose of distinguishing its poetry from its non-poetry and then the determination of the nature of that non-poetry. The poem, we are told, must not be treated like something limited and transitory, like a philosophical problem, a moral need, a political aspiration of this or that time; for

to treat a poem like such things is to lose its individuality and universality, that divine character of creators, which is their power to submerge every practical determination and particular thought in the serenity of contemplation.[11]

The poem, or at most all the genuine poetry of a single poet, must not be put into a context broader than itself. It cannot, in fact, be put into such a context, although it is possible to abstract parts of it and put them wherever one desires. It cannot be put into such a context just because it is a union of individuality and universality and just because the whole universe and the whole of history is harmonized within it in a single, unique form. The critic must limit himself to monographs, he must

submerge himself in the object which in a determined moment interests him and allow himself on no condition to be distracted, because in the single he finds all that interests him; in sum, he finds the Whole.[12]

He finds all that interests him by re-making the internal dialectic of the poem, by moving from its individual feeling to its cosmic harmony and by uncovering the point of union between the individuality of the poem and its universality or "cosmicità." Like the poet the critic must identify, dialectically, individuality and universality; he must, that is, identify his characterization of the dominant feeling of the poem and his judgment of the aesthetic success of the poem and its parts. At this time, Croce in no way implies that characterization and evaluation are separate or even "distinct" aspects or moments of criticism; and he is right to avoid this implication. For one's characterization determines his evaluation, and the evaluation determines the characterization. If the critic fails, for example, to grasp the individual feeling which dominates and harmonizes a poem, if he lights upon a minor and subordinated feeling and claims that it is dominant, then he will be forced to claim that all those parts of the poem not dominated by this erroneously exalted feeling are non-poetic. Or if the critic fails to respond to certain poetic aspects of a poem as poetry, if he judges them erroneously to be non-poetry, then his characterization of the unique feeling of the poem will inevitably be narrower than it should be, since he has ruled out part of it as not worthy of his response. The new criticism, then, is single and indivisible: the critic re-creates the poem, moving from its unique characteristic to its beauty, from the single to the whole. He can do this only in a monograph; he must do it in this form not because Croce's general approach to poetry is at odds with the sociological approach of the past century, but because of his own radical shift from a conception of poetry as individual to a conception of poetry as cosmic, as the dialectical identification of individuality and universality.

Actualism in the New Aesthetics

Croce did not think of himself as prone to making radical shifts. It should not, then, be surprising that the very essays in which he develops his new conception of art are full of thoughts in conflict with it, thoughts out of the past which are strong enough to pull the whole conception down within a few years. Before considering these destructive elements, however, we should recognize that, in its novel aspects, Croce's conception of art as cosmic is fundamentally actualistic. Croce has stolen the fire of genius from Gentile and has developed an actualistic aesthetic with none of the actualistic weaknesses which were touched upon in the last chapter.

If one were not opposed to actualism, he might describe Croce's new conception of art in the following way. Croce has finally, he might say, conceived of art as a three-term dialectic. The immediate feeling with which the poem begins is the thesis; it is the immediate subject. Its antithesis is the whole multiple world of the poem, all the feelings and images which the ruling feeling is in the process of dominating. The synthesis, the mediate subject, the *pensiero pensante,* is the sense of cosmic harmony, aesthetic coherence itself; it is that awareness by means of which one determines at every point of the dialectic whether the objective moment is adequate to the immediate subject, is its identical opposite, is dominating the multiplicity of the object as the unifying feeling. But, one might continue, Croce avoids every hint of a crude actualistic identification of art with philosophy and history and science by weighting the dialectic heavily toward the immediate subject. Poetry is the same as philosophy in the sense that both are fully dialectical; but, whereas philosophy is weighted toward the mediate subject, toward the judgmental determination of universal proportion, poetry is weighted toward the immediate subject, toward feeling and the love of harmony. Even the mediate subject of a poem is like a feeling; and, if it is a thinking, it is a thinking suffused with the warmth of emotion, it is not so much a judgment of proportion as it is a sense of harmony. Poetry is also the same as science since both are fully dialectical: but science is weighted toward the

objective moment of the dialectic, its multiplicity is accentu-
ated, it is primarily analytical; whereas the parts, all the diverse elements, of a poem are relatively slighted, they all feel
the same, because they are caught up in the heavily accented
feeling which dominates them. The poem, then, is dialectical:
it moves from the immediacy of feeling through the multiplicity of analysis to judgmental mediation, to the active thinking
which is the beginning and the end of all reality and which
gives every action its real form. But the accent of the poetic
dialectic is so heavily upon the immediate feeling that even the
ultimately real action of a poem may be referred to as an
aesthetic synthesis, not simply as thought thinking. The actualists themselves had left the relationships among the moments
of the dialectic in so crude a form that it was impossible to
distinguish art from philosophy. Croce was the first to show
how their dialectic might be developed aesthetically.

Criticism itself, according to Croce's reform, would be a
three-term dialectic, but more heavily weighted toward the
objective and synthetic moments of the dialectic than poetry
ever could be. The critic would emphasize the immediate,
subjective moment of the poem, concentrating on the poem as
weighted toward the thesis; but he himself would be objective
and mediate, he would strive to show how the immediate
feeling of the poem, its individualizing characteristic, suffused
and unified the many elements of the poetic cosmos in such
a way as to realize aesthetic harmony. He would, in effect,
be showing just how the individuality of the poem was identical with its universality.

Remnants of the Earlier Aesthetics

As the arch opponent of actualism, however, Croce was not
likely to present openly and boldly a position like the one
just described as though it were his own. In all his important

essays of this period he dampened the fire of his new insight with a sprinkling of old ideas inconsistent with the new. We are repeatedly told, for example, that art is "pure intuition," free of judgment and concept. "Art is the making of an image; thought is the making of a judgment." [13] Rhetoric and sentiment may call for such claims, but not thought. If art is mediate in the new aesthetics, then Croce has no solid grounds for continuing to call it "pure intuition." "Intuition" may well deserve so respectable a definition as "the immediate cognition of a concrete object in its determinations of space and time." [14] But it is certainly inseparable from immediacy independent of all mediation. Furthermore, quite apart from whether the notion that art is free of judgment may be reconciled with the new notion that art is the positing and resolving of a problem, Croce's failure to connect the two ideas and at least try to reconcile them forces me to believe that the older idea is no longer a thought, but only a sentiment. One might keep the new idea of art free from a fully developed philosophical judgment by saying that the artistic problem and solution, the dominant feeling and the full poem, are indistinguishably one, whereas the subject and the predicate of a philosophical judgment are distinct though unified. [15] Although that distinction would not hold up in Croce's old scheme, as our earlier analysis of his *Logica* indicated, it would hold up within an actualistic framework. Only philosophically, only with the accent upon the mediate subject, can the distinction between the thesis and the antithesis of the dialectic be clearly discerned and thus their judgmental nature exposed. Artistically, accenting the immediate subject, one may feel that they are indistinguishable.

Croce, to be sure, is not obscuring his new insight deliberately; he simply has not conceived it lucidly. Clarity of thought is not always his main objective. He goes so far at one point, for instance, as to claim that the union of individuality and universality to be found in cosmic art may also be found in "every form and act of the real." [16] Particularity and finiteness, he momentarily feels, come from the failure to complete the movement from "immediate feeling" to its "mediation and resolution in art." But elsewhere and far more consistently he speaks of the "cosmic afflatus" and the "imprint of totality" in art as contrasting with the immediacy and particularity and finiteness of practical activity.[17]

Despite all the isolated statements about the dialectical nature of art, about its movement from immediacy to mediation, Croce has not securely possessed himself of a three-term dialectic. Beyond the dominant feeling and the dominated world of multiplicity, Croce must posit some form of balancing and harmonizing activity. One may infer that this mediating form is aesthetic activity itself, an element in all activity but here dominant as identical with the artist's own awareness. And one may infer that this active form is somehow related to the artist's own particular love of cosmic harmony, the very feeling which sets him off from the inartistic. Or one may, as I have done, think of the two as one, as the mediate subject of the aesthetic dialectic, a dialectic weighted toward the immediate subject so that its mediate subject seems most intimately at one with the immediate subject. Croce asserts no one of these three possibilities more clearly than the others, though all are reasonable inferences. He is obscure here, I believe, because he does not wish to introduce something judgmental into his notion of art. He suggests it, however, because he knows he must. If only art could be dialectical and not dialectical at the same time, Croce's sailing would be smooth.

But he is in even more difficulty with his reformed conception of literary criticism. He has argued that criticism must be monographic, must be limited to a poem or a poet, if it is to avoid chopping up the miraculous union of individuality and universality which distinguishes "the divine character of creators." [18] The critic, we are told, must submerge himself in the single object of interest and there discover the Whole. But if Croce continues to maintain a sharp distinction between the poem and criticism of the poem, as he most certainly does,[19] then the poem, at least when it is discussed, is limited by something other than itself, by the critic's own activity and judgment, so that it must have a very limited kind of universality and *cosmicità*. As soon as one allows that the critic's thinking is distinct from the poem, as soon as one admits a more inclusive form of thinking than the inclusiveness of the poetic cosmos, then one's reason for limiting the critic's inclusive thinking to a single poetic cosmos collapses. If he can include within his own thinking one "universal cosmos," then why should he not include two or a dozen? And why should he not go on to write a history of Italian poetry, not a monograph at all? His history would have all the individuality and universality that any thinking can have, and he could respect the limited "universality" of the poems about which he wrote as well as the Crocean writer of monographs could respect that of the single poem which he included within his thinking. In sum, Croce's new theory of criticism as monographic demands a more intimate relationship between poetry and criticism than his older notion of these forms of activity allows for.

The Theory Applied to Ariosto

Croce could not for long preserve his precariously balanced theory of cosmic art, and within five or six years he retained nothing but its pieces. Before this breakdown is complete, however, he demonstrates the strength of the theory with a series of what most would call his finest critical studies, those on Ariosto, Shakespeare, Goethe, and Dante. By far the most brilliant and enduring of these, his study of Ariosto, is so intimately related to the theory of cosmic art that the breakdown of the theory cannot be understood until we look to this critical study as the most integral and meaningful manifestation of the theory itself, an amazingly perfect realization of both its strengths and its weaknesses.

The heart of the study is Croce's critical *macchia*, his intellectual *intúito* into the identification in *Orlando Furioso* of individuality and universality, of the dominant sentiment of the poem and its aesthetic form. The entire essay is a sustained union of Croce's individual insight and his philosophical concept, of characterization and evaluation. Croce counters De Sanctis' claim that Ariosto had no definable content and simply expressed over and over his love of expression, his love of art, by arguing that Ariosto was giving aesthetic form to a single unique feeling just as all genuine artists and poets do. De Sanctis was misled reasonably enough, however, because Ariosto's dominant feeling is nothing other than an individual counterpart to universal aesthetic form, to beauty. The dominant feeling of *Orlando Furioso* is, according to Croce, "the love of cosmic harmony" itself.[20] And, to be sure, according to the new theory of art, aesthetic form is nothing else than the expression of cosmic harmony.[21] The poem, then, is a movement from an immediate love of harmony to the mediate expression of harmony; and one might very easily think that the identity of the poem was an identity without a difference, of art with art or harmony with harmony, rather than a dialectical identification of opposites. But for Croce, who in the past has proved so prone to collapse opposites into undifferentiated identities, this close similarity between the individual feeling of *Orlando Furioso* and its aesthetic form is a wonderful advantage. For he is enabled to speak about both form and content when speaking only of one. The more he individualizes the dominant feeling of the poem, the more he universalizes; the more he evaluates, the more he characterizes. Ariosto's love of harmony, we are told, is utterly sensuous, it has no conceptual or religious element to it and thus provides no resistance to the universal harmonizing form of aesthetic activity.

Now according to Croce's conception of art as cosmic, every poet has a particular love of cosmic harmony; otherwise he would not be a poet. But usually the poet's dominant feeling is different from his love of harmony. It could be a sense of vital and irreconcilable opposition, as Croce finds it to be for Shakespeare; or it may be a sense of strength of will, as he finds in Dante. Whatever they may be, such feelings could not be immediately identified with aesthetic form as Ariosto's dominant feeling can be. Even among poets whose love of harmony is at times dominant, one is apt to find their love intellectualized, as Croce claims Petrarch's love of harmony is, so that there is opposition between the individual and the universal.[22] Ariosto, then, is proving to be the uniquely fitting poet for Crocean criticism, for with him alone is it possible to discuss the difference between poetic individuality and universality with almost total neglect of the difference!

Furthermore, when Croce comes to discuss the material of *Orlando Furioso,* that is, all the subordinate feelings of the poem when abstracted from the dominant feeling, they turn out, in all their multiplicity, to be closely similar to the dominant feeling of the poem itself. In his practical life Ariosto was always in love, always in love with the bodily beauty of a woman; and his amorous torment was gentle and controlled rather than raging or hopeless.[23] Even in politics his feelings are of the same kind, feelings of kindness and generosity. Now as a consequence of the harmonious nature of the multiple feelings which make up the material of the poem, they cannot but be gently and smoothly dominated within the poem by Ariosto's love of harmony. The antithesis of the poetic dialectic, although multiple and thus opposite to the thesis, could certainly not offer less opposition than it does.

To be sure, I must not make Croce's job of criticism sound too easy. His discussion of the miraculously close identity of the individuality, particularity, and universality of *Orlando Furioso* is elaborate and detailed. Separate attention is given to Ariosto's irony, to his octave, to his personages, and to his habit of interrupting incidents in the middle of their course.[24] My point is simply that no matter what aspect of the poem Croce is discussing, he is enabled to say much the same thing because everything about the poem is so much like everything else. The interruptions, for instance, have to do with Ariosto's love of balance, for they express his care not to give undue importance to any one story or any one character. His octave Croce calls "smiling" (*sorridente*), in a special sense, "as the manifestation of a free and harmonic life, energetic and with equilibrium, beating in veins rich with good blood and contented in this incessant beating."[25] His irony is found to be nothing else than the sustained victory of his fundamental motif, his love of cosmic harmony. Croce says that

one may call Ariosto's irony similar to the eye of God who observes the movement of creation, of all creation, loving everything equally, both good and evil, greatness and smallness, loving creation both in man and in a grain of sand, because he has made all, and taking in nothing but the movement itself, the eternal dialectic, the rhythm and the harmony.[26]

This is one of the many glorious statements in Croce's essay which refer equally to the individual feeling dominating the poem and to its universal aesthetic form. Croce is able to make such statements so simply and clearly, he is able to discuss the full dialectic of the poem without stress and struggle, primarily because all three moments of the dialectic of Ariosto's work approximate an identity with no differences among them. In other words, Croce has found the poem which allows him to work with his new theory in such a way as to avoid giving up the old. He can discuss the dialectic of the poem as though it were no dialectic. He may imply that the poetic synthesis is judgmental and also that it is not, because, even though he compares Ariosto's awareness to the eye of God, even though Ariosto may seem to be judging his whole world as worthy of love, everything like a judgment in the poem may also be taken to be nothing more than a feeling, for in Croce's eyes the judgmental synthesis and the dominant feeling are in this one poem indistinguishably identical. The poem is dialectical and involves mediation, but nothing could be closer to an immediate intuition without actually being one.

This first test, then, of Croce's new theory of art as cosmic proved to be a painless one. Croce could write brilliantly of *Orlando Furioso* without swinging away from his notion of poetry as having only two terms, of being a feeling imagined, because the immediate subject and the mediate subject of the poem were so closely similar. In fact, he was not even forced by Ariosto to depart from his deeply ingrained feeling that poetry has only one term, is immediate emotional awareness, for the elements of the world of *Orlando Furioso*, the objective moment of the poem, are practically the same as its immediate-mediate subject. The poem is a perfect illustration of Croce's ambiguous theory, which is partly new and partly old. The fact is that Croce never went further with the theory than he did at this time and with this poem. He retains as part of his vocabulary all the new terms for poetry as dialectical, as cosmic, as moral, as a union of individuality and universality, and for criticism as monographic evaluation and characterization; and certain capsule descriptions of poetry in the later *Ultimi saggi* and *La poesia* are as precise and as stirring as anything to be found in the *Nuovi saggi*. But most of his serious thought about poetry and art in these later works is opposed to whatever is novel in the theory as it was formulated in 1917 and 1918.

The Retreat from the New Aesthetics

The most important evidence of Croce's retreat from the new aesthetics may be found, as early as 1922, in what appears to be no more than a minor change in his description of literary criticism and history. In several essays written in 1922 and 1923 and in a note written in 1923 and appended to an essay of 1919, Croce describes criticism as composed of two operations, evaluation and characterization.[27] Although at one point Croce will assure us that the two operations are only abstractly distinct,[28] it seems clear that he is thinking of them as quite separate. Characterization, he tells us, is only empirical, only approximate, for one can never define precisely that *individuum ineffabile* which every genuine poem is. He even goes so far as to admit modestly that his "formulas" in the essay on Ariosto were merely instances of psychological classification and at best no more than approximations to the individuality of the poem.[29] Furthermore, Croce asserts that characterization has to do only with the content of the poem and not with its form, which is universal and identical in all poems. As for evaluation, it of course remains absolute; a poem, a line, a word is either poetic or it is not, and that is all there is to it. One may use different words in order to describe the form of a poem, but they are nothing more than synonyms. In 1922, criticism is still described as monographic and as concerned with the individuality and the universality of poetry, but it clearly is not concerned with the union of individuality and universality of a poem as it was in the theoretical and practical essays of 1917 and 1918. Croce has discarded the critical fusion of individual insight and universal conception as part of his more energetic past. The critic is now seen as first experiencing a poem in its unknowable individuality, then judging it as having universal poetic form or as not having it, and finally as describing in approximate terms the individuality of whatever parts of the poem he finds to be poetic. All the ingredients of the more integral and demanding form of criticism remain, but they have been torn apart and placed side by side.

In effect, this change is a retreat by Croce from a momentary unification of universality, particularity, and individuality to his old distinctions of the pure concept, the pseudo-concept, and the intuition. Evaluation is purely conceptual, it is an historical judgment; characterization is a form of empirical judgment carried out with pseudo-concepts; and, of course, the poem to be evaluated and characterized is the intuition. Once this retreat is made, Croce is back in all the trouble he was having before his controversy with the actualists; only now it is more irritating because he has been free of it temporarily. It is no longer possible to think about the poetic union of individuality and universality because the means for doing so, the moment of particularity, all the endless distinctions of thought which make up the objective moment of the three-term dialectic, have been set off from genuine thought as nothing more than pseudo-concepts. Even worse, one is now forced to do all his genuine thinking about something unthinkable, about that *individuum ineffabile,* the unthinkable individual-universal poem. One's absolute judgments, then, are to be predicated of inconceivable subjects; and this means that they must be taken on faith by every one except the judge, since that which is judged is undiscussable.

It is true that Croce asserts that we can all re-evoke poems of the past and therefore would all have the poetic cosmos before us by means of which we could check the judgment of another as to whether it is truly poetry. Whether one man's cosmic *Divine Comedy* is identical with another man's, Croce will not even consider seriously. He simply affirms that they are identical, granting that something magical is involved.[30] Exactly why one should have faith in this magic when he is forbidden to believe in the identity of the very greatest translation with its original is another matter which Croce does not set his mind to.[31] Working under the general historical notion of development which disallows any identical repetition, he asks us to believe at one and at the same time: words, millions of words, may be repeated identically over and over, yet the imaginative experience captured in one group of words cannot be repeated identically in another group of words. It would seem clear that Croce must drop his belief in magical re-evocation. But if he did, then his absolute judgments would be predicated of unsharable subjects, and he would simply be forced once again to integrate characterization and evaluation so that the subject of the evaluation would be something thinkable. If he did that he would also be forced to overcome the empirical and approximate limitations of the characterization in order that the historical judgment itself might be something more than approximate. We are now struggling over the very difficulties which tormented Croce in those years before Gentile originated actualism. Is the subject of an historical judgment, the poem as a critic thinks about it, identical with the original imaginative intuition? If it is not, then how can the judgment give knowledge of the imaginative intuition? And if it is, then how is it that an intuition which is unthinkable by definition has suddenly become the subject of the only kind of genuine thinking, the historical judgment? At this time in

Croce's career it should surprise no one to find him writing articles to the effect that Italy has had too much philosophy, and that its thinkers should get down to the job of writing history and criticism.[32]

Unfortunately, however, a botched theory mars practice. The deterioration of Croce's aesthetics following upon his retreat from the full implications of his new theory of cosmic art also affected his practical criticism. Essay upon essay is full of his solemn efforts to pronounce judgment on a particular passage as poetic or non-poetic; for example, the whole study of Dante turns upon the distinction between the poetry and the non-poetic structure of the *Divine Comedy*. His volume of essays on European poetry of the nineteenth century is entitled *Poesia e non poesia*. The weakness of these studies is surely not that Croce is insensitive: "How could one miss his exquisite taste? *I* know those poems, let me tell you, and *I* know he is right!" One is proud, of course, to share Croce's magic, to be sensitive enough to know just how sensitive he is; but if literary criticism is to be as philosophical as Croce would have it, certainly something more than inexplicable insights might be expected from it. In his evaluations Croce gives us nothing more.

Consider, as an example, his notorious article on Leopardi in *Poesia e non poesia*. In that study he asserts that Leopardi is poetic only when "pure and healthy." When he is polemical, ironic, and satiric, when he laughs wickedly, he is not. When he is exposing a series of thoughts, a pessimistic catechism, when he is asserting a desperate resignation, then he is quite outside poetry. Most of "La Ginestra, o Il fiore del deserto" and all of the "Epistola al Pepoli" are supposedly dominated by a didactic tone; the "Bruto" and "Canto notturno" are oratorical, ruled by a tone of accusation; even the stupendous "A se stesso" is declared to be "not poetry, but a notation of feelings and of resolutions which do not go beyond the circle of the individual." [33] Leopardi's true poetry, we are then told, is limited to his idylls. Now these are fascinating opinions, shocking, blasphemous, the very kind of intuition that might set a great critic in motion, as De Sanctis was set in motion by his belief that Ariosto is not a poet, but only an artist. But Croce has ruled himself out as a great critic. He has no way of justifying his opinions. He may say that in "La Ginestra" Leopardi is primarily exposing a series of thoughts; but that justifies nothing. The question remains, is that series of thoughts dominated by an individual feeling which reaches toward and attains cosmic form, or is it not? Croce will not consider the question, for he has separated evaluation and characterization and will not bring together detailed discussion of the poem and his judgments upon it. Nor is his claim that the highly intellectual "Pensiero dominante" and "Amore e morte" are genuine poetry and not didactic, even though in a meditative form, any more interesting, for he gives us nothing but this general opinion, just as his broken-down theory suggests that he should. Even his later essay on "Amore e morte," [34] in which he looks at the poem part by part, saying that certain lines are poetic and others are not, is worth little because he can present no individualized explanation of his judgments. His unsupported and arbitrary assertions cannot but seem arrogant folly even though they are in accord with a feeble theory.

It should be admitted that after 1922 Croce devoted less and less time to what he considered to be genuine poetry. He gave most of his intellectual energy to political and ethical history; and when he did write about non-poetic literature, it was with much greater tolerance than before. This new tolerance may, I think, be traced back to the breakdown of his theory of poetry and poetic criticism. The separation of evaluation and characterization, of one's consideration of the universal form of poetry and the individual content, was just the right preparation for *La poesia*, Croce's homage to all beautiful expression which is not truly aesthetic or poetic. All non-poetic prose, according to the argument of *La poesia*, may or may not be beautiful, depending on whether the author has cloaked it with a pretty dress abstracted from genuine poetry. Literary expression, we are told, is a form of civility and gallantry, a harmonization of one's non-poetic expression and a style stolen from poetry. Only one who had become accustomed to experiencing aesthetic form as distinct from its individual manifestation could have given such prominence to that form as distinct from its individual manifestation, that is, as separate from genuine poetry. Croce's theory of poetic criticism as composed of two distinct operations, evaluation and characterization, and his practice of judging the form of poems before even considering their individuality, in effect made the poems under his scrutiny all too similar to the many different forms of literary expression enumerated in *La poesia*, to oratory, entertainment, emotional effusion, and didactic works, all appareled prettily. In theory, to be sure, the form and content of poetry remain indistinguishable, whereas the form and content in all literary expression are distinct. But given Croce's separation of evaluation and characterization in his theory of criticism and his separation of them in practice, one would be in no position to think or talk about poetry in a way different from his thought and speech about literary expression.

Even though Croce wrote infrequently and weakly of genuine art during the last thirty years or so of his career, the very cause of that weakness freed him to write about literary expression with far greater appreciation than he had before. His studies of sixteenth-century Petrarchism, of "poets" and writers of the full and late Renaissance, and of the Baroque age in Italy are informative, judicious, morally enlightening, and entertaining. There is none of the strife and struggle which one recalls from Croce's earlier writings, when he was trying to overcome his errors; nor is there any of that sense of almost miraculous accomplishment which accompanies his first essays on art as cosmic and his study of Ariosto. But if true intellectual ripeness may be described as making even one's errors bear fruit, then the Croce of these late literary studies earns that praise.

Chapter Five
Gentile's Mature Aesthetics: Art as Self-Translation

*A*lthough Croce worked out an actualistic aesthetics in his theory of art as cosmic, and took it seriously enough for use in his monograph on Ariosto, in retrospect his success seems that of a dilettante. It is overly generous to assert that he had thought through the relationship between the dominant feeling of a work of art and the judgmental sense of its cosmic harmony, and that he had in truth set the artistic act into dialectical movement. To be sure, he had glimpsed this relationship, and his awareness of it is evidenced by his application of it to *Orlando Furioso*. But the theory of art as cosmic is not articulate and coherent, and its implications are not drawn forth rigorously; nor was Ariosto's poem shown to be dialectical in an unambiguous way. Notwithstanding the brilliant flowering of Croce's mature aesthetics, then, it is only with the publication of Gentile's *La filosofia dell' arte* in 1931, and with Gentile's late critical essays on Leopardi, that actualism was to achieve its maturest aesthetics and criticism. *La filosofia dell' arte* was Gentile's next-to-to-the-last genuinely philosophical work; and it is the one in which he most fully overcame the perils and limitations of actualism. Resting as it does upon his theory of art as self-translation, as *autotradursi,* and upon his concept of the thesis of the dialectic as feeling, as *sentimento,* this work overcomes the tendency in earlier actualism toward empty abstractness, toward a static relationship among the moments of the dialectic, and toward the collapse of the three terms of the dialectic into two. It is also true that, as an achievement of secondary importance, *La filosofia dell' arte* improves upon Croce's maturest aesthetics, much as Croce's own aesthetics of 1917 and 1918 improved upon his earlier work. But, primarily, it represents Gentile's transcendence over himself, his triumph over his own weaknesses and those of his school.

Surprising as it may seem, however, *La filosofia dell' arte* has been repeatedly dismissed as no more than an attack upon Croce. Guido Calogero, whom one cannot associate with blind hatred of actualism, simply refuses to talk about its aesthetics, claiming that aestheticians like Gentile are so insensitive that their ideas on art are beneath discussion.[1] Adelchi Attisani claims that Gentile had nothing essential to say in aesthetics after a slight essay written in 1909. Of *La filosofia dell' arte* he says:

This is more than anything else the fruit of ambition, and a wretched ambition too: that of checking the Aesthetics of Croce, of breaking down the more than thirty year long dominion of that Aesthetics in order to replace it with his own. The harshly polemical, not to say aggressive, tone of the work stems from this fact.[2]

Thereupon Attisani repudiates the book peremptorily as sterile and archaic. Even Armando Carlini, in an article most sympathetic to Gentile, seems forced to concede that *La filosofia dell' arte* contains nothing new and that it was meant to contend for the field with Croce's aesthetics. The kindest thing Carlini can say is that, "contrary to Gentile's habits, here the polemical tone dominates."[3]

Without a doubt, *La filosofia dell' arte* is superficially polemical. Probably one could accumulate over a hundred passages in which Gentile points up one of Croce's errors. Croce's failure to achieve a principle of unity; his distinctions between thought and action, between historiography and history, and between pure thought and empirical thought; and his notion of the pseudo-concept with all its corollaries concerning technique, literary genres, and artistic media: all these are scornfully rejected. The notions that theoretical activity is universal whereas practice is particular, that intuition negates the will, that art has a special material called feeling, and that a genuine a priori synthesis can be realized as the unification of the initially separate image and feeling, these too are repudiated. Gentile cannot find enough opportunities to deny Croce's distinction between art and knowledge, between beauty and truth, between poetry and criticism, and, in general, between poetry and non-poetry. One might think that Gentile was trying to exorcise everything Crocean from his system.

The hostile tone, furthermore, in which these exposures are made is quite disagreeable; and one might for this reason alone prefer that E. F. Carritt's translation of the book remain in manuscript as it has for the past thirty years.[4] Consider, for example, the way in which this preliminary statement is made:

Distinguish, yes, but within the synthesis, and hence always holding firmly to the initial principle. And this, I am sorry to say for all the zealots of the holy ark of distinction (of false distinction, which multiplies today like fungi from the fertile soil of that journalistic philosophy of facile production and of facile selling), is unity. . . . Without the plant, with its strong root planted in the earth, from which it sucks its vital juices; without the living plant, and without the principle of its life, you might have some beautiful fruit to look at, but it would be made of painted oakum and canvas.[5]

The absence of Croce's name (according to official policy, H. S. Harris tells us) intensifies this antagonism as it bursts forth again and again during the course of the book. Ordinarily such fury does not affect Gentile's argument itself and is used only incidentally or for transitions. For example, it is only after he has made a point that Gentile says:

> This observation should be useful, but one knows a priori that it will be of little profit to the ordinarily facile philosophers of belles-lettres, who continue in their melancholy (oh, the infinite melancholy of the non-theologizing philosophers!) not only to distinguish but to separate the temporal and the eternal, empirical thought and pure thought; and, if they do not turn their backs on philosophy, which they have proclaimed a simple methodology, in order to embrace the coarse things of history and of experience coarsely conceived, they believe they can grope among the shadows of a dark abyss without bottom, where there is no respite and living is impossible.[6]

If such open malice had been confined to asides like this one, its only effect would probably have been to embarrass Gentile. But it is possible to sense his antagonism even at the heart of his most serious arguments. For example, as he works out one of his more brilliant distinctions, that between the man of genius and ingenious men, it is not merely fanciful to sense, as a kind of undertow, a suggested contrast between the genius of Giovanni Gentile and the ingenuity of Benedetto Croce. If the undertow is allowed to work with full force, the whole book must go under, as it apparently did for Calogero, Attisani, and Carlini.

Gentile wrote the book at a very difficult time for him. After 1929 actualism ceased to be the official philosophy of Fascism. At the seventh national congress of philosophy in 1929, of which Gentile was the president, it was argued by Father Gemilli that no thought was less Christian than Gentile's, and that Italian youth should not be taught idealism. Said he: "we are not to bring Kant into accord with St. Thomas." [7] With the Concordat of the same year neo-scholasticism and "realism" became officially dominant; and for one so concerned with action as Gentile was, such a defeat must have been the source of intense grief and anger. Nonetheless, although the personal pain is a kind of stylistic cloak of fire which wards off serious readers, I believe *La filosofia dell' arte* is a philosophical triumph. It is clearly a rhetorical defeat: Gentile tries to shame Croce and in fact shames only himself. In substance, however, it is a success: Gentile goes well beyond earlier actualistic aesthetics, and only as a consequence of this is he in a position to point out the inferiority of Croce's aesthetics to his own.

Art as Self-Translation

The most radical idea of *La filosofia dell' arte* is the idea of art as self-translation, as *autotradursi*. The immediate subject of a poem, sheer feeling or pleasure, in its very assertion of self denies itself by becoming object to itself. In plainer words, in his attempt to express his feeling, the poet denies it as immediate feeling by asserting it as verse. This experience, like all human experience as seen from Gentile's point of view, is self-conscious. The poet observes himself deny himself by objectifying his feeling; he observes the immediate pleasure of oneness break into the pain of multiplicity; and he struggles critically to make the objective moment of the experience equal to the original feeling, to win his way to a synthetic unity as complete as the immediate unity of feeling. Every new line of a poem then becomes a translation of the original feeling, as it has been expressed in the lines thus far composed, into a new unity in which the poem as object is closer to being adequate to the feeling of the poem. As formulated here, Gentile's theory takes account of the sensuousness of art by establishing feeling as its initial principle; it emphasizes the constructive aspect of art, for feeling cannot be expressed at all except through the making of a world with that feeling as its form and unity. The brooding and critical eye under which every step of the constructive process occurs, the self-conscious judgment as to whether the feeling as objectified is adequate to the original feeling, is presented as the cognitive element of the poem.

This conception of art and poetry as self-translation had its actualistic anticipations, tentative and incomplete as they were. Gentile's own article on the Right and the Wrong of translations, published in 1920, provides the grounds for the theory. Gentile claims in that article that translation is the condition of all thought and learning, not only between two languages, but also within one:

But what is translation—not in the abstract, but in the concrete, when someone is translating and when one considers just what he is doing—if it is not an interpretation in which one passes from one language into another because they are both known to the translator, and, that is, the translator has put both into relation within his spirit and can pass from one to the other, as from one part to the other of the same language? And that language is truly single, it is truly there for the translator: it is neither one nor the other, but the togetherness of the two in their relation or unity. Whoever translates begins to think in one way, from which he does not cease, but which he transforms, continuing to develop, to clarify, to render always more intimate and subjective to himself that which he began to think. And in this passage from one moment to another of his own thought, in his single language, that which takes place, considered empirically, is called translating, as a passage from one language to another. And does not the same perhaps occur when we read that which is written in our own language, by others or by ourselves? [8]

This passage is a significant advance over Gentile's earlier notion that

the book which is read is not . . . the book of the first author, but the *book of the reader.* In other words, every book can be said to have as many authors as it has readers. Whoever does not take this point of view and deludes himself into thinking that the book exists in so far as it has been written or printed, as the exteriorization of the spiritual life of its author, will tend to make use of the book in school as an instrument of compression rather than as an incitement and spiritual elevation.[9]

In this earlier passage Gentile's attention rests too heavily upon the act of comprehension and slights the act of assertion itself. In the later article on translation he concentrates upon the movement from initial assertion to a further assertion which, in effect, comprehends the first one. But still the emphasis is upon a situation like this: Dante's having made an assertion, we then by our very reading of it translate it. The original assertion is clearly slighted; the nature of the thesis is not precisely enough defined to allow for a significant opposition between it and its identical opposite. Without the sense of difference, the need to unify is missing, and as a result the self-conscious effort to make the translation an "objective correlative" is slighted, if not ignored. Along with this, one loses any criterion by means of which the translation may be judged, and the translator or reader lacks a way to read responsibly rather than irresponsibly. Subject to the same criticism is Guido De Ruggiero's "Arte e critica," an article which he dedicated "To my friends R. G. Collingwood and A. H. Hannay in memory of our conversations at Oxford." [10] Because De Ruggiero too readily assumes the artist's assertion, just what it is that the artist criticizes and interprets is not at all clear. The immediate subject, the thesis of the artistic dialectic, is repeatedly neglected, here as in so many other actualistic statements.

The problem, then, which Gentile faced in *La filosofia dell' arte* was to establish the nature of the immediate subject, the thesis of the dialectic, so that there would truly be a self for the artist to translate. Once before, Gentile had grappled with the immediate subject, in his *Sommario di pedagogia come scienza filosofica*, his first unified book after the birth of actualism. In *La filosofia dell' arte* the immediate subject is feeling, the transcendental principle of art, in fact "the living principle itself of the life of the spirit," "the universal productive center." But in the *Sommario* the immediate subject is the very opposite of vital and productive. Considered apart from the full synthesis, it is the abstract "I," empty and undetermined. It is, curiously enough, self-consciousness, what one would assume the synthesis, the mediate subject, to be; and it is nothing at all except as concretely synthesized with the empirical "I," the "I" as object among objects. As it is within the synthesis itself, within the mediate subject, within the real "I" as the unity of self-consciousness and consciousness, nothing at all can be said about the thesis because it has become indistinguishable from the synthesis. The unity of subject and object, the relationship between them, is not thought of as self-consciousness, as the consciousness which the subject has of itself as positing its opposite; for the thesis, the initial subject, has itself been defined as self-consciousness. And the self of which it is conscious within the synthesis is the self objectified, not the self positing itself as object.[11] The consequence of this error is that through much of the *Sommario* Gentile's dialectic has only two terms, the subject and the object, act and fact, and they are discussed as static and immobile. Oddly enough, the immediate subject eludes Gentile just because he tries so hard to conceive of it in *motion,* as part of the dialectic, and as nothing in itself. As a result the whole dialectic grinds to a halt. Gentile had rejected the Hegelian dialectic because the only kind of Becoming which could synthesize Being and Nothing is thinking, and Hegel had ruled thinking out of that elemental stage of his dialectic. With the act of thinking itself as the ultimate synthesis, Gentile believed he could avoid reducing thesis and antithesis to an identity without a difference. But at the heart of his argument in the *Sommario* the thesis has become indistinguishable from the synthesis; and the only other term, the object, takes on the aspects of either Being or Nothing indiscriminately, and whether as history or nature or the empirical "I," it is always a fixed fact.

The major difficulty for Gentile is that he must conceive of the thesis as essentially nothing except as it turns into its opposite; but he must not conceive of it as having already turned into that opposite. How, then, could he conceive of the thesis without reducing it to the antithesis or to the synthesis? It must, of course, be nothing outside the synthesis, for in actualism there is no substance outside or prior to the function, there is no actor except within the act. The self, the ego, is nothing except as part of the dialectical action itself. But one should have expected that, within the synthesis, Gentile would carry out an analysis of the difference between the opposites of the synthesis and between each of them and the synthesis itself. The fact that he accomplished this in *La filosofia dell' arte* but not before is marked by his rejection of "sensation" (*sensazione*) as "the absolutely immediate psychic act" [12] and his substitution of "feeling" (*sentimento*). The trouble with the word "sensation" as a possible thesis for Gentile's synthesis is that neither of its basic meanings has anything to do with "immediate subjectivity." "Sensation" can refer to something given, some immediate datum, and thus it is in accord with the objective moment of the dialectic. It can, furthermore, refer to the sensing of something given, something objective, and thus it harmonizes with the mediate subject, with the sensing which contains the sensum. The word lends itself, in sum, to the terminology of form and content, but in no way to dialectical terminology, to thesis, antithesis, and synthesis.

The word "feeling," on the other hand, is perfect for dialectical use. It most frequently refers precisely to "immediate subjectivity" (as examples, consider "an eerie feeling," and "a feeling of uneasiness"). But it may also be used with a strong element of objectivity ("When you touch that you will experience a feeling of warmth"). Finally, it works well as a term for synthesis ("While I was feeling for his pulse, he awoke"). The word lends itself to the conceptualization not only of immediate subjectivity, but also of subjectivity as actually existing not immediately, but within the dialectical act. A word which could carry its immediacy within its mediacy is just what Gentile needed. With it he established the thesis of the dialectic as the transcendental principle of art, as the non-actual essence of art, and defined the artistic experience, the existence of art, as the full dialectical act.

The Artistic Dialectic: Thesis

The advantages of Gentile's theory of art as *autotradursi* over Croce's theory of art as cosmic are substantial, although not entirely obvious. Gentile himself did not argue against Croce's cosmic theory; in fact, he ignored it, probably because it was so close to his own and he was not interested at this time in any similarities between Croce's thought and his own. In truth, however, the theory of *autotradursi* may be characterized as the deepening and sharpening of the theory of art as cosmic.

Beginning with the first moment of the dialectic, we cannot deny that Croce's ideas about the element of feeling in art were ambiguous and that they made feelings unduly passive. The feelings which are supposedly brought into oneness with images are said to have been the passive elements of practical action, or desires unrealized in action, or, finally, desires and actions not discriminated from one another. The feeling which dominates the poem, the "aesthetic feeling," was not very clearly distinguished from the feelings contained within the poem, and its relationship with all the multiplicity that it unified was never precisely described.

The feeling which Gentile establishes as the principle of art is not as such a particular or specific feeling; it is feeling in its unmultiplied and unmediated oneness. As the principle of artistic form, it is neither actual nor dialectical:

It animates the body of art, but is unseen. What is seen is the body animated. To read a poem, to penetrate into the soul of its livingness, one must sense its *fremito,* one must intuit or divine the internal principle which puts our soul in motion and which lives again in us; but one cannot look it in the face, one cannot fix it and make it the material of experience to be thought about. It is a *nescio quid,* a *Deus absconditus* though present, which masters us and moves our tongue and draws us like that mysterious force which rouses dreams that at times test our faith, like divine revelations or true signs of warning.[13]

Feeling as a transcendental, non-actual principle is basically pleasure. It is the heart of nature as experienced from the inside out; it is genius, that *vis interna naturae,* that working force that gives life to all that has it; it is beauty in the sense that it is the unity which makes any multiplicity pleasurable. Furthermore, its relationship with the world to which it gives unity is one of necessary opposition, according to the logic of the dialectic. As Gentile points out, feeling can assert itself only as its opposite, as, for example, the question, "Do I have this feeling?" or the assertion, "I have this feeling." The feeling as principle is one, it is pleasure: as asserted it is multiplicity, it is at least two elements, the "I" and the feeling in either the above question or assertion. The multiplicity resulting directly from the assertion of feeling is thought, or distinction; and as the opposite of feeling as pleasure, it is pain. In its most elementary form the artistic dialectic may be described as follows:

The relation of two opposites is dialectical, not only in an abstractly logical sense, but in a metaphysical sense, that is, really and concretely. Their duality is the opposition of a unity in itself, of something unique which lives, develops, becomes, and is in so far as it is not, and vice-versa; and thus it posits itself as an identity of opposites. A stable, fixed pleasure, always itself and nothing else, is a dead pleasure. . . . Its life is nothing if it does not issue continually from its opposite. Thus from Epicurus to Kant, those who have looked most acutely into the dialectic of feeling have defined pleasure as a cessation of pain.[14]

Even though feeling as a transcendental principle is character- ized by Gentile in a most general way as sheer pleasure; it al- ways exists in a localized and unique form because it is un- thinkable apart from its opposite, the multiple world of thought and distinction. It exists not as pleasure, but as this unique pleasure giving artistic form to its opposite, the world of pain which is its articulation.

The Artistic Dialectic: Antithesis

Turning now to the antithetical moment of the dialectic, we find that Croce's conception of the world of a poem, of that multiplicity which is unified by feeling, is severely limited by the questions which it raises but does not answer. Like his conception of feeling, it is not so much erroneous as it is am- biguous. Often he calls the body of the poem an image and describes the poem as a cosmic intuition in which image and feeling are fused. Are we to infer from this that the world of a poem, and not just its formative feeling, must be sensuous, visible, and audible, with its odors and tastes and touches? Has Croce fallen into the error of raising a modern predilection for sensuous poetry into a necessary aspect of all poetry? Has he excluded all philosophical discussion from poetry unless it is coming out of the mouths of characters sitting about in imagined space and time? If he has not, then we must ask why he has excluded what he calls "pseudo-concepts" from poetry? What is the difference between "man," "dog," and "cat," as they are used in poetry, and those words as they are used prac- tically, for classification, as general concepts framed for our convenience? Croce's response to such difficulties never goes beyond the re-statement of his general distinctions.

Gentile's concept of the world of a poem as the objective moment of the artistic dialectic overcomes these difficulties. The assertion of feeling, the expression of feeling, is the world of the poem, a world which is not limited to the sensuous, visible, and audible:

The Imagination will be bodily, but not with that fictitious and incomprehensible bodiliness which opposes bodies to bodies and which would separate the soul from things and from other souls themselves. Rather it will be so with that intimate, profound bodiliness of the "I," which extends from the so-called sensations—which are no other than thoughts but turned toward spatial and temporal things—to the purer ideas concerning infinite and eternal things.[15]

Any words and any thoughts, no matter how brutish or how angelic, no matter how fluid or how systematic in meaning, may be part of the world of a poetic experience. The fact that the world is dominated and unified by the subjective moment of the dialectic, by feeling, gives to Gentile's conception of the poetic act all the sensuousness needed to distinguish it from other forms of activity. One is not, then, placed in the uncomfortable position of denying that most of Leopardi's "La Ginestra" is poetry on the grounds that it contains arguments.

More important, Gentile can cope with the problem that, despite Croce's efforts to exclude matters of technique, convention, literary genre, and artistic media from the aesthetic experience because they are "pseudo-concepts," most readers continue to include them, to respond to them, as part of their experience of art itself. Gentile allows us, for instance, to treat the idea of pastoral elegy as an important part of the body or world of Milton's "Lycidas." The idea is not in itself poetic; but no idea, thought, image, or word is poetic in so far as it is part of the objective moment of the dialectic, of the moment of multiplicity.[16] When unified by the subjective moment of feeling, the complex, systematic idea of the "pastoral elegy" is as poetic as any sound or rhythm or image in the poem. One may, it is true, think of a genre, say, tragedy, as abstracted from the dialectical movement from subject to object, may, that is, conceive of it as purely objective. And one may write a play not to express his feeling, but simply to illustrate the idea of tragedy. But the presence of the verse form, thought of as just that, as a verse form, does not mar the poem as poetry any more than it makes the poem poetry. The feeling of a poem cannot exist apart from words and ideas, images and generalizations. The objective moment, all multiplicity, is essentially non-poetic: whether its presence makes a poem non-poetic depends upon whether it predominates. The greatest poetry is impure. What makes it poetry rather than philosophy or history is not the dialectical moments of its existence, since all the moments are present in every experience. It is poetry if its essence is poetic, and its essence is poetic if the subjective moment of the dialectic dominates over the objective and the synthetic moments of its experience. Not the mere presence, then, but the predominance of the subjective moment determines that an experience is poetic. With this notion of all the moments of the dialectic as present in every experience, but with one of the three prevailing, Gentile admittedly loses the neatness gained by Croce with his sharp distinctions between poetic verse and non-poetic verse (which may be useful, entertaining or whatnot). If all verse is non-poetic and poetic at the same time; if every judgment of a law court written in the most plodding style is both poetic and non-poetic, then we shall be unable to make qualitatively absolute judgments as to whether any experience is poetic. I believe, however, that common sense, the proposed touchstone of *La filosofia dell' arte*, is here on Gentile's side, although common people may at times be intimidated by a literary dictator who announces that one play is mere entertainment while another is true art.

The Artistic Dialectic: Synthesis

With the third moment of the dialectic Gentile makes his most significant advances over Croce's theory of art as cosmic.

It may be recalled that Croce's "sense of cosmic harmony" came close to being a synthesis of the feeling and the world of a genuine poem. "Cosmic harmony," however, was not thought of as an active moment in the making of the poem itself. It was rather a predicate affixed to the poem by its judge: even as experienced by a reader the poem is a fusion of two terms only, the feeling and the image, and there is nothing that can be said about the fusion itself, the intuition, that is not already applicable to the image or the feeling. The judgment, then, is imposed from without; logically it must have been present within the poem, but Croce could not articulate its presence there because to do so would violate some elements of long-standing faith. Poetry is not, according to his view, self-conscious; the poet is not aware of his assertion as he makes it, hearing, understanding, evaluating, and revising as he progresses.

That, however, is just what the poet is doing according to Gentile's conception of art as *autotradursi*. Poetry is a dialectical act, it is fully self-conscious: as mediate subject the poet hears his own assertion made as immediate subject; and, acting as his own critic, he senses just where the movement from immediate subject to object, where the splitting up of the oneness of feeling into the multiplicity of words, is incomplete. Riding the wave of the dialectic, he then becomes asserter, his new assertion being a translation of the unfolding poem completed up to that point, with each new assertion being a modification of all that has gone before.[17] At every stage in its growth the poem is both a speaking and a hearing, a making and a knowing; it is both art and criticism. When Gentile identifies genius and taste, then, he means to identify them dialectically, in the moment of self-consciousness, in that effort by the poet to bring about a triumph of his feeling over the world of pure objectivity, in his effort to animate the body of the poem with its soul.

The poem in its very making, it should be recognized, is being thought of as a dialog; this is what Gentile's notion of self-consciousness requires. Woe, then, to the poet who is alone, who does not split into two personae, the speaker and the hearer, both one in the self-conscious effort to make the feeling and the world adequate to each other.[18]

Probably the most important aspect of Gentile's new artistic dialectic, especially when it is compared to the earlier dialectic of the *Sommario,* is its open-endedness. The overarching consciousness of the earlier work was thought of as something complete: the real "I" is the unity of the pure "I" and the empirical "I"; and that means that the active "I," the thinking of the present moment, has interiorized, has comprehended, the fact of the empirical "I," has, that is, understood its own past. In fact, at one point Gentile identifies the real "I" with memory: the thinking of the present sees itself in its own past, sees its own identity in its opposite.

In the new dialectic, what had been self-consciousness in the *Sommario* has become nothing more than consciousness. The immediate subject asserts itself as object: I am this fact. As mediate subject, however, as the new self-consciousness, one is observing the inadequacy of this assertion and is striving for a fuller assertion than one has just been making. The dialectic is opened up toward the future, and the present has become a movement from past to future. Or, as Josiah Royce said of an analogous theory, the present is the interpretation of the past for the future. In Gentile's words:

One may say that this portentous energy which dominates our lives and in whose explication our living consists, is indeed finite; but different from all things which are finite and are destined to be and remain such, it is conscious of its own limits and is not content with them and aspires to go beyond them. This is a manifest sign that it *is not, but ought to be infinite;* or it is not so immediately, but is becoming such.[19]

Life—and here we are thinking mainly of the life of a poem—
is conceived of as a movement of interpretation very much like
that worked out by Royce in the second volume of his *The
Problem of Christianity*.[20] It is even closer to Karl Vossler's
conception of all speech as theomorphic; as man's endless effort to understand what he hears by an interpretive assertion
which he then tries to understand by further interpretation; as
his endless effort to overcome his finiteness by including it in
a more comprehensive assertion.[21] Man is not infinite, in one
sense, for he clearly has limits. But in another sense he is, for
by recognizing his limits and understanding them, he goes beyond them.

Literary Criticism

The implications of this concept of poetry as self-transcendence and self-translation are important for Gentile's
theory of literary criticism not only as straightening out difficulties in Croce's thought, but also as breaking down some
absurdities in Gentile's own thinking. In his *La riforma dell'
educazione* (1919) he had argued that the *Divine Comedy*
which we know is that which is within the criticism that interprets, understands, and judges it. In a Hegelian fashion he
implied that art is not important in itself, that in fact it does
not even exist except as philosophy, as the full dialectical act
of which literary criticism is one form.[22] This in turn implies
some rather high-handed negligence about the work of art itself. But with the theory of art as self-translation Gentile overcomes the anti-aesthetic implications of the idea by showing
the exact sense in which art is identical with, yet different
from, philosophy. Although the essence of art is feeling, its
existence depends upon the artist's self-conscious efforts to
criticize, to think about his feeling and thus by means of his
very criticism to express his feeling more and more fully. The

Vichian notion that man can know what man makes acquires experiential sense through this new conception. It becomes: man can know what man makes because man's making is a knowing and his knowing is a form of making.

Croce's problems with his theory of literary criticism stemmed from his exclusion of self-consciousness from poetry and from his notion that the poem must be complete before its criticism begins. There is simply no way for the critic to enter into the completed poem and gain knowledge of it and judge it when his very entrance and his self-consciousness would be introducing into the poetic experience elements which, by definition, are excluded from that experience. Although he had exciting flashes of insight during the period of his theory of art as cosmic, Croce quickly fell back into a theory of criticism maimed by these very weaknesses. The critic, he says, begins his act by entering into the poem *magically*. During this stage he senses *intuitively* which parts of the poem are poetic and which are not. In stage two—not necessarily separated temporally from the first but separated nonetheless—he judges the poem and its parts as aesthetic or practical or whatnot. In the third and final stage he characterizes the poem in an empirical and only approximate way, using all sorts of pseudo-concepts like "This is a tragedy, it is Elizabethan, it is a revenge play, and so forth." The trouble with the theory is that there is too much magic and intuition to it and no knowledge. Gentile avoided such irrationalism.

By his discovery of the self-translating element in poetry, he was enabled to see the incompleteness of every poem and of every work of art. The poem is seen to be the movement from feeling, to feeling being asserted, to feeling as asserted being interpreted by repeated assertions. Criticism is a part of all poetry, just as poetry is a part of all criticism. Poetry is essentially feeling but existentially it is self-conscious: criticism is essentially self-conscious, but existentially it involves feeling.

As Gentile conceived of it, criticism includes three stages integrally related. The critic begins by a study of the objective moment of a poem, studying the literary conventions, the language, the social and political and philosophical implications of the poem. His entire study at this stage, however, is directed towards understanding this part of the poem as its antithetical moment, as springing dialetically out of its opposite, out of the thesis, the feeling of the poem. And even in this first, philological stage of criticism the critic has entered into an interior dialog between the artist as he understands him and himself as the one who is doing the thinking. This interior dialog contains all the crucial aspects of Gentile's concept of the interior community, as he conceived of it in his last book of philosophy, the *Genesis and Structure of Society*.[23] And this dialog should be thought of as a continuation of the poem itself, which was a dialog within the poet, who asserted himself as artist and heard himself as critic.

In the second stage of criticism the critic enters into the state of artistic grace from which the poem originated, the moment of immediate subjectivity:

And he no longer deduces or reasons further, nor does he analyze coldly, for having entered into this state of grace he touches the depths of nature and is stirred by the warmth of its creative energy. No more analysis, but rather synthesis. The discursive and rational moment, in which the recollection of analogies and also those polemics with other critics and philosophical discussion or historical reconstruction was permissible, is now transcended. . . . The world has been possessed and has become blood of our blood, all one with us, with our feeling, in which is the first root of our being. Around us, there is nothing else: no more care, no thought. In the joy of this infinite power of ours, we are not now face to face with the artist, but we have transcended every difference and all duality between him and us. We have restored within ourselves that profound humanity which is his humanity, that humanity through which everyone who speaks to us with sincerity and who moves us is our brother, and which draws us there where we feel ourselves to be sons of one alone, with the same heart and eyes to look around us, seeing the same world.

Precisely thus: the same eyes and the same world. Once you have entered into the feeling of the poet, that same world which was his, infinite or with illimitable boundaries, behold it arising again in all its particulars: it rises again as a living, warm, logical, luminous world, the beautiful world animated by the spirit of the poet.[24]

In the third stage, which issues directly from the second, the critic writes an exposition of the poem, a reconstruction of its concrete content:

The exposition of the work of art . . . is not a prosaic summary, analytic and explicative, but a creation of feeling. The content previously transcended rises again; but it is no longer that insipid, abstract content, which is seen but not touched, or is touched as *per manum alienam et absque gustu,* as our Campanella said; rather it is the concrete content wholly suffused with the taste of feeling.[25]

It is within this process of criticism that the poem itself endures; the criticism is the immortality of the poem as it is realized in history. The critic and the poet are at one, although as the critic realizes his expository act, he is distinct from the poet, whose essence he shared in the oneness of feeling. The relationship between poet and critic is thus explicated by Gentile as that historical community of poetic making and critical knowing, of speaking and hearing, which is the very existence of poetry, a true identity with significant differences.

It has been said that Gentile's entire philosophy is modelled upon the classroom, and that the dialog between teacher and pupil is his root metaphor. Certainly his theory of literary criticism illuminates startlingly the nature of classroom discussions of poetry, at least at their best. The poem endures and is enriched through critical discussions, even through classroom discussions, of it. Of course, the "discussion" includes intensive reading of the poem; but because poetry exists only through self-conscious criticism, talk about the poem is itself the life of the poem. It is not, let me repeat, the essence of the poem. But it is its existence. Where if not with teachers and talkers and writers about poetry had one thought poems endured? In poets? Yes, in so far as they think as critics. In readers? Yes, in so far as they think and talk. In books? Yes again, in so far as they are read by people who think critically. In heaven or with God or the Spirit? But should one be so optimistic? Ought not the critic to bear his burden as the poet bears his? Poetry is communal; it exists only in dialog. What, if not this, have teachers of poetry thought they were about?

Gentile's Criticism of Leopardi

Although Gentile was a much less prolific critic of poetry and literature than Croce, he does have a small group of lectures and essays on the poetry of Leopardi which bear out my claim that the theory of art as self-translation is the heart of *La filosofia dell' arte*. Were it not for these essays I should hesitate to give the theory such prominence in Gentile's thought, for at least in Italian aesthetics theory and practice are almost always wedded. If an Italian philosopher were not writing criticism in harmony with his aesthetics, then it would be doubtful that he actually possessed the aesthetics which was being attributed to him. Croce's monograph on Ariosto is proof that he had actually thought through a theory of art as cosmic much as I have described it. Two lectures on Leopardi, given in 1927 and published in 1928, three years before *La filosofia dell' arte*, prove Gentile's possession of the theory of poetry as *autotradursi*. Especially when compared with his earlier pieces on Leopardi, these two reveal Gentile as unmistakably thinking of Leopardi's poetry as a three-term poetic dialectic and as himself thinking in the form of a three-term critical dialectic. Contrary to the belief that Gentile tended to form a theory before putting it to work, it would appear that the theory of art as *autotradursi* may have grown directly out of Gentile's criticism of Leopardi's poetry.

Gentile's two earliest articles on Leopardi, published in 1907 and in 1911, may be dismissed as derivative. The first is Crocean, organized around the idea that Leopardi presents not a philosophy, but a state of mind in his poetry, and around the idea that whatever philosophy one may find in his poetry must be treated as merely instrumental to his artistic interests.[26] The second article is based upon the idea of there being a sharp De Sanctian distinction in Leopardi's writing between "heart" and "head," upon a contradiction "between the feeling —not elevated to a concept—of human greatness and the concept (the content of Leopardi's poetry) of man as standing opposite nature, and therefore of the absolute fatality of grief."[27] In both articles Gentile is accepting as dogma Leopardi's lack of self-consciousness: in the first, we are told, he picked up highly dubious propositions without questioning them; in the second, Gentile says, he never achieved a consciousness of the opposed motives which make up the "forma leopardiana."

The first sign that something new is going on in Gentile's thinking about Leopardi is to be found in a long article of 1916 on the *Operette Morali*. De Sanctis had rejected almost everything intellectual in Leopardi's poetry on the grounds that it was heady and that Leopardi's poetic essence is idyllic, calm, and serene, a lament over lost innocence, a fusion of the joy of love and the sadness of death.[28] He found the *Operette Morali* to be a series of only loosely related essays most of which were frigid and artificial, promising an imaginative fulfillment which they did not realize.

In opposition to this point of view, Gentile argues that one can penetrate to the heart of the *Operette Morali* only by treating them as a unity, a single prose poem, rather than as a disconnected series. If a translation of his thought into the language of the much later *Filosofia dell' arte* is permissible, one may say he is arguing that the critic, in order to win his way to the essential feeling of the work, must take its entire objective moment seriously, not just those parts of it which strike him as poetic. For, in fact, the entire objective moment of a poem, and not just those elements of sarcasm or close logic, is non-poetic. Out of his study of the objective moment of the work, Gentile makes his way to the idea that the *Operette* have a triadic form and that Leopardi possessed this form from the start, from 1824 when he composed the first twenty essays of the book.[29] The first of the three groups which constitute the triadic form of the *Operette* Gentile finds to be idyllic: its dominant implication is that simple, unconscious life is happy, and that the more one thinks the sadder he becomes and the more intensely he yearns for his lost innocence, or unconsciousness. The second group of the triad is said to be organized around Nature's command to the Soul: "Live, and be great and unhappy." The suggestion of this group of essays, in contrast to the first, is that one should strive to be great, to achieve glory, to understand life without comforting illusions, to risk one's life with heroic action, to sing poetically. Such efforts would lead to unhappiness because one would discover through them the vanity even of those things which appear to be great. In the third group, composed of the opening piece, the "Storia del genere umano," and the original conclusion, "Dialogo di Timandro e di Eleandro," Gentile finds Leopardi affirming the worth of the bitter knowledge of one's own littleness and feeling a love and pity for all men in their littleness and wretchedness. The triad is not presented as dialectical. The second and third groups follow as advances over the first group, but the connections among them are rather loose and each part of the triad is restricted to certain essays only.

In the lectures of 1927 Gentile applies what is essentially this same triad to Leopardi's poetry proper, and he conceives of it here in a dialectical form. The whole triad is found in each poem and its moments are related as thesis, antithesis, and synthesis. The moment of the idyllic is like the thesis of the dialectic, like immediate subjectivity. So long as the shepherd does not think, he can be as quiet and content as his sheep. But the very assertion of this joy breaks into pain, into "that negative moment of detachment and opposition" which some find more clearly characteristic of Leopardi than the idyllic moment, the moment in which Croce found Leopardi's true poetry. According to Gentile:

This pain is materialized . . . from the sweetness of the idyll. *Odi et amo.* The negation would never have its lyric significance if it did not correspond to a vigorous and powerful affirmation. Precisely because life is so beautiful in the eyes of the Poet, and he feels its fascination so strongly in his heart, he grieves so much not to possess it.[30]

Gentile finds a self-consciousness in Leopardi's mature poetry, a thinking, a synthesis, which goes beyond the thoughtless pleasure of nature and the pain of thought:

This thought which devastates and destroys the original unity of man with nature becomes itself a new nature. It is the nature of that soul great because unhappy and unhappy because great, the grounds for which the Poet takes pride in himself as above the crowd of fools. . . . Leopardi becomes conscious of that superior happiness in which his spirit is purified and re-invigorated through thought and song. For, as he says, "nothing shows better the greatness and power of the human intellect or the height and nobility of man than the power man has to know and entirely comprehend and strongly feel his own littleness." Thus he feels that that very infinity in which he is sweetly shipwrecked is itself contained within his own thought, his thinking which embraces it as it expands ever outward. Then he, little and exiled flower on the arid back of exterminator Vesuvius, is inebriated with his own poetry, which consoles the desert.[31]

As a critic Gentile has worked through the objective moment of Leopardi's poetry, its abstract content, until he has been lifted into its opposite, that state of grace, that fount of feeling. In his utter oneness with the poet, in that fusion of pride and love, he finds the whole dialectical act to arise before him and he sees the world of the poet with the eyes of the poet. As critic, however, as the explicator of the poetry of Leopardi, he thinks with a self-consciousness and articulateness and coherence that go beyond the poet's; and he discovers that that poetic fusion of pride and love is a dialectical synthesis of the clash of innocent pleasure and experienced pain. This critical insight illuminates what was before fused feeling. The insight was present in Leopardi's own poetic dialog, but it was dominated by the feeling; the feeling is present within Gentile's critical dialog, but it is dominated by his insight.

Walter Binni is undoubtedly right in condemning Gentile's triadic scheme for the *Operette* as arbitrary; but his claim that Gentile remained loyal to the De Sanctian thesis that Leopardi's poetry is idyllic is imprecise.[32] Once the triad had been worked out dialectically, its arbitrariness was gone and Gentile was no longer compelled to force any particular poem or essay into a single moment of the triad. Furthermore, the presence of the full dialectic in all Leopardi's poetry does not exclude the possibility of there being development from one poem to another. In fact, contrary to Binni's opinion, Gentile was not incapable of "historicizing" Leopardi's poetry. He sees the poems as a development of Leopardi's self-consciousness and finds a much heavier element of mediation in the later ones, in the "Aspasia" group and "La Ginestra" especially, than in the earlier poems. He does not, to be sure, break all

Leopardi's poetry into two parts, as Binni does; with the idyllic poems being those written on or before April 9, 1830, the day on which Leopardi completed the "Canto notturno di un pastore errante dell' Asia," and the heroic poems being written afterwards, after the breakdown of the "myth of Recanati," of a youthfulness which had endured as a nostalgic possibility.[33] But such a cleavage between the earlier and the later poetry seems like "historicizing" carried to excess. In his *Titanismo e pietà in Giacomo Leopardi* Umberto Bosco has worked successfully against Binni's bifurcation of Leopardi's poetry and has done so from a position very close to Gentile's.[34] The "titanism" which Bosco discerns in much of the poetry is essentially a pride in the bitter knowledge of man's littleness. The *pietà* which Bosco finds to be a pervasive element in Leopardi is close to the love and pity Gentile attributed to the poet as a dominant feeling toward men in their misery and helplessness. These qualities do not characterize different periods in Leopardi's poetic development; they are at the basis of all his poetry. Such a claim does not mean, for Gentile any more than for Bosco, that the individual poems cannot be characterized as distinct from each other. All that it means is that changes and development are to be viewed in the light of this single, complex feeling which is the essence of Leopardi's poetry.

The success of Gentile's criticism of Leopardi is the more impressive since Leopardi's general outlook and basic sentiment are so very different from Gentile's own. Croce seems like the perfect critic of Ariosto because spiritually akin to him: Croce keeps aloof from the material he works with, just as Ariosto keeps aloof from his characters; Croce's easy banter, his ironic joviality, his at times Olympian joy spring from anguish no more than Ariosto's harmony and love do. But Leopardi was a materialist, battling endlessly with *noia*, with ennui, and with his sense of man's futility, whereas Gentile was an idealist, vibrantly enthusiastic, boring at times to be sure, but never bored, full as he was of the sense of man's infinite possibilities. If constitutive criticism of a poet alien to oneself is most difficult, then Gentile's essays on Leopardi are nearly miraculous. But his very theory of criticism, it should be noted, requires that the critic identify himself with his opposite. The objectivity obtainable within this conception of criticism is greater than in most theories, because Gentile is demanding so much self-consciousness. In explicating the life of a poet's feeling, the critic would be required to ponder at length over the *differences* between the poet's feeling and his own; only then could he avoid unintended confusion between the poet's sense of life and his own; and only then could he attain genuine oneness with the poet in a state of pure feeling. The impressiveness of the critic's achieved identity with a poet almost his opposite remains; but it is explained as a characteristic of all successful criticism, which is by definition the difficult realization of what Blake summed up in the proverb, "Opposition is true friendship." In fact, one may wish to attribute the inferiority of Gentile's criticism of such artists as Dante, Alfieri, and Manzoni to his overly close spiritual affinity with them. He may well have seen too much of himself in them. Gentile believed himself his brother's keeper; he believed as intensely as man can believe in the oneness of all men. It would be only natural, then, that in writing of those spiritually like himself, his sense of oneness might obscure significant differences.

Flaws in Gentile's Criticism

The most serious weaknesses to be found in Gentile's criticism cannot be quite so simply explained. As we have seen, he conceived of every poetic experience as the unfolding of the immediate "I" into the world of that "I." Now the individuality and universality of the act are formal, as they are in Croce's theory of art as cosmic. That is, they are attributes of the immediate "I," not of any element in the world of the "I." Or they are attributes of the mediate "I," but as dominated by the immediate "I" in the poetic dialectic, so that the two are almost indistinguishable. The immediate "I," the feeling which gives form to a poem, is, furthermore, impersonal, in the sense that it is quite distinct from the empirical "I" of the poet, from his self as one among many selves and as different from those other selves. *La filosofia dell' arte* takes account of the fact that a poet may write egotistically, in the common sense of the word. That is, he may work against the impersonality of the poetic form; he may try to exclude some of the feeling from his poetic world; he may even begin to think of himself as being, in the very act of creation, one self cut off from other selves and as writing for them or in spite of them or to work upon them. Such thoughts could be caught up in the poetic form, it is true. But if pushed far enough, if the corruption became extreme, then the act of writing would be polarized toward the objective moment of the dialectic, the moment in which even selves are objects separate from each other; and it would no longer be essentially poetic.[35] Though Gentile took account of such poetic failure in a theoretical way, he almost wholly ignored it in his practical criticism. Realizing that there is an element of non-poetry in every line of even the greatest poetry, he simply ignored the fact that even according to his own theory there are two kinds of non-poetry. There is the genre which is dominated by the immediate subjectivity of the poetic act; but there is also the genre which itself dominates, so that the objective moment of its dialectic becomes essential and the act does not simply include the non-poetic moment but is essentially non-poetic. Certainly it would be likely that in a fairly long poem a few lines would prove to be essentially non-poetic, with the egoism of the poet overcoming his subjective "I." Even the recognition by Gentile of one empty rhyme, one hurriedly composed because a famished poet heard the dinner bell, would be satisfying in its humanness. But Gentile will not demean himself by distinguishing non-poetic lines within a poem which is essentially poetic. Once he has decided that a poem is poetic, then it is a poetic unity and all its elements are contained within it. If something stands out against the unity, that means that the critic is simply not translating well enough. In other words, Gentile is a chronic over-reader, even though his theory should have cautioned him against it.

This error, by far the most serious in his criticism, is evidently caused by something merely personal, some egoistic flaw in his nature. Possibly his very exuberance made him trust those he trusted at all in a wholehearted way, poets as well as politicians and tyrants. But that may be an overly generous interpretation. He may have been reacting antagonistically against Croce, who erred in the opposite way of breaking down poems line by line into the poetic parts and the non-poetic parts. More probably the flaw stems from a combination of these two weaknesses, the one generous, the other petty. This combination may be seen quite openly in Gentile's distinction between the man of genius and the ingenious scholar, a distinction made toward the end of *La filosofia dell' arte* as part of his analysis of genius and taste. Pettiness lies in the implied identification of the ingenious scholar with Croce, the genius with Gentile. The implication is unavoidable if the passage is considered in the context of the entire book. On the other hand, Gentile's very definition of a genius suggests that he would be an overly generous reader of poetry, one who slid over single bad lines for the glory of the whole. An analysis made by an ingenious man, Gentile says, will show that ingenuity is

clarity of thought, it is knowledge and skill in technique, it is doctrine and erudition, it is that sharpness of intellect which perceives
the littlest things, the least apparent particulars and the most fleeting aspects. It is completeness of description. It is the cleverness
and wit of one who, not being within things, feels himself to be on
the outside and smiles and lightly passes and escapes. But it is not
profundity of thought, it is not warmth of inspiration, it is not the
force which draws souls along with it mastering them and raising
them to the vision of a superior world, one no longer visible. Ingenuity belongs to exegetes, genius to creators. Ingenuity does not
aspire to originality, since for it things are already there in front of
one and the job required is to distinguish them well and recognize
them in their order and by their signs. And vice versa, the genius
does not know things already there before him: tormented by his
anxiousness for a world to be created and which he will create. In
this anxiety particulars do not matter, he does not have eyes for the
parts, fixed as he is on the whole, on the synthesis of the elements,
on the vital. In his profundity he is obscure: material of study for
commentators, like that nature which gives its investigators so much
to do.[36]

There is nothing objectively accurate about the distinction,
but it can be said to present a contrast between Gentile's own
ideal for himself and the worst possible picture one could
draw of Croce. The obvious truth is that both men were
geniuses with a good bit of ingenuity at their command. But
emotionally Gentile allied himself with those who seek, with
those whose novelty makes them obscure, with those who love
the object of their study with a passion, with those who will
neglect a flaw for the greater truths.

Gentile's deep-seated attachment to the distinction between
the genius and the ingenious one and his association of it with
Croce and himself is curiously borne out in a tribute which
he wrote for Giuseppe Pitrè, a Sicilian physician and folk-
lorist. He tells of the close friendship between Pitrè and Salva-
tore Salamone-Marino, also a Sicilian physician and folk-
lorist. He tells how their friendship ended, with a break as
violent and bitter as their friendship had been intimate. The

break was not caused by any mere occasion, Gentile tells us, but because of a profound spiritual disparity:

Salamone-Marino was the student of positivistic methods; the naturalist in search of the so-called objective truth. To ascertain the facts, all, in so far as they can be ascertained, of equal value, as the elements of that truth in whose discovery and definition is the whole interest of scientific research.[37]

Pitrè was very different. He loved Sicily and studied it with a passion and tried for as much critically valid knowledge as possible:

But he never had the absurd pretense of detaching himself from the material of his studies, as if it would move and speak for itself, once it was brought to light. And he did not have this pretense because against such an ingenuous and unintelligent form of inanimate and empty objectivism his nature rebelled. It led him to live with all his intelligence and culture, within the Sicily of his heart, within its memories, within its pains, within its passions.[38]

Salamone-Marino's form of thought kept him aloof from the object of his study, even when it was Sicily, the beloved country. Pitrè, in contrast to this, took whatever he studied into himself and made it live with a vitality at least partly his own. The implicit analogy to which I am referring is, of course, that between Pitrè and Salamone-Marino in Sicily and Gentile and Croce in Italy. And Gentile wrote his tribute to Pitrè at a date late enough to indicate that he must have sensed with great bitterness the contrast between Croce's aloof integrity and his own sacrifice of himself to an Italy plunging toward ruin.

In truth, however important so absolute a separation may be in politics, in aesthetics its significance does not go beyond the distinction of Croce's frequent under-reading of poetry and Gentile's inveterate over-reading of whatever poetry he took to be worthy of his thought. For us to consider the aesthetics of Croce and that of Gentile as simply opposite, without an underlying unity, or for us to concentrate upon one to the neglect of the other, whatever partisan comfort it might give, would entail the emasculation of the aesthetics of both.

For in all that is crucial to criticism and aesthetics, the differences between Gentile and Croce cannot be understood apart from the fundamental oneness of their thinking. Croce's theory of art as cosmic is a translation of his own earlier aesthetics in the light of Gentile's actualistic logic. Gentile's theory of art as self-translation is, similarly, a translation of early actualistic aesthetics in the light of Croce's mature aesthetics. The differences between the theories of art as cosmic and of art as self-translation, apparent as I hope this chapter has made them, are indeed relatively slight. Apart from Gentile's aesthetics, Croce's is confused; apart from Croce's, Gentile's is arid. But if their aesthetics are considered together and as fundamentally at one, in spite of the fierce antagonism of the two men, nothing in the entire history of aesthetics comes close to the richness and clarity of their theories of art as both knowledge and action.

Chapter Six

R. G. Collingwood's
Early Aesthetics:
Art as Contradiction

*S*uperficially, the aesthetics of R. G. Collingwood seems to develop in a direction opposite to that of Italian aesthetics as we have interpreted it. Collingwood appears to move from an actualistic position in his *Speculum Mentis* of 1924 to a Crocean form of thought in *The Principles of Art* of 1938. Beneath this appearance, however, the movement of his thought is quite different. In truth, Collingwood's early position is a bizarre combination of Crocean aesthetics and actualistic method; his final position is an impressive though unsuccessful combination of the mature aesthetics of Croce with that of Gentile. Unbelievable as it may sound to anyone acquainted with *The Principles of Art*, Collingwood first explains art not as knowledge, but as error, not as active, but as passive, not as emotional, but as unemotional. Even so, his first theory of art should be viewed within the tradition of neo-idealistic aesthetics, as a worthy parody entitled not "Poetry as Knowledge and Action," but "Poetry as Error and Inaction." Most amazing of all is that from so strange a beginning he worked his way to a major expression of the theory of art as active, cognitive, and emotional. His final position is not, at least conceptually, an advance over either Croce or Gentile. In fact, this first of two chapters devoted to Collingwood is given over to his early position mainly so that the deep rifts in the thought of *The Principles of Art* may be understood as something other than inexplicable lapses. But even in its errors Collingwood's final position is serious enough so that much may be learned from it.

Warned as he now should be that Collingwood does not make a significant advance over earlier neo-idealistic aesthetics, the reader might properly question whether our study provides his theory of art with an appropriate context of thought. After all, it may be said, a recent book concerning Collingwood's later philosophy has all but ignored Italian idealism; and it is certainly true that Collingwood brings to his studies of art some ideas which are closer to the thinking of F. H. Bradley, Bernard Bosanquet, E. F. Carritt, and H. Wildon Carr than to Italian aesthetics. Given the complexity of the Italians' thought, and its diversity from one period to another, reducing Collingwood to Croce's or to Gentile's position cannot be our intention. In answer to any claim that Collingwood's aesthetics is either Crocean or Gentilean, one must raise the question: With which particular Crocean or Gentilean aesthetics is his thought being identified? The reductive, unhistorical thought which leads to facile identifications of Collingwood with either the actualists or Croce is as gross a blunder as the belligerent notion that Croce and Gentile were utterly antagonistic to each other. For all that, Croce and Gentile were antagonistic and Collingwood was Italianate. If his early position recalls the quip "Inglese Italianato è un diabolo incarnato," his mature aesthetics redeems him without ceasing to be closely related to Italian thought.

The external evidence for Collingwood's affinities with Croce and with Italian actualism is impressive, but may be only briefly noted here, since it has been adequately considered by others.[1] Collingwood translated Croce's study of Vico, his autobiography, and his "Aesthetica in nuce," of the *Ultimi saggi* (1935).[2] He translated two works by De Ruggiero, his *La filosofia contemporanea* (with A. H. Hannay) and his *Storia del liberalism europeo;* and he revised the translation of a long passage from Gentile's *La filosofia dell' arte* by E. F. Carritt, a passage appearing in Carritt's *Philosophies of Beauty* (Oxford, 1931).[3] Furthermore, the evidence that Collingwood shifted emotionally from actualism to Croce is unequivocal. His early attachment to actualism is attested by the comical conclusion to his article "Croce's Philosophy of History," which was published in 1921 in *The Hibbert Journal*. Collingwood rounds off his actualistic demolition of Croce by suggesting that Croce may, by deserting philosophy for history, "reach the point of absolute idealism to which his successors Gentile and De Ruggiero have already carried his thought." [4] On this reference to Croce's "successors," which is repeated in the *Speculum Mentis,* Croce comments amusingly that Collingwood's confusion of his "predecessors" with his "successors" was only a temporary error.[5] It is plain that by 1928 Collingwood's allegiance had shifted from the actualists to Croce. In a letter written in that year to Croce, he expresses his plan to dedicate himself to philosophy as the methodology of history. And in a letter written ten years later, he tells Croce that *The Principles of Art* follows Croce's aesthetics in all essentials (a kind acknowledgment, but what, one wonders, could it mean?).[6] Finally, in his own *Autobiography* of 1939 Collingwood refers in a veiled way to his belief that when Gentile became a Fascist he ruined himself as a philosopher.[7]

All these points assure us that the proper context for Collingwood's theories of art must include Italian neo-idealistic aesthetics. He belongs here and cannot be understood elsewhere. The external evidence tells us little more than that; and, to be sure, we must use care not to reduce him to this context, for his failures grow out of certain predilections which he shared with other English philosophers.

Art as Contradiction

Considered apart from its Italian context, Collingwood's early aesthetics, as it is presented in the *Speculum Mentis* (1924) and in the *Outlines of a Philosophy of Art* (1925), is almost incredible. Reduced to a bare and unpalatable form, Collingwood is saying that art is a contradiction between what it is *for* itself, what it is for the artist who experiences it, and what it is *in* itself, what it is for the philosopher who analyzes it. As an error, as a contradiction, Art, he finds, is simply absurd—which explains why only savages, children, and dreamers are artistic. Collingwood's manner of expression contributes to the air of folly which hovers about so odd and antiquated a theory. He writes as though what art is *for* itself were really what art is *in* itself. Having misled his reader in this way, he then shifts to what art really is *in* itself, and thus seems directly to contradict what he has just been saying. Disturbed, as he should be, the reader is then in need of the argument which shows that, though art is in truth contradictory, the philosopher who sees this truth is only being paradoxical. The style seems offensive even as paradoxical rather than contradictory, because it is a way of playing with the reader, leading him to the truth circuitously, by way of apparent contradiction and shock. If the reader of such a book is prepared simply to remain passive while he is being amused, he can endure it more easily than if he reads actively, striving to reconstruct the author's thought and to translate it in his own mind. For when he reads in the second way, he is not simply being played upon, he discovers that he is being played upon, and ought to be put on guard against tricks. It is all too obvious that the author of serious thoughts, however humorous, wry, and witty he may be, is unwise to play with his serious readers, although he may join with them in playing upon those certain to misread him. Collingwood assures us that he has no intention of putting our noses to the dialectical grindstone; but his style nudges us in that direction, toward that flimsiest and most fanciful kind of dialectic, the dialectic of paradoxes. Whatever his success—and we shall see that it was not much —Collingwood did have a serious purpose in his early aesthetics, a purpose plainly visible when viewed against a background of Italian aesthetics. It will be recalled that early actualistic aesthetics, as represented by Fazio-Allmayer and De Ruggiero, was inclined to reduce art to criticism and poetry to philosophy. In fact, in his article dedicated to Collingwood and Hannay, De Ruggiero asserts that the art of Dante should be approached in exactly the same way as the philosophy of Thomas Aquinas. This argument provoked Croce's hilarity:

For De Ruggiero the true and real categories are not art, philosophy, science and such, but persons, and, without incommoding Dante and Thomas Aquinas, those of our daily acquaintance, Peppino, Giovannino, Gaetanino, Michelino, and so forth. It is serious, but it is thus.[8]

Early actualism, as we have seen, tended to reduce everything to philosophy. In the *Speculum Mentis* Collingwood tried to present an actualistic and logic-centered position—as all admit, even Croce—without reducing everything to logic and philosophy. Looking back upon the book after seven or eight years, De Ruggiero—who had ceased by then to be an actualist—was able to praise it for accomplishing just that:

Like few others, Collingwood has a profound sense for dialectical opposition and adheres to the richness and variety of the forms of human experience. Reading his book, we do not encounter that mere formalism characteristic of the final stage of that Italian idealistic school which has taken the name of actual idealism.[9]

Collingwood's plan is to present the position of Croce's early *Estetica* as the way art is *for* itself. Art as it is experienced by artists and as they think about it is, Collingwood tells us, "pure imagination," the subject immediately at one with its object:

The experience of beauty is an experience of utter union with the object; every barrier is broken down, and the beholder feels that his own soul is living in the object, and that the object is unfolding its life in his own heart.[10]

Art as pure imagination—though with paradoxes flying thickly about us we must not expect neatness of language—is basically what Croce meant in the *Estetica* by contemplation. One *sees*, and the object one sees is neither real nor unreal, for to such a distinction the imagination is indifferent.[11] As in the *Estetica*, the imagination as described by Collingwood is concerned only with the individual, and not with relations among individuals, which are the concern of the intellect. Art, we are told, creates out of nothing, simply by attending to an object—Collingwood is largely ignoring feeling and emotion just as Croce did at first. Furthermore, Collingwood allows that for the artist art is identical with language; it is expressive and its meaning is immediately identical with the vehicle of expression, with that which carries meaning.[12] Finally, like the early Croce, Collingwood presents this conception of art as a concrete activity,[13] as experiential, and as self-contained and autonomous. Art, in essence and in existence, is thought to be primitive and pure, the simplest of human activities.

When art as it is *in* itself becomes his subject, however, Collingwood shifts from a mock acceptance of Croce's early aesthetics to an actualistic position. Art is in truth a complex activity mistaken by those who indulge in it for something simple and primitive. Art is not pure imagination; it is rather thought mistaking itself for pure imagination.[14] The artist possesses a concept of relevance and of coherence, and it is in the light of that concept that he imagines just what he imagines and ignores what he ignores. Art seems immediate to the artist and his sense of beauty is an emotional coloring on the object imagined. In truth, however, art is mediate and the artist alternates between his concept, which determines the beauty of his images, and those images themselves.[15] Put in a slightly different way, it may be said that the artist erroneously imagines that he does not think, that the thinking which controls and disciplines his imagination is some outer force. He calls himself inspired, and in the aesthetic experience his thinking is present simply as a feeling of *givenness*.[16] In fact, however, he is thinking, and he is his own muse. Furthermore, art does not really create out of nothing as the artist fancies it does. His imaginings rest upon and stem from the facts of his own life and environment.[17] He ignores his dependence, and his ignorance makes him an artist rather than a critic, a critic being one who traces the connection between a work of art and its factual basis. In another sense, however, the artist is a critic mistaking himself for an artist. In addition to connecting image and fact, the critic judges whether an image is beautiful or ugly. Although unaware of it the artist, like the critic, judges his every image in the light of his concept of relevance: if it does not fit the concept he rejects it as ugly; if it fits he accepts it as beautiful. Furthermore, art is not truly language; it is thought mistaking itself for language, for the opaqueness resulting from the erroneous belief that a word and its significance are immediately fused into one. Form and content, the principle of oneness and the many images included within it, are moreover imagined by the artist to be immediately identical. In fact, however, they are not only distinct, but contradictory. The artist works out his principle of oneness beforehand, and that is an act of thought. He then shifts from this abstract thought to his equally abstract imagination.[18] Contrary to Croce's identification of expression and intuition, Collingwood views them actualistically as contradictory.

From such an analysis it should be evident that art does not even exist. Its very birth is its death. Instead of being self-contained, it is, as contradictory, endlessly self-transcendent. What does exist is thought mistaking itself for art. According to Collingwood's own analogy, art *in* itself is like a man mistaking himself for a poached egg.[19] The imagined poached egg does not exist, but the man and his error do. The error does in truth make a difference: the man is not simply a man, he is a man with a delusion. If the error were wiped out, art would be philosophy. Art is not philosophy, it is erroneous philosophy.[20]

It should be emphasized that art, as it is being conceived of here, is truly contradictory. Collingwood is not presenting an erroneous view of art, that of the early Croce, and then correcting it with the actualistic truth. Instead he is presenting the true view of art as error, as an activity available only to those who are mistaken. To learn the truth about art is to lose the art. One cannot, it should be granted, know that one is a man mistaking himself for a poached egg and continue making that mistake. Once the mistake is gone, so is the egg. With the truth comes an end of art: if one knows the difference between the real and the unreal, then one cannot fail to distinguish between the real and the unreal. Since that very failure is the essence of the imagination, one's knowledge must obliterate his imagination. Art is either art or philosophy mistaking itself for art. Once one knows which it is, he is cut off from art. And, in truth, it is a good thing. As Collingwood says, the artist is like a man who turns himself into a werewolf whenever he can. He cannot be a werewolf all the time since he must do the insipid, daily chores; but, living in his error, he thinks that being one is the only thing worthwhile. No wonder then, Collingwood concludes, that "the artistic temperament" is a term of reproach! [21]

In effect, Collingwood has erected the most destructive contradiction to be found in Croce's aesthetics as late as 1913 into the fundamental truth about art. Art is simple awareness; that is the truth about art as artists experience it. But the truth about art for artists, what is explicit for them, is only an appearance. In reality, art is complex; it is both knowledge and action. But the reality of art is only implicit in art itself, and thus art is reality mistaking itself for an appearance. Now, setting aside temporarily the chance that such a *tour de force* is an imitation of the method used by F. H. Bradley in his *Appearance and Reality* (In his *Autobiography* Collingwood claims that Bradley had the most deeply critical mind in European philosophy after Hume),[22] we may ask, how could a discriminating student of art like Collingwood allow himself to be led into so anti-aesthetic an interpretation of art?

The Absurdity of the Theory

The *Speculum Mentis* is a distressing book because it is meant to be actualistic and yet is weakest at that very point where the actualists distinguish themselves from Croce; that is, at the point of self-consciousness. Collingwood's plan is to improve upon Italian actualism by retaining as part of its dialectic five forms of activity given prominence in Croce's Philosophy of the Spirit. Like Croce and unlike the actualists, he allows that, in a sense, the forms are separate from each other. But each is separate for Collingwood not because of what it is formally—as at least some of them are for Croce— but only because it erroneously claims, against the other forms, to be the sole repository of the ultimate truth. Apart from its error each of the first four forms, art, religion, science, and history, is really the fifth, philosophy. The artist—to remain within our subject—claims that his specialty embodies the truth. But for its erroneous claim to a separate possession of the truth, however, art is nothing but an element in philosophy.

The perversity of Collingwood's position becomes immediately apparent when one asks, Do any artists or poets who experience art in the way described by Croce as "aesthetic contemplation" actually claim the ultimate truth for art? Collingwood includes art in his dialectical series only on the grounds that they do. But they obviously do not, because Croce's early aesthetics was framed specifically to deny the ultimate truthfulness of art. In the early *Estetica* art is presented as primitive, and that means that it is *not* truthful, useful, or good. Folly, then, is the very basis of Collingwood's consideration of art. He is asking us to believe that "the artist as such" goes about asserting: my art, of course, has nothing to do with truth and goodness, and that is why it is the sole repository of ultimate truth. We are being asked to hear this typical artist say: yes, I alone possess the ultimate truth, knowledge of what is truly real, because I alone refuse to distinguish between the real and the unreal. Such a statement sets practice and theory at odds. It suggests that an artist who experiences his art as ultimate truth thinks about it according to a theory which explicitly denies that, as beauty, art has anything to do with either truth or goodness. Such an idea is more absurd than the absurdity it attributes to artists. Collingwood, or at least so it would seem, had no good reason for thinking that artists were so utterly cut off from theories of art as truth. Setting aside theories of art as pedagogic because they are unduly ancient, we may expect that romantic theories like those of Coleridge and Shelley were still current. For that matter, in one of his finest essays Croce opposes Shelley's claims for art as excessive. If an existent artist, in contrast to a non-referential type ("the artist"), claims like Shelley that art attains truth, then he will think of the imagination as a form of *insight* that penetrates beneath surfaces and into some inner reality. If another artist claims that art does not attain truth, he may well think of the imagination as a form of *seeing* which concentrates upon surfaces. To claim that all artists as artists mix up these two positions does not follow.

The most devastating consequence of this illogic is that most of the talk about art in both the *Speculum Mentis* and the *Outlines* lacks an experiential basis. Nobody except the mad artist who thinks he is a poached egg experiences and thinks about art as Collingwood says "the artist" does. Repeatedly we read phrases like "the artist as such," "the aesthetic experience," and "the concrete activity of art" without being able to relate them to any conceivable human experience, let alone to any which we ourselves have had.

How, one may ask, could a serious thinker use a phrase signifying a type of person, "the artist," as if it referred to individuals, to certain artists, in such a way that it could not possibly point to anything existent or experiential? In the Italian aesthetics which we have been studying the answer would be, Impossible! In British aesthetics, however, the answer would rather be, But that is just why aesthetics is not a respectable branch of thought; for some British aestheticians talk about non-existent types as though they exist. If I. A. Richards and other "new critics" had any effect at all, surely they must have shamed such academicians out of existence. In British aesthetics just prior to Collingwood's *Speculum Mentis*, however, confusing the type and the individual is habitual, as the works of F. H. Bradley, Bosanquet, and Carritt, among others, make manifest. Now if one can talk endlessly about the intimacy between an artist and his medium, confusing the class-term "medium" with the actual and individual material with which a certain artist is working at a certain time; if one errs in this way as Bosanquet repeatedly does, then one is well on the way to talking about types which lack experiential reference as though those types were themselves existent individuals.[23] Confuse the individual and the particular, confuse an existent artist at work and the abstract idea of "the artist" long enough, and a tradition of aesthetics may develop with no existential significance whatsoever. Croce, as we have seen, blundered logically into confusing "an individual poem" and "the poetic"; but because of the solid experiential basis for everything he said, because his daily reading and criticism of individual poems lay behind his comments about "the poetic," there is always something existential to be learned from his most confused abstractions. British aesthetics, however, lacked a critical and experiential basis. The most obvious evidence for this lack is the plethora of poetic quotations in works by Carritt and Bosanquet, writers desperate from the lack of real experience, who strive to fill the gap with the appearance of experience, with lines of poetry only vaguely pertinent to the immediate fancy under discussion. Italian aestheticians avoided excessive quotation because a reader who is understanding their thought is led constantly to relate the meaning of their general terms to individual artistic experiences.

Collingwood's failure, then, is in the tradition; he is simply following a pattern. He can refer to "the artist" without regretting the absence of individual artists, without being disturbed that his types cannot have existing instances, because British aesthetics had been anaesthetized against contact with individual artistic experience. Bradley himself, with his deeply critical mind, could pull out of nowhere the phrase "Beauty is the self-existent pleasant," and then prove that the experience of beauty is self-contradictory in that it is just one more appearance on the path to ultimate reality.[24] G. E. Moore's common-sense reaction to such phantasies was sensible.

The Inconsistency of Collingwood's Thought

Collingwood had plenty of personal experience with art; but, as an aesthetician, he could not think in such a way as to connect his thought with that experience. Behind his theory of art as contradiction lies a contradiction in his own thinking. Within one and the same argument he has put two contradictory dialectics to work. Explicitly, the *Speculum Mentis* is organized around a Hegelian dialectical series, a movement from thesis to antithesis to synthesis, a movement modelled upon that from Being through Nothing to Becoming. Implicitly, however, the book is actualistic: it is the unfolding of the thinking subject becoming aware of itself as identical with its opposite, with its object. At the end of his lengthy argument, Collingwood asserts that philosophical thinking is ultimately truthful because it is the discovering of itself in its object. Having passed through an analysis of art, religion, science, and history, the philosopher Collingwood discovers this truth about his own thinking. It goes beyond the contradictory claims of those other forms of activity and discovers their genuine reality within itself:

Concrete philosophy is therefore art. That beauty which is the fleeting quarry of the artist is no stranger to the philosopher. His thought must clothe itself in speech, and to him all the quire of heaven and the furniture of earth becomes a divine language, symbolizing in sensuous imagery the eternal truths of thought.[25]

Observing the movement of his own thinking as it objectifies itself, the philosopher, according to this actualistic argument, would discover the pure imagination as the first moment of his own thinking, as immediacy contained within the mediation of his thinking. But once Collingwood has reached this peak of self-consciousness, he fails to show us that he has really been there all along. To do so, he would have to return to a consideration of each form of activity and to show us how it is integrated within the dialectic of active thinking. He does not do so, partly because he is not quite that self-conscious, and partly because his original presentation of art is anti-actualistic: he saw art not as a form of immediacy contained within mediate activity, but as immediacy which was excluded by mediation. To think about art is to recognize it as thought mistaking itself for imagination. Once it is recognized as error, the imagination cannot be experienced as immediate. Without immediacy, there is no art to experience. All the immediate identifications, of subject and object, of word and meaning, of form and content, of intuition and expression, evaporate into error as soon as one knows the true nature of art. This approach to art contradicts Collingwood's brief actualistic comments at the end of his text. Collingwood did not begin at the beginning of the actualistic dialectic; he began at the beginning of a Hegelian or Bradleian dialectical series.

Now this series begins not with the mediate subject, but with the immediate subject. This moment, Collingwood says, is presupposed by all the others in the series, each of which springs out of the internal contradictions of the moment which precedes it. Instead of beginning his study of the dialectic with the act of thinking, Collingwood begins by identifying himself wholly with the first moment of his series. Then, by experiencing that moment from the inside out, he seeks to express its contradiction, that between intuition and expression, a contradiction which forces art, the moment of immediacy, to transcend itself and become religion, the assertion of the imagined object as real. "Art as such" and "Art as understood" contradict each other not as part of the actualistic dialectic: in that dialectic the immediate moment would be preserved as synthesized. They contradict each other as part of a series which destroys the first moment in the birth of the second. Understanding art and experiencing it are utterly incompatible. Croce had said that the Hegelian transcendence of the concept of art is truly the death of art, not its preservation in a higher form. Although the same cannot be said of an actualistic conception of art, it can be said of art within Collingwood's dialectical series. Collingwood says very little about art within the dialectic of actual thinking, which is at work only toward the end of his book, presumably because he has taken care of its preservation as part of the dialectical series. In truth, he has not.

Gentile, in pursuit of a tentative insight of Spaventa's, had discovered that unless one turns Hegel's dialectic upside down and begins with Becoming as actual thinking, the movement from Being to Nothing must be arbitrary, so that the dialectic cannot be set in motion unless one surreptitiously introduces an element of thinking. The arbitrariness of Collingwood's series bears this out. At first, it is true, he presents his series as though it were meant to be as logically rigorous as Hegel's series was meant to be. He introduces it as a "natural" order,[26] and De Ruggiero was misled into believing its order to be "irreversible and progressive." [27] Collingwood admits that the order of the series, which he has presented as "dialectically necessary," had simply been used by him as a matter of convenience.[28] Although we may be grateful for the admission, it contradicts everything prior to it. If he did not mean the series to be taken seriously, then possibly his arbitrary use of actualistic reasoning within the series, thinking introduced surreptitiously in order to make the series move, is not meant to be taken seriously either.

One illustration of such idle actualism should suffice. It is an argument used to reduce the individuality of art to something quite inferior to anything seen thus far in neo-idealistic aesthetics. It will be recalled that, in discussing art, Collingwood means to be thinking from the inside out. Now he asserts that the "work of art as such," as experienced by the artist, as it is *for* the artist, is a windowless monad.[29] By this he means that the artist is absorbed entirely in his imagined object and that there are many other imagined objects which he ignores. This claim is clearly nonsense when made from within the artistic experience itself. If the artist imagines, as part of his imaginative experience, that he is ignoring things, then his very ignoring of things becomes part of his experience, and it is not a windowless monad at all. Tennyson's "Now Sleeps the Crimson Petal, Now the White" is a superb example of a pure, exclusive poetic experience weighed down by all the reality it is "ignoring." An artist need not ignore all other poems during his creation of a new poem. Consider William Collins' "Ode to Evening," which is so richly allusive that it seems to include elements of all kinds of English poems from Spenser's up to the moment of its own composition. What then can Collingwood mean? He has unjustifiably shifted his point of view from within a poetic experience to one external to it. From a center of activity outside the artistic experience, he then views that experience not as an activity, but as a fact, not as a process, but as a product; and, as one fact among many, as one empirical object among many such objects, it appears to involve a neglect of its relationships with other experiences. It appears self-centered, not inclusive, but exclusive. In the same way, every kind of experience could be shown to be neglectful of other experiences. The only inclusive experience is the present activity of thinking itself, whether artistic, historical, or philosophical. Collingwood has introduced the distinction between act and fact in a wholly illegitimate way simply to assert his prejudice that artists are self-absorbed and solipsistic. Artists, he feels, are egocentric children; and, as he says elsewhere, unlike us historically trained philosophers, artists can be genuinely interested only in contemporary art.[30] Although the prejudice is patently false, Collingwood makes his claim as though his dialectical series requires it. The only grace saving him is that we may doubt whether he really takes either his dialectical series or the actualistic distinction between act and fact with any seriousness.

Collingwood could not take the thought of his *Speculum*

Mentis seriously because both his dialectics, the Hegelian and the actualistic, are truncated forms. Each is composed of two terms rather than three. In the dialectical series there is no mediation whatsoever. Art is simply a contradiction between intuition and expression. There is no mediation between them, and the artist wanders confusedly from one to the other. Furthermore, there is no mediation between art as such, as pure imagination, and the truth that art is thought mistaking itself for imagination. Nor is religion a synthesis of the contradictions of art. Instead it is just one more contradiction to art, an opposite which does not include, but which excludes art by repudiating the artist's indifference to the reality of his images and asserting its own image as real. The entire series moves in just this way, each new form denying not just the error in what precedes it, but whatever intrinsic form it has, everything that makes it distinctive, until one reaches the final form of philosophy. From this fifth form one should have reason to expect the synthesis missing thus far. But at this point, where Collingwood tries to shift from his series to an actualistic dialectic, the third, mediating moment is missing as much as ever. Whereas the fourth moment, history, had asserted the absolute fact, the object, as an all-inclusive reality, philosophical thinking exposes the historian's failure to consider himself, the observer, as part of that reality.[31] The philosopher corrects the historian by showing that the historical object is in truth included within the observer's own awareness. The philosophical observer is no solipsistic artist; he does not exclude from his awareness anything real, for he knows that the real world is his identical, though opposite self. From this peak of self-awareness Collingwood then asserts that the dialectical series, as he has presented it, is the objectification of philosophical thinking. The philosopher is the one who thinks through the entire series; the series as object is identical with his thinking; and he, as the final, mediate thinking, is

aware of this identification. But there is nothing active or dialectical about this final relationship: it is composed of nothing
more than the inclusive awareness and the included object,
the series, which has been laid out spatially as an ascension
from one error to the next. The final dialectic is made up of
act and fact, of truth and error. There is no way to re-vivify the
series, because neither it nor the abortive actualistic dialectic
has a truly immediate subject; that is, Collingwood has allowed
the subjective immediacy of art to slip away from him, and he
has conceived of it as no more than the lowest division of a
purely objective series. As a result, there is no way to return
to art and to experience it as a genuine part of the final synthesis, as the immediate moment of the dialectic of thought.
Collingwood may assert that the artistic moment, as subjective
immediacy, is a part of this pseudo-dialectic of thought; but
he has not presented it as such. And if we return from the
final synthesis to the series as Collingwood originally constructed it, all we can say is that the most obvious thing which
it excludes is that self-awareness characteristic of thinking, of
the mediate subject. There is a subject thinking through the
series, obviously enough; for Collingwood is at work writing
out the book. But this subject lacks articulated mediation; it
is indistinct and unattended to; and opposite it is the first link
in an objective series which is composed of arbitrary contradictions and which is, therefore, not the identical opposite of
synthetic thinking, but its contradiction. Collingwood's object and subject are at one only in the sense that they are
both arbitrary and both contradict the final philosophical synthesis which is meant to overcome all contradiction.

If all thinking as real is a three-term dialectic, if all thinking is the mediate subject aware of itself as asserting its opposite but identical object, then Collingwood's failure in the
Speculum Mentis is precisely the characteristic failure of early
actualism. He has slighted the first moment, the immediate

subject, treating it not as the asserting of the moment of objectivity, but rather as indistinguishable from that moment. And such a reduction in his dialectic provides us with another explanation for his conceiving of art as an inactive, unemotional, windowless, and egocentric monad. Art for him is merely one fact among many, there to be dissected as a product rather than to be re-created as an action. And with the moment of immediate oneness reduced to a part of the objective moment, it becomes clear why Collingwood could get caught up in a series which might have been continued indefinitely, but which he stops conveniently after moment number five. For he has ignored the fundamental problem of actualism, the need to explain the relationship between the one and the many. His final subject must bear all the oneness since he lacks an immediate subject, while the whole series makes up the moment of multiplicity. He unites them only with a dogmatic assertion that they are identical opposites. Thinking through the series, we find that it directly contradicts any subjective mediation, so that, when we turn to the unadulterated thinking of philosophy, we discover it to be unable to find itself in what is supposed to be its opposite, the objective series. In order to assert it as finding itself there, Collingwood must falsify even that thinking, turning it into an act which cannot vitalize its object, but which turns everything it touches into a dissected corpse. Its triumphs are lonely since the victims are not around to share the celebration.

An Essay on Philosophical Method

Any notion that the *Speculum Mentis* is no more than the folly of Collingwood's youth, as he himself implies in his *Autobiography*, is disproved by his *An Essay on Philosophical Method*, a treatise published in 1933 when he was at the height of his intellectual powers. For a brief consideration of this,

Collingwood's major effort to systematize his philosophical method, reveals the same vacillation between two incompatible dialectics that we discovered in his youthful work. Throughout the book Collingwood wavers between an objective dialectical series like the five-form series of the *Speculum Mentis* and an actualistic dialectic of the act of thinking itself. In contrast to his earlier work, the conflict in this one is not exposed, but muffled: Collingwood's basic idea, that every philosophical concept—or act of conceiving—is a scale of forms, is vaguely and loosely enough constructed, so that it applies equally and indiscriminately to either of the two incompatible dialectics. Curt Ducasse's repudiation of the book on the grounds that it glorifies philosophical imprecision pierces to the heart of Collingwood's argument.[32] He reconciles irreconcilables by ascending to mistiness.

Ostensibly, the scale of forms is an objective series to be imagined spatially as an ascending ladder without an absolutely fixed bottom or top. Beginning from a low position one finds that, as we move up the scale, each form is closer to its full realization than the one below it. According to the planned imprecision, Collingwood refuses to unify his analyses of the relationships between one form on the scale and the form which precedes or follows it. All forms of the scale constituting Collingwood's philosophical concept are said to be species of a genus which bears the name of the concept or scale of forms in which they have a place. Unlike the relations of co-ordinate species in scientific classification, however, these species overlap. Using the *Speculum Mentis* for purposes of illustration, one may say that the two lowest species of the genus Truth are art and religion, and that these two overlap because an imagined object is an essential element of both of them. Collingwood would define their "overlap" in this way: both are the same in the sense that both embody their generic essence, both claim the truth with their imagined object; but they differ both in degree and in kind.[33] Religion embodies more of the truth than does art, and its embodiment of the truth differs in kind from that of art; for not only does it imagine an object, but it also asserts it as real. Furthermore, these forms of the scale are related according to distinction and opposition, a dual relationship presented as distinct from that of degree and kind, although the difference seems largely verbal.[34] This relation, stated simply, is the notion that that opposite which comes after *A* in the scale is not only not-*A*, but also a distinct form which performs what *A* only promised to do. *A* or art claims truth as the imagining of an object without regard to its reality. Not-*A* or religion is opposite *A* because it does not disregard the reality of the imagined object. Furthermore, it is distinct from *A* because as a refusal to disregard the reality of its object, it asserts its object as real. By using a definite illustration one shows, in my opinion, that, as Collingwood presents the terms, there is no working difference between degree and opposition, nor is there one between kind and distinction. He makes no effort to distinguish either pair. Kind and distinction are, I think, being used without a significant difference, although the real problem in Collingwood's analysis is that no effort is made either to distinguish or to unify them. And since degree as he thinks of it in philosophy is immeasurable, all that it means is "greater"—which, translated into the scale, becomes "closer to the top." Not-*A* is greater in degree than *A* as containing more of the generic essence than *A*, as being closer to the top than *A*, as being, that is, in the diminished sense of the word "opposition" as Collingwood is using it, opposite to *A*. Collingwood is multiplying distinctions in excess of his need.

More important, our illustration indicates that the forms on the scale cannot be distinguished, as Collingwood distinguishes them, unless one already possesses the full concept, the articulated generic essence of the scale. If one knows that the assertion of an image as real is closer to the truth than is an image without such an assertion, it is not because one is asserting the image as real, but because one has a criterion by means of which he can make this judgment according to the relationships of degree, kind, distinction, and opposition. One can make the judgment, that is, only if he possesses within his act of thinking a clear concept of truth itself. The possession of this criterion is concealed from Collingwood only because of vagueness, only because of his refusal to attend to the nature of his own thinking. Once again, the arbitrariness of the relation of the lower forms of the objective dialectical series becomes apparent; and Collingwood has only seemed to overcome it by an illegitimate introduction of the concept fully articulated from the very beginning.

As a matter of fact, however, Collingwood himself has much to say in the *Philosophical Method* in support of this actualistic interpretation of the scale of forms which I have just been using to criticize his conception of the scale as no more than an objective series. At several points, for example, he refers to the highest form on the scale, thus far thought through, as a theory in the light of which the lower forms are seen to be not theories, but experiences, not the living truth, but error transcended.[35] This description of the scale parallels closely Gentile's earlier conception of the dialectic as composed of two terms, act and fact. No part of the objective series of the *Speculum Mentis* but rather the act of thinking which gives the *Philosophical Method* itself its essential form provides a fitting illustration of this conception of the scale. The erroneous "experience" against which Collingwood presents his theory is, according to my judgment, no other than Croce's circle of distinct forms. Croce's forms are distinct, but they are not opposed to each other and they do not differ in degree. Each is as full an embodiment of their generic essence, of the *actus purus,* as are the others. With no explicit reference to Croce, Collingwood offers at least one interpretation of the concept as a scale of forms, as a sustained critique of Croce's notion of thought as distinction.[36] Such a critique cannot be made with the scale interpreted as an objective dialectical series; for such a series has been irrecoverably refuted by Croce himself. It can be made only with an actualistic dialectic.

The real novelty of the *Philosophical Method*, however, is a third shape which is given to the scale of forms; and it is this shape which Collingwood has most clearly in mind. Interpreted in this third way, the scale is not an objective series in which one moves according to a "natural" order from one error to the next until he reaches the true form, a form actually present from the beginning, though playfully concealed from the reader. Nor is it a scale composed of only two forms, one's own present thinking which contains the *logos*, the criterion of truth, and that erroneous thought which one is transcending. It is really no other than the layout of Collingwood's book. He begins the *Philosophical Method* with a relatively low form of the concept of philosophical method, with what we know about it from common experience. We all know, he says, that species in philosophical thinking do not remain separate, but overlap. Having set forth this imprecise idea, Collingwood then raises himself to the higher level of the scale of forms itself. This level may be said to differ from that of the overlap in degree and in kind; but it cannot be said to oppose it unless one reduces "opposition" to "degree." The lower level is not opposed by the higher in any fuller sense of the word "opposition" because Collingwood asserts that one appeals to the lower for verification of the higher. We are asked to accept the higher level, the scale of forms, just because it is a case of overlapping. In harmony with G. E. Moore's appeal to common sense, Collingwood would have us verify our refined forms by reference to the form of common experience.[37] The higher form differs from the lower only in the sense that it is more precise and articulate. The higher form is true to the extent that it explains the lower. Finally, if the layout of the *Philosophical Method* has a third level to its scale beyond the notions of the overlap of species and of the scale of forms, it is Collingwood's act of thinking through the book itself, including within it the levels of overlapping and of the scale of forms and transcending, by means of them, Croce's conception of thought as distinction. If this third level is presented only in an ambiguous way, it is because here too Collingwood refuses to choose between an objective series and an actualistic dialectic. In this particular case, the choice is between a series beginning with imprecision and concluding precisely and a dialectic which can begin only with precise thinking, only with self-awareness, only with a sense of what one is doing as he actually thinks. The layout of the book is an imaginary form of thinking: one moves from what is obvious, common, and imprecise to what is erudite, elevated, and precise. The essential and truly existent form of the book, however, is the form of its actual thinking, the form of philosophy as the history of philosophy, the form of Collingwood's argument as an analysis and transcendence of Croce's philosophical method.

Collingwood's failure to choose between the two forms is, in fact, an argument against his conception of philosophical method as a movement from imprecise common sense to precise knowledge. He begins imprecisely; he concludes, not precisely, but imprecisely. With actualism there are no half-way houses; they had all been demolished at least by the time of the publication of Gentile's *La filosofia dell' arte,* a work which Collingwood must have known. Collingwood was not, however, convinced one way or the other,—a point made by Professor W. G. De Burgh in a review of one of Collingwood's later pieces. To my mind, he could not be convinced because what he saw of actualism was a static and sterile two-term pseudo-dialectic of act and fact, truth and error, present and past. Seeing no more than this in the concept of the act of thinking as the ultimately real, he wandered among shifting and antiquated phantasms.

In justification of his wandering, it should be said that he may have added a form of thought, the scale moving from common-sense imprecision to precision, to his other two dialectics, just because there was no living environment of common sense in England for which his own thinking could provide some refinement. Croce's sense was not British common sense, even though many of his ideas were well known through translations and through the work of such philosophers as J. A. Smith, Bosanquet, Carr, and Carritt. Gentile was able to begin at the highest and most precise level of thought possible just because all thinking Italy—even Mussolini, according to a near-deathbed admission—knew its Croce thoroughly. The context of imprecision existed and all he had to do was think rigorously. If Collingwood never thought in such a way, it may be because he felt forced to include within his own book a context of imprecision as a basis for the more serious thinking which he hoped to do. It is undeniable that a bitter sense of intellectual isolation permeates Collingwood's *Autobiography*. His choice may well have been between these two things: writing to himself in the hope that others would refine themselves enough so that they could hear him without that incomprehension which can turn anything to dust and ashes; or letting that R. G. C. who was "a man of action" loose upon the world in an effort to speak its language and at least to lead it a little way on that path of thought much of which he had already travelled in the *Speculum Mentis*. That he chose the second alternative, the overt form of the *Philosophical Method* and that of *The Principles of Art* conclusively demonstrate. And if this is the sacrifice which he made, certainly he paid dearly for it through exposure to ridicule and refutation. Given

the obvious popularity of his books among philosophical lay-
men, however, who can say that such a sacrifice made in an
effort to reach the "people" may not be redeemed by some
future fruition, unrecognizable as its appearance must be?

Chapter Seven

The Principles of Art:
Art as Communal

*I*n his effort to explain how it is that artists actually
work with "intellectual apprehensions," the very
idea of which he opposed throughout most of *The
Principles of Art*, Collingwood has this to say about one intellectual poet:

> Donne (and this is why he has become so congenial to ourselves in
> the last twenty or thirty years) has expressed how it feels to live in
> a world full of shattered ideas, *disjecta membra* of old systems of
> life and thought, where intellectual activity is itself correspondingly
> shattered into momentary fulgurations of thinking, related to each
> other only by an absence of all logical connexion, and where the
> prevailing emotional tone of thought is simply the sense of this
> shatteredness: a tone expressed over and over again in his poems,
> for example in 'The Glasse', and in the shape of a moral idea by his
> many verses in praise of inconstancy.[1]

The Principles of Art is itself broken into three different forms
of thought, with almost no logical connections among them.
There are, if I may echo his *Autobiography* of a year
later than the *Principles*, three R. G. C.'s who keep a rather
distant company in this book. There is a Crocean R. G. C. who
thinks of art as the pure contemplation of the individual and
who sets up an objective series of forms, each distinct from

the others and autonomous, but all occupying unalterable places in the series. There is a Gentilean R. G. C. who knows that art is knowledge and action, who envisages art as a self-conscious activity in which intuition and expression are opposed and synthesized. And there is a third R. G. C., "a man of action" whose "gloves-off philosophy" is "meant to solve a 'practical' problem," whose business is to "make the world better." [2] It is this third Collingwood who laid out *The Principles of Art* as a movement from imprecise common sense about art to what he hoped would be a precise theory of art. This Collingwod exhorts his readers to action, even if unsupported by consistent theory. This is the R. G. C. whose heated and enthusiastic style gives his shattered thoughts whatever unity they may have.

The Principles of Art is not, however, of social significance only as mirroring, with its own inconsistencies, the inconsistencies of the world around it. The Gentilean and "gloves-off" forms of Collingwood's thought combine to solve the problem of how it is that the artist and his community come to know their innermost feelings only in artistic activity. Because of this solution *The Principles of Art* is clearly the most important work in neo-idealistic aesthetics by a non-Italian author and the most significant English work in aesthetics written during the present century. Collingwood solves the problem only in a practical way, it is true; he may make the world better, but without letting it know exactly why it is being so; for his forms of thought do not combine harmoniously, and their inconsistencies are compounded by the pervasiveness of the third form, his Croceanism.

Crocean Elements in The Principles of Art

Surely Collingwood was not intentionally exaggerating when he told Croce that the doctrine taught in *The Principles of*

Art "is in all essentials your own," [3] for the Crocean form is the most openly and systematically presented of the three forms making up the book. Put as concisely as possible, it may be said that according to this form of thought all experience falls into three "levels," the psychic, the imaginative, and the intellectual, with possibly a fourth level involving the activity of craftsmanship. The spring of contradiction which made the series of the *Speculum Mentis* into a dialectical series, of which each form turned into a higher through its own inconsistencies, is quite gone from this series. Even that faint nudge towards self-transcendence in the *Philosophical Method,* the sense of opposition which a lower form on the scale has towards the one directly above it, is gone from the *Principles.* The "levels of experience" are distinct and autonomous. Their order, however, is unalterable just as the order of Croce's forms of the spirit is. The imaginative level presupposes (a word dear to Collingwood from now on as its equivalent always was for Croce) the psychic, and the intellectual presupposes the imaginative. Although this order is fixed, although psychic experience provides the material for imaginative experience, which in turn provides the material for intellectual experience, Collingwood does not assert, as does Croce, that one must move from one level to the next. And here he is close to Gentile's notion that dialectical necessity must be kept out of all series elaborated within the objective moment of the dialectical act.

Collingwood's concept of psychic experience, of that which presumably must be the material for all art, is like the "psychological fact" of the first edition of Croce's *Estetica.* Collingwood allows, however, as Croce did not, for the analysis of this level, following, it would seem, Gentile's analysis in the *Sommario* of "sensation" as bearing emotion. Psychic experience, we are told, is an evermoving flow of sensa which are charged with emotion; it is what Descartes called "the immediate experience of the union of the mind and the body" and what

Alexander regarded "as a relation to ourselves which is too intimate to be knowledge." [4] More sophisticated here than Croce was, Collingwood says we must presuppose this level of experience, because we cannot know it directly as we can know the higher levels, all of which involve consciousness and self-consciousness. We know of the existence of feeling (a word whose meaning Collingwood strives to use as synonymous with "psychic experience") only as it is *given* to our consciousness and only as we observe it in others.[5] Psychic experience is mere sentience; it is below the level of consciousness, although Collingwood hesitates to call it unconscious.

In many ways, the imaginative level of experience is like the "pure imagination" of the *Speculum Mentis*. It is the conscious attending to one feeling (a sensum charged with emotion) or to one sensum, to the neglect of all others. Using one's imagination means ignoring the difference between reality and unreality; it means the absence of all relations whatsoever, the fusing of all that one views into an "individual fact." Poets and artists do not distinguish themselves from their world; they do not distinguish themselves as subject from their world as object, any more than they distinguish one sensum from another within their world. Collingwood does join Croce and Gentile in the *Principles,* as he did not in the *Speculum Mentis,* by recognizing "emotion" as part of the imagined object. Since he conceives of "emotion" as utterly passive, as simply a "charge" which hangs onto a "sensum," the word "emotion" is preferable to "feeling" for him, as it is not for either Croce or Gentile. Much that Collingwood says, furthermore, lends itself to an immediate identification of expression and intuition. Attending to a feeling is considered to be an expression of it. Actually looking at an evening sky and experiencing an emotion of tranquillity is itself an expression of that one feeling. Finally, since psychic experience raised to the imaginative level is transformed, it may be said that, in art, there is no content distinct

212 | *Neo-Idealistic Aesthetics*

from form: the two are immediately identical, just as expression and intuition and subject and object are. Immediacy and individuality, then, are the outstanding characteristics of imaginative experience, just as they were in Collingwood's earlier aesthetics and just as they usually were for Croce.

Intellectual activity, as the third and last level of experience strictly so-called, must come after and presuppose attention to individual sensa. For it is the relating of already existing sensa, and of sensa with relations, and relations with relations, and so forth. Unlike a poet, who by nature concentrates on one feeling and only one feeling in any one experience, an intelligent critic compares one imagined feeling with other such feelings and, through his comparisons, arrives at judgments as to whether a particular verse is poetry or non-poetry.

Finally, just like Croce, Collingwood recognizes a level of experience into which almost all non-poetry and pseudo-art may be packed, the level which Croce calls "practical activity" and Collingwood "craftsmanship." Both think of such experience as a perversion of art, as the use of art for an ulterior motive, as the arousal of a pre-determined emotion. The very act of attention by a genuine artist is the discovery of a feeling, and this discovery itself is the making of a work of art. The craftsman, in contrast, begins his work by putting some emotion which has already been expressed into a particular class. He then produces an item the purpose of which is to arouse that *kind* of emotion in a particular audience. The experience of arousal is largely passive for the audience, whereas an experience of true art is active; in arousal there is no heightened awareness, only the increase of emotion. Finally, if the craftsman arouses a type of emotion in such a way as to purge the audience of it on the spot, Collingwood calls it amusement, and Croce "intrattenimento"; if he sends his audience out of the theater, not purged, but all charged up, then Collingwood calls his craft magic, and Croce calls it "oratoria."

Gentilean Complications in the Principles

Fortunately, this Crocean conception of art and of an inalterable series of levels of experience does not come out neatly in *The Principles of Art*. For Collingwood is anything but a slavish imitator; he combines his Crocean position, as I have already said, with a conception of art which contradicts it, a conception rather close to Gentile's. The presence of a double direction to his thought may be sensed in the following distinction,—and a curious one it is—which Collingwood sets forth as innocently verbal:

The activity of consciousness . . . converts impression into idea, that is crude sensation into imagination. Regarded as names for a certain kind or level of experience, the words consciousness and imagination are synonymous. . . . But within a single experience of this kind there is a distinction between that which effects the conversion and that which has undergone it. Consciousness is the first of these, imagination is the second. Imagination is thus the new form which feeling takes when transformed by the activity of consciousness.[6]

In the *Speculum Mentis* the contradiction between the "pure imagination" and the expression of the imagination is thought of as a contradiction within art. In *The Principles of Art* a similar contradiction may be found, but it is not a contradiction in the nature of art. It is rather a contradiction in Collingwood's thinking about art. When thinking in a Crocean mode, Collingwood uses "consciousness" and "imagination" as indiscriminately the same; for, after all, he means there to be no distinction between expression and intuition, or form and content. When he is thinking as an actualist, he keeps the terms distinct, opposed and synthesized, and his shifting from one mode of thought to the other is simply an arbitrary response to the needs of the moment. Before considering the details of this contradiction within the *Principles*, I think it fair to say that his arbitrary inconsistency is part of a pervasive diminution in Collingwood's self-awareness. It is reflected elsewhere in his retreat from the belief, presented in the *Philosophical Method*, that the philosopher can justify his own starting-point critically, to the sceptical notion of *An Essay on Metaphysics* (1940) that, like everyone else, the philosopher must simply accept his starting-point as an "absolute presupposition." It is also reflected in a shift in the essays of *The Idea of History* (1946) from the notion that philosophy transcends historiography in its critical method and self-awareness (in the essays of 1935-36) to the Crocean theory of philosophy as the methodology of history (in those essays finished in 1939-40). These changes do not, of course, justify contradictions in the *Principles*. At best they give external reinforcement for my theory that Collingwood has shifted from a fantastic though moderately consistent theory of art as contradiction to a self-contradictory theory of art as communal.

If the object of the imaginative experience "is never a plurality of terms with relations between them, but a single indivisible unity: a sheer here-and-now," [7] then the artist could never make the assertion "This is my feeling" and the denial "That is not my feeling." Yet such an assertion and denial is presented by Collingwood as the basis for those theories stemming from his second and third modes of thought: of that struggle by means of which the artist overcomes the temptations which would lead to a corruption of his consciousness; and of his duty to express for his community the feelings which its ordinary members are afraid to consider as their own. [8] If the artist is asserting, "This is my feeling," then he is distinguishing and relating a "feeling" and his "self." Collingwood qualifies this notion of art as assertion by saying that the artist really knows nothing about himself except that the feeling is his. But this qualification cannot wipe out the relational, assertive aspect of this part of his theory: all that is needed for it is a possessor and something possessed. If one retreats to a claim that there is no distinction whatsoever between the possessor and the possessed, then the artist could not possibly be asserting, "This is my feeling." If, instead, one says: the object of imaginative experience, not the experience itself, is an indivisible unity, then one is forceably thrown into a position of distinguishing experience from the object of experience in such a way that all claims for the immediacy of this level in the series of experience must be abandoned. The experience as expression (or as consciousness) is distinct from the object of imagination, the vehicle of language from its tenor, the form from its content, the expression from its intuition, the subject from its object; all are distinct though unified, and one's conception of art is evidently not Crocean, but Gentilean. Collingwood certainly accepts this position; the trouble is that he also accepts the Crocean position which contradicts it, without taking note of the contradiction. In other words, Collingwood is presenting the theory of art as contradiction as he did in the *Speculum Mentis*, but without realizing that he is doing so. As a result, the contradiction lies in his thinking rather than in his subject-matter.

Collingwood sets forth his theory of "the corruption of consciousness" as though it fits his Crocean position; but he does so only by loading it with Gentilean implications. The artist headed for corruption, he says, begins by attending to a feeling. Now according to the Crocean position, by that very attention to a feeling, the artist would have expressed it. But Collingwood claims that the initial attention is broken off because, for some reason, the artist wishes to disown the feeling. His final work could not then be an indivisible unity, for the fusion which he worked out between himself and his "imaginative vision" would be related, as incomplete in itself, to that psychic experience which he disowned. One could say, within the Crocean framework, that utter fusion characterizes only successful art, not unsuccessful. But, with his analysis of artistic failure, Collingwood has implicitly introduced relations into the successful work of art. "Attention" is being presented as a triumph over the temptations of inattention. At every step after the first glance, it requires the steady assertion, "This is my feeling, I do not disown it." The very idea of "attention" itself, which is at other times spoken of as immediate awareness, is here being expanded into a dialectical synthesis in which the "I" of the poet watches himself attending to a feeling and refuses to let his self follow any natural inclination to disown something unpleasant or embarrassing. Although he is doing so in Crocean language, Collingwood is presenting a concept of art as a dialectical action composed of three terms.

There are passages, furthermore, in which Collingwood explicitly describes attention, or consciousness, as necessarily involving self-consciousness. At one point, for example, he says:

What we hear . . . is merely sound. What we attend to is two things at once: a sound, and our act of hearing it. The act of sensation is not present to itself, but it is present, together with its own sensum, to the act of attention. This is, in fact, the special significance of the *con-* in the word consciousness; it indicates the togetherness of the two things, sensation and sensum, both of which are present to the conscious mind. A man *conscius sibi irae* is not one who simply feels anger; he is one who is aware of the anger as his own, and is aware of himself as feeling it.[9]

Although Collingwood may say elsewhere that the artist is not aware of himself as something other than his feeling,[10] simply by allowing him to recognize himself as the owner of the feeling Collingwood has elevated his notion of consciousness to a form of self-consciousness, at least according to actualistic thinking. For the self of actualism is always an act and never some "thing," some substance. To be self-conscious is not to be aware of one's self as an isolated entity; it is to be aware of one's self as the asserting of one's opposite but identical object. To be aware of one's self as sensing a sensum is unequivocally to be self-conscious. With all this, one may still claim that there is a stronger sense of oneness in artistic self-consciousness than in any form of intellectual activity. Gentile himself accounts for this by his analysis of art as a form of action in which the first moment of the dialectic predominates.

Actually, however, in some passages Collingwood allows for even more awareness on the part of the artist than any we have considered thus far. He argues that, whatever our theory may be, we must somehow account for the fact that an artist, in the very act of creation, can distinguish successful from unsuccessful expression. He says:

A person who on one occasion fails to express himself is a person quite accustomed to express himself successfully on other occasions, and to know that he is doing it. Through comparison of this occasion with his memory of these others, therefore, he ought to be able to see that he has failed, this time, to express himself. And this is precisely what every artist is doing when he says, 'This line won't do'. He remembers what the experience of expressing himself is like, and in the light of that memory he realizes that the attempt embodied in this particular line has been a failure.[11]

Such a description of the artistic experience directly contradicts the claim that the object of such experience is a "single indivisible unity." The artist in the passage possesses critical intelligence. He relates and compares at least two expressive experiences, the one in process and a past one, and evaluates the first in the light of the second. Art is not immediate, imaginative unity at all. It is a dialectical unification of imagination and the conscious expression of that imagination.

It might seem a simple solution at this point to say that Collingwood meant to distinguish between the activity of the artist as ephemeral, as lasting only so long as it takes him to create his work, and the work itself, the imaginative vision as enduring so long as it exists as a product and has viewers to appreciate it. But Collingwood repeatedly repudiates such a "realist" position, saying that when we come to view a painting, what we come to view is not a product at all, but an "imaginary experience of total activity which we find in the picture because the painter had put it there." [12]

It might also be felt that such an actualistic interpretation emphasizes a few phrases here and there to the utter neglect of what is the most sustained and coherent analysis in the entire *Principles*, Collingwood's analysis of the difference between imaginary sensa and real sensa and between these two and illusory sensa. Although what I have said is inconsistent with a Crocean interpretation of this analysis, it is not necessarily inconsistent with the analysis itself. After an elaborate historical review of the question, especially as Locke and Hume had worked on it, Collingwood arrives at the conclusion that sensa are not to be distinguished by anything in themselves, but only according to the manner in which we think about them. Sensa are imaginary if we have not interpreted them, if we have not thought about whether they are produced by ourselves or by something outside ourselves. The artist, Collingwood says at one point, does not try to decide whether the appearance of a woman disgusts him because of something about the woman or because of something in himself; he simply expresses the appearance of the woman as disgusting. Real sensa are sensa interpreted according to the kind of distinctions which the artist ignores; and illusory sensa are those sensa which have been misinterpreted.[13]

Now such an analysis does fit with the Crocean notion that the artist sees without thinking, that he views everything as fused into one, making no distinction between the real and the unreal, or between this imagined sensum and any other sensum. But, given what Collingwood says elsewhere, we may approach his analysis of sensa in an actualistic manner. We may say: an artist who is struggling to express all his feeling truthfully and to deny none of it; an artist aware of himself as expressing an individual feeling; and, even more, an artist who is comparing this expression with a past expression and judging its success in the light of that other must also be aware that he should avoid interpreting his sensa as either real or illusory. Knowing what it means to interpret sensa, he avoids such interpretation to the extent that it interferes with his effort to make his sensa expressive of emotion. Such intellectual and relational awareness would seem essential to all serious art. Only freaks of beauty could be created without such knowledge.

If we turn now to Collingwood's theory of art as identical with language, we might well reverse ourselves and say that *The Principles of Art* is so overwhelmingly Gentilean that its Crocean elements must be mere fragments of some past wreckage in Collingwood's mind not yet swept away. For even though he wrote to Croce that he accepted his identification of art and language, the words Collingwood uses in the *Principles* suggest that he is closer to Gentile's notion of expressiveness in art as self-translation.

It may be recalled that for Gentile the language or expression of art is the whole bodily activity of the artist, and that this activity is his whole world, with all its articulations and discriminations, no matter how brutish or how angelic, no matter how sensuous or how conceptual. Now in his description of that language which is artistic language, Collingwood means to describe the essence of every particular language, though he is not so clear about this as Gentile was. He says that this essential language

is nothing but the totality of our motor activities, raised from the psychical level to the conscious level. It is our bodily activity as that of which we are conscious. But that which is raised from the psychical level to the conscious level is converted by the work of consciousness from impression to idea, from object of sensation to object of imagination. The language of total bodily gesture is thus the motor side of our total imaginative experience.[14]

For Gentile, only as one's feeling is given bodily expression does it cease to be merely a transcendent principle, and come into existence. For Collingwood, only as feeling is given bodily expression does it cease to be a mere presupposition, and take on a conscious form. In the aesthetics of both men this particular linguistic act is the act of artistic creation itself. These likenesses should not be allowed, however, to conceal two points of divergency. Collingwood's "feeling" is tied to sensation, to images, as Gentile's is not, so that he, like Croce, must be forced to prefer imagistic or sensuous poetry, at least if he would remain loyal to his original notion of art as the expression of feeling. Furthermore, by his emphasis upon "motor activities," Collingwood may intend in another way to reduce and confine the nature of the expressive world of the artist.

As though in support of these warnings against our bringing Collingwood too close to Gentile, his notion that one can speak only because one can hear himself speak takes a surprisingly different turn from that theory of Gentile's which it resembles so strikingly. Gentile's notion led straight into his theory of art as self-translation: feeling is expressed only if its expression is listened to and understood. The process of expression circles in wider and wider sweeps as assertion is heard, understood, and interpreted by further assertion. The genius and the taste of the artist, furthermore, are dialectically identified by Gentile: one's expressiveness and his capacity to listen appreciatively develop inseparably. Finally, it is on the basis of Gentile's theory that all speech is an internal dialog that he can argue so persuasively for the oneness of a reader's experience of a poem with the poet's. This oneness results from his idea that

there is no end to the expanding circle of expression and interpretation which is initiated by the poet. The reader merely
continues this process, opposite though at one with the most
advanced re-creation of the poem which he transcends in his
own reading. The poem lives and grows in history only as it
is read with feeling and with a critical eye. All remnants of
nineteenth century "aesthetic individualism" are abandoned in
such a theory. To use a word of Collingwood's, every reader
of a poem is "concreative" with its poet. The poem which I
have read critically does not, to be sure, become mine; rather
it becomes ours. It becomes "La Ginestra" as made and criticized by Giocomo Leopardi and as made and criticized by
Umberto Bosco.

Now at first glance Collingwood is quite close to this theory.
To paraphrase him: only because one hears and understands
his own expression of feeling is he able to express it; only, that
is, because one's poetic action is also knowledge is it either
action or knowledge. But here are Collingwood's own words:

When language is said to express emotion, this means that there
is a single experience which has two elements in it. First, there is an
emotion of a specific kind [This last phrase is a sheer mistake for
'a unique emotion,' which everything in the book requires him to
say], not a psychic emotion or impression, but an emotion of which
the person who has it is conscious, and which by this consciousness
he has converted from impression into idea. Secondly, there is a
controlled bodily action in which he expresses this idea. The expression is not an afterthought to the idea; the two are inseparably
united, so that the idea is had as an idea only in so far as it is expressed. The expression is speech, and the speaker is his own first
hearer. As hearing himself speak, he is conscious of himself as the
possessor of the idea which he hears himself expressing. Thus two
statements are both true, which might easily be thought to contradict each other: (1) it is only because we know what we feel that
we can express it in words; (2) it is only because we express them
in words that we know what our emotions are. In the first, we describe our situation as speakers; in the second, our situation as hear-

ers of what we ourselves say. The two statements refer to the same union of idea with expression, but they consider this union from opposite ends.[15]

There is one devastating weakness to this translation by Collingwood of Gentile's concept of art as self-translation; and this weakness is a direct consequence of his still vital belief in Croce's doctrine of art as immediate intuition. Now it seems reasonable to interpret this passage as follows: through his consciousness the poet attends to a feeling, and his attention is an awareness which gives shape to, which expresses, that feeling; furthermore, since consciousness necessarily involves self-consciousness, the poet hears his own expression or speech and understands and evaluates it in preparation for further expression. In fact, however, the last sentence of the quotation reveals a blurring of this complex situation so that instead of hearing his expression, as Collingwood has said he does, his poet may really "hear" no more than the unexpressed feeling which he thereupon expresses. If he does not hear his speech at all, if he merely "hears" the psychic feeling which he is about to express; then self-consciousness is reduced to consciousness, and speaking and hearing is reduced to the act of attention. Then the whole notion of an inner, artistic dialog is being used as nothing more than a misleading, grandiose, and fanciful metaphor for the immediate identification of attention and expression. Although a relationship of immense importance in Gentile's aesthetics is being presented here as though it meant something, it may well be no more than a set of empty words.

Obviously, Collingwood is closer here to establishing a meaningful relationship between speaking and hearing than he was, in the *Speculum Mentis,* to bringing together art as pure imagining and art as thought mistaking itself for pure imagining. Despite his Gentilean language, however, Collingwood is still loyal to the Crocean notion that "imagining" and "expressing" feeling occurs in some kind of fused, immediate way. After all his talk about hearing and knowing what is expressed as part of the experience of artistic expression, he can fall back to saying:

Language in its original imaginative form may be said to have expressiveness, but no meaning. About such language we cannot distinguish between what the speaker says and what he means. You may say that he means precisely what he says; or you may say that he means nothing, he is only speaking. . . .[16]

Here, in an effort to distinguish genuine or artistic language from symbolism or intellectual language, Collingwood openly retreats to a Crocean notion that artistic language, like the imagined object, is immediately at one, fused and without internal relations. The whole notion that the artist speaks, hears himself, understands, and then tells what he means with a further assertion is gone without a trace. Even when he is speaking of language as an interior dialog, Collingwood is infected by the idea of expression as immediate, at least to this extent: if he is not reducing the act of hearing to an indistinguishable part of speech, he is at best thinking of the act of speech as being completed, in its "fusedness," before the hearing begins. In the whole of *The Principles of Art* there is no grasp of the idea of an interior community of language. At some points Collingwood can imagine a person's saying something and then becoming a hearer and listening to what he has said. But he cannot go so far as to allow for an interior dialog, an interplay between my self as speaker and my self as listener, or for a widening circle of assertion and interpretation. In other words, he has missed the heart of Gentile's theory, the idea of self-translation as a developing activity in which art and criticism, the artist as genius and the artist as appreciator, interchange expression and reflection.

The Third R. G. C. of the Principles

Collingwood's handling of the relationship between the artist and his community is the most solid evidence that he has not truly grasped the theory of art as self-translation, but has merely used it for his momentary convenience as one more fragment among the ruins of his intellectual world. Occurring intermittently throughout the *Principles,* his discussion of the communal nature of art reaches its climax in an impassioned plea that author, performer, and audience all act as co-authors in the creation of every work of art. Opposing the individualistic approach to artists as self-sufficient gods, Collingwood argues that artists create only through collaborating with other artists, with those who perform their work and with those who listen to it. At least superficially this theory of art as collaboration, as communal, seems to be derived theoretically from the Gentilean notion which Collingwood partially adopted: "The aesthetic activity is the activity of speaking. Speech is speech only so far as it is both spoken and heard." [17] Now this derivation could have been properly drawn. For Gentile conceives of both the original creation and all subsequent re-creations of a work of art as the self-conscious elaboration of an interplay between speaking and hearing, assertion and interpretation, and art and criticism. But Collingwood's derivation of it verges on parody.

In order to assure the need of performers and audience in the creation of a work of art, not only does Collingwood deny that the artist can truly listen to himself and criticize himself, but he heaps ridicule upon those artists who try to do so. Mozart is praised for leaving it to his soloist to improvise the cadenza in a concerto! [18] And "Mr. Bernard Shaw" is roundly condemned for prefacing his plays with elaborate stage-directions (It should be pointed out that this example is illicit, because elsewhere Collingwood has said that Shaw is no artist anyway!).[19] On what grounds, one may ask, is the artist commanded to be incomplete, to stop short of what he thinks he ought to do in order to express his feeling? Certainly, Gentile's theory provides no basis for the command. From his point of view, the artist interprets as thoroughly as he can, revising for the sake of precision, adding all the qualifications he can think of in order to make his expression as full as possible. Every new performer, every new audience, must strive to return to the original creative feeling and to interpret it more fully than has ever been done before. Just as the artist is obligated to be as critical an audience for himself as possible, so his audiences are obligated to move as close as they possibly can to the creative center of his work.

Collingwood's rejection of both obligations has, then, no basis in the theory from which it appears to be derived. There is, however, an intrusion by the third form of his thought which may explain his relinquishment of the second. Even though in theory his artist is expected to listen to himself, Collingwood argues at one and the same time that he cannot and that, even if he can, he should not. On the one hand, practical-minded R. G. C. is providing reasons for the artist's cutting his thinking short, even though he need not do so. It is not that the artist cannot think, but that, if he does so very much, he will stifle the originality of his performers and audience. Helpless souls that they are, if the artist pushes his thought too far, they will see nothing else to do. This is the counsel of a man generous with the sacrifices of others for the good of still others. In other words, Collingwood would have his artists be a little humbler, a little more incomplete, for the convenience of those slavish performers who need the thrill of feeling that they too can do something original. On the other hand, Collingwood mixes into these patronizing arguments some others which suggest that the artist *cannot* develop his original feeling or intuition critically. Printed literature, we

are told, suffers immeasurably from the distance between author and audience, a distance increased "by every new mech-
anization of art." [20] The patent implication is that an author
cannot, in truth, listen to himself and criticize himself, and
that his audience cannot, without his actual presence, work its
way back to his original feeling. All this talk about co-author-
ship, then, would seem to be based upon the inadequacies of
author and audience: the author can only express himself, the
audience can only listen. But there is no theoretical basis for
this, at least according to what we have seen. Its basis is a
pious wish for humility, and the shift from "the artist should
not listen" to "the artist cannot listen" is a rhetorical trick.
The Gentilean theory is directly contradicted by the practical
wish masking as a necessary limitation of the artist. The wish
takes this form: Be as little as you really are. The theory suggests that you can be much bigger than this desired littleness.

Collingwood's wish that artists would be humble seems to
arise from a deep-seated sense of their being worth less than
they aspire to be, a sense which dominates his discussion of
art in the *Speculum Mentis*. He is not, to be sure, suggesting
that artists and performers and listeners are like werewolves
or like a man who thinks he is a poached egg. But he does
seem to be going back to the Crocean notion that artists express themselves in an immediate way and that the true artistry
of what they do is accessible only to those others who listen
to them. For example, he claims that dress-rehearsals are artistically dead because they lack an audience, as though the
performers could not hear themselves. Furthermore, he con-
temns the phonograph on the ground that "the performers
and the audience are out of touch." [21] But surely the performers can hear themselves and trained listeners can hear the
music expressively through a phonograph record. Whether such
a record can convey "the total bodily activity" of any serious
music is, of course, quite another matter. It might be argued

that the contribution to the music which is made by the musicians' bodily activity can never be recreated even by the best trained listener to a record. That, however, is not Collingwood's argument. He rejects the phonograph and the cinema too—as useless where genuine art is the concern, because "the audience is not collaborating, it is only overhearing."

In fact, audiences earn no more respect from Collingwood than do artists. It is indeed curious that, in a book so passionately opposed to the indulgent and passive nature of mass entertainment, Collingwood can assert that even artistic audiences do not grasp the original feeling of an author at all, or at least that doing so is no concern of theirs. For him, genuine art has nothing to do with our going beyond ourselves in order to experience and understand the feeling of someone else: "Whatever value we set on . . . a poem is due to its expressing not the poet—what is Shakespeare to us, or we to Shakespeare? —but ourselves." [22] In other words, art is that activity in which we find out about our own feelings, not about those of others. Other people matter, Collingwood would seem to imply, only if they are just like ourselves!

Gentile's theory of art as self-translation rests, it will be remembered, upon a conception of man not as a finite individual, but as a self-conscious person who strives to widen that interior community of which he is ultimately composed. Man is finite, but strives to be infinite. Another person is not simply given to us as a part of our community. Unless we try to understand that person and to feel at one with him, through going beyond the differences which separate our empirical ego from his, that person remains a rejected object, dead to our community. Our responsibility, according to Gentile's theory, is to act ceaselessly in such a way as to approach a dialectical oneness with others, distinct and opposed, though in harmony. Collingwood's emotional thrusts against those who would set artists up as gods and as infinite do not strike against

Gentile. His theory calls for action, for a movement away from one's finiteness, but explicitly denies the possibility of any arrivals at infinitude. At most, he would conceive of moral activity as man in the act of becoming godlike; and, of course, he believes that art is a moral activity.

Collingwood does not, then, in his practical fervor, repudiate only what he openly repudiates; that is, the glorification of the individual artist as a god. He also rejects any notion of art as a movement toward godliness. For him man—at least artistic man—is not really a person, capable of splitting into many personae while remaining one as self-conscious; he is a finite individual. In artistic activity he is very close to what he was seen to be in the *Speculum Mentis,* a windowless monad. Collingwood exhorts him to be a little more considerate in his selfishness, to leave his poem undone so that a reader of it may mould it more easily to express his own feeling; and he even urges the artist to acquire the feelings of his community so that his expressions will reveal their selves as well as his own. Since, however, no one knows his feelings until he has expressed them, it is difficult to understand how the artist is to go about "having" the feelings of his community before they have been expressed at all, so that his expression of them will have communal significance. Collingwood thinks that he is telling them how to go about it when he demands that they no longer isolate themselves as their nineteenth-century prede-cessors did. Does he think that, as a superior philosopher, he can understand feelings even before they have been expressed, and that he has come to know that the feelings of his com-munity do not include those feelings which ripen in expe-riences of isolation? Is humility to be only for artists? Did Leopardi's isolation make him less of a communal poet than he would have been otherwise? Who knows, in actual truth, just which expression will miraculously make sense of the deepest feelings of an entire community? My point is simply this: it is no business of the aesthetician to tell artists how to go about acquiring the right kind of feelings, especially when their very own theory suggests that no feelings can be known except through artistic expression.

Even when Collingwood seems to turn upon his conception of the artist as a selfish little man and to suggest, like Gentile, that the artist is rather a person in the making, he manages to twist his comments in a belittling way. We are, Collingwood admits at one point, interested in others, even in our artistic affairs. One becomes aware of himself as a person, we are told, only to the extent that he also becomes aware of others as persons.[23] Now since this awareness is achieved only through artistic expression, it might provide a solid basis for the notion of art as communal. In effect, however, all that it means is that the artist cannot hear himself very well and needs the assurance of others that what he hears is truly his person as he has expressed it. Collingwood's artist may justly be imagined to say: How do I know what I hear myself saying until I hear other persons say what I said? This artist will show an interest in his community, not because of a moral responsibility to enlarge his own interior community, but rather because of his need to assure himself of his own nature and worth.

In summary, Collingwood's treatment of the artist and his community should be recognized as primarily an expression of his third mode of thought. He uses Gentile's theory of art as self-translation in order to set forth the communal obligations of artists as having a theoretical basis. But the nobility of this conception of the artist is severely qualified as Collingwood first takes away his power of hearing and then reduces him to something just short of a windowless monad. All in all, the distance between the orator Collingwood and the artists of whom and to whom he declaims is almost as great as that separating the poet from the philosopher in the *Speculum Mentis*. Ultimately, it is true, such a statement can refer only to the tone and style of *The Principles of Art*. Certainly the theories behind even this relationship between the artist and his community point in both directions, one exalting the artist, the other debasing him.

Art and the Intellect

There is no great distance between the contradictions just considered and those undermining Collingwood's analysis of the relationship between artistic activity and intellectual activity. If anything, his way of viewing the relation between art and intellect is more openly contradictory than what we have seen thus far. More than anything else in Collingwood's thought, it may help us understand why intelligent men might wish to reduce philosophy to the mere analysis of words separated from that non-verbal context of which they are presumably a part. Collingwood's downward descent into the limbo of contradiction may strike some as tragically noble; but the contradictions in his handling of this particular relation between art and intellect are at best a cause for astonishment. Collingwood says that art concentrates upon "a single indivisible object," whereas the intellect probes among the relations of objects to each other: it is also Collingwood, however, who presents art as making connections just as the intellect is said to do. Collingwood says that the material of art is psychic experience whereas the material of the intellect is that experience only when it has been raised to the level of conscious artistry: but he also says that the material of art includes not only conscious, but also intellectual experience. At least, Collingwood will affirm, the way in which art expresses intellectual emotions differs from the way in which they are expressed by the intellect itself: but he gives even that distinction up, saying that he sees no reason why the two forms of expression should differ at all. In sum, he is saying that art and the intellect are distinct levels of experience, and he is saying that they are not distinct levels of experience. At all times, of course, he means for there to be an overlap between art and the intellect: that is, although art is free of intellect, the intellect incorporates art into its activity. But even this overlapping distinction is abandoned as Collingwood finds one aspect after another of his Crocean mode of thought to be inadequate.

For our purposes, the first of these contradictory aspects of Collingwood's analysis of the relation between art and intellect has already been considered sufficiently. When Collingwood says:

The truth it [art] pursues is not a truth of relation, it is a truth of individual fact. The truths art discovers are those single and self-contained individualities which from the intellectual point of view become the 'terms' between which it is the business of the intellect to establish or apprehend relations. Each of these individualities, as art discovers it, is a concrete individual, one from which nothing as yet has been abstracted by the work of intellect. Each is an experience in which the distinction between what is due to myself and what is due to my world has not yet been made.[24]

we know that he is reducing art to mere imagination as separated from consciousness, self-consciousness, and expression, a reduction which so belies the nature of aesthetic experience that we know he cannot remain loyal to it, any more than Croce could. The very idea that any experience can be purely immediate, that there can be any conscious experience in which the one excludes the many, in which there are no parts to be unified, is wholly alien to the tradition of thought in which Collingwood is working. He misses the absurdity of his claim, however, for a not incomprehensible reason. Although he is striving to avoid the fanciful dance of ideas unrelated to experience which he staged in the *Speculum Mentis,* although his thinking is weighed heavily toward art as existential, toward art as it is when actually experienced, he remains the captive of his notion that in some sense art is "pure imagination." Bolstered by his knowledge that, at least at some time, Croce had proclaimed such a belief, he rashly asserts that art even as experienced and even as it exists is "pure imagination." In the *Speculum Mentis* he never said anything so palpably false. When he described art there as "pure imagination," he meant to be false to the nature of any real artistic experience. In effect, he was saying: this is just what foolish artists and aesthetes like Croce think is going on; in fact, part of the same experience, artistic expression, directly contradicts this imaginative purity. The "truth" of art in the *Speculum Mentis* was, of course, a falsehood. To approach truth art had to cease to be itself and had to become more complicated forms of activity. In *The Principles of Art* Collingwood means to concentrate upon the full aesthetic experience and to attribute to it a strength to discover truths that are not mere appearances. But time and again he is victimized by a ghost from the past and describes the aesthetic experience and its truth in a manner which was originally intended to be only partial, to be a kind of stunt played upon his readers, a cruel exposure of the presumptuousness of artists. Collingwood could not help contradicting so foolish an error; and when he does so, he has wiped out a distinction between art and the intellect: both are recognized to involve relations.

They do, however, remain distinct for what appears to be a much more solid reason, that is, the difference in their respective materials. To this distinction Collingwood is clearly more faithful than he is to the first one. According to the inalterable order of the "levels of experience," artistic experience presupposes psychic experience. As a result, art is essentially imagistic and sensuous. Formally, to be sure, we may now say freely that it is a way of looking at things, conscious and self-conscious attention, the making of oneself out of one's feelings which is at the same time a knowing of oneself. But the material, what becomes within the work of art the imagination as distinct from consciousness, is feeling, or sensa charged with emotion. By Collingwood's own clear-cut definition, feeling is never "emotion"; it is always sensa charged with emotion.

Although this theory stands Collingwood in good stead through much of the *Principles,* and especially when the existent art work of which he is thinking is music or painting, it breaks down when he turns to look seriously at drama and poetry. The facts, as observed, are that the subject-matter of a play like "Romeo and Juliet" or "King Lear" and the poetry of such poets as Dante, Donne, Shelley, and Eliot is heavy with "intellectual apprehensions." [25] Given these facts, Collingwood must make one of two choices: he must either break down the order of his series so that intellectual activity may, at least sometimes, be prior to art and thus available as its material; or he must say that art need not be art at all, but may be intellectual activity. Collingwood clearly leans toward the first choice, for it would seem to leave his distinction between art and the intellect standing, even though it would break down the order of presuppositions. The artist, we are told, may do more than express feeling, an action which is consciousness charged with its own nonpsychic "aesthetic" emotion; he may also express the emotional charges on both artistic and intellectual activity.

Collingwood, however, has analyzed intellectual activity, its emotions, and its own form of expression in such a way that he cannot rest comfortably with the first of his two choices. Intellectual activity, the relating of imagined sensa, is always emotional; it has its own peculiar emotions just as art and psychic experience have theirs. Now each activity is said to have its own special form of expression for its emotions; and no emotions go unexpressed, at least by that form of expression which is natural to them. Intellectual emotions, then, must exist as expressed; and they must be expressed by language raised to the level of symbolism. They exist, then, as expressed by "total bodily activity" which has been raised artistically to the level of consciousness and which also points, symbolically, to relationships, the essential part of all intellectual activity.

Suppose, for a moment, that an artist set about expressing such an emotion. By his act of imaginative expression he would be raising to a level of consciousness an emotion already attached to a "total bodily activity" previously raised to the level of consciousness and already pointing beyond itself to relational thinking. Such a weighty expression would, of course, lack immediacy and indivisibility because the expressed emotion would be pointing to relations: but Collingwood never really cared about that, even in its sacrosanct form in which expression and intuition are identified. But, as a more serious difficulty, there would seem to be no reason for the artist to express himself in this way. Why should he express consciously what has already been expressed not only consciously, but also intellectually? Collingwood may suggest that there are intellectual emotions of which one is not conscious; but he cannot mean anything so contradictory to all that he has said of that highly conscious intellect, its emotions, and its symbolism.

Collingwood's only choice is to say that art need not be art at all, that it may instead be intellectual activity. Although this may demolish a distinction at which he has labored,—although perhaps rather hastily—it simply must be so. The artist, then, who works with intellectual emotions, is in fact *the* one who expresses them. In other words, he is the intellectual who does some relational thinking, experiencing along with it a certain emotion, and who then uses emotional, that is, expressive words to symbolize the thoughts which he has had. Troublesome as this fact may be, this description of intellectual art does not differ from Collingwood's description of intellectual activity. Where, then, has Collingwood arrived but at the starting point of Italian actualism, at the conclusions of those thin articles by Fazio-Allmayer and Guido De Ruggiero proclaiming that art is philosophy?

He might have avoided such embarrassment had he learned from Gentile to distinguish between the essence and the existence of art, and had he avoided existentializing his concepts of art, intellect, and feeling. But how could he avoid it when he was calling them "levels of experience" and when he was trying so to overcome the aridity of the *Speculum Mentis* by bringing his concepts and actual experience as closely together as possible? If that unique work of art *King Lear* is intellectual, then the concept of artistic activity may also involve intellectual elements. Thus, just as Croce did in his early struggling, so Collingwood in his late floundering is failing to distinguish a particular concept from a fully existent act. Such an error is more clearly pardonable when committed by an erstwhile philologist than by a professional philosopher who has had the benefit of the philologist's mistakes.

Overwhelmed by the monstrousness of particular concepts which he has been confusing with existent acts, Collingwood is forced to go down to defeat in his own stalwart way. That is, he openly and honorably thinks through his own disintegration. Having found that the same things go on in most artistic activity as go on in intellectual activity as he has defined it, he tries to distinguish the *way* in which they go on by means of an old Croceanism. Let the difference be put in this way:

The poet converts human experience into poetry not by first expurgating it, cutting out the intellectual elements and preserving the emotional, and then expressing this residue; but by fusing thought itself into emotion: thinking in a certain way and then expressing how it feels to think in that way. Thus Dante has fused the Thomistic philosophy into a poem expressing what it feels like to be a Thomist. Shelley, when he made the earth say, 'I spin beneath my pyramid of night,' expressed what it feels like to be a Copernican.[26]

But Collingwood had left "fusion" behind long ago, with his first error, his identification of art with "pure imagination." As a result, he does not even try to make this mysterious word go to work for him here. No effort is made to distinguish thought as fused from thought which is not fused. And after one paragraph he simply drops the matter.

How then can Collingwood distinguish the manner in which intellectual poets think from the manner of intellectuals? Is Dante to be as much a philosopher as Thomas Aquinas, and Aquinas as much a poet as Dante? After several feeble suggestions which are immediately rejected, Collingwood tries the notion that whereas genuine philosophers are actually in the process of exploratory thinking as they express themselves, poets may simply take over thinking which has already become thought and then expound it:

For the poet, there is, perhaps, none of this dynamism of thinking. He finds himself equipped, as it were, with certain ideas, and expresses the way in which it feels to possess them. Poetry, then, in so far as it is the poetry of a thinking man and addressed to a thinking audience, may be described as expressing the intellectual emotion attendant upon thinking in a certain way: philosophy, the intellectual emotion attendant upon trying to think better.[27]

But Collingwood is too honest to maintain so arbitrary a distinction. He simply gives up, hedging only a little with his pretense that the distinction which he has been unable to draw is only one between two species of "literary composition":

I do not know how else to distinguish the two, as species of literary composition, except either by substituting pseudo-philosophy for philosophy (or pseudo-poetry for poetry, or both), or by using distinctions which I know to be false. But the distinction I have stated is, I would insist, arbitrary and precarious. I see no reason why the intellectual experience of building up or criticizing a philosophical view should not afford the poet a subject-matter no

less fertile than that of merely holding it. And I am sure that a
philosopher who expressed the experience of developing a view,
without making it clear to himself and his readers what view he
was developing, would be doing only half his work.[28]

There is nothing more to say except that this is breath-taking
honesty. In the very next chapter, it is true, all these disturb-
ances over the relation between art and the intellect have been
set aside, and Collingwood is writing as though the only material of art is psychic experience. After all, the worth of one's
work depends on its results, not on its logical consistency, or so
at least the third R. G. C. might have said.

Literary Criticism

In deference to the lack of perfect patterns in experience, we
must admit that on one subject of thought in _The Principles of
Art,_ the subject of literary and art criticism, Collingwood is
not contradictory. There is no equivocation or uncertainty in
his description of the critic's business. It is

to establish a consistent usage of terms: to settle the nomenclature
of the various things which come before him competing for a
given name, saying 'this is art, that is not art,' and, being an expert
in this business, performing it with authority. A person qualified so
to perform it is called a judge; and judgment means verdict, the
authoritative announcement that, for example, a man is innocent
or guilty. . . . The critic knows, and always has known, that in
theory he is concerned with something objective. In principle, the
question whether this piece of verse is a poem or a sham poem is a
question of fact, on which every one who is properly qualified to
judge ought to agree.[29]

It may be that Collingwood is consistent on this subject only
because he says so little. If he had said more about the authority with which a critic performs his task about the objectivity
of critical judgments, he might well have gone beyond the

simple idea of criticism as judgment and tried to relate its judgmental and its creative aspects, as both Croce and Gentile did in their maturest thought. Surely if he could recognize the concreative nature of performing and observing a work of art, he was not far from discovering something similar in serious criticism. If he had made such a discovery, to be sure, he probably would have fallen into one more contradiction: that between criticism as mere judgment and criticism as both concreative and judgmental. Because he stopped short, his theory of criticism is simple and consistent.

In the popular and deliberately imprecise first section of *The Principles of Art* Collingwood illustrates his simple theory with a number of verdicts. The following examples should remind the reader how delightfully "authoritative" Collingwood's verdicts are:

Mr. Bernard Shaw is another devout follower of Horace. There has never been any damned nonsense about art with him; he has careered through life most successfully as an entertainer, careful always to keep a few ball cartridges among his blank, and send his audience home indignant about the way people treat their wives, or something like that.

Mr. Galsworthy began his career by putting so much *utile* and so little *dulce* into his stage-puddings that only very determined stomachs could digest them at all. So he gave up playing with magic, and specialized in entertaining a rather grim class of readers with the doings of the Forsyte family.[30]

It may already be clear that Collingwood is modelling his verdicts upon the decadent form of Croce's criticism, a criticism largely devoted to draining the poisons of rhetoric and entertainment off the gardens of art proper. Like Croce's Collingwood's judgments are immediate, intuitive, and absolutistic. One recognizes intuitively whether a work is art, expressing feeling fully, or bad art, expressing it inadequately, or pseudo-art, that is, not expressing feeling at all, but rather arousing it. On the basis of this intuition, one then pronounces sentence, committing the work to one cell or another or allowing that it deserves to live on the golden ground of art proper. Making this pronouncement "with authority" means no more than doing it in a style which expresses "absolute confidence," or so Collingwood's own examples indicate.

Collingwood's schemes of classification do not, however, justify quite so much confidence. When he is keeping his particular concepts of amusement, magic, and genuine art distinct from individual, existent works of art, he can recognize that magic and amusement may exist as containing elements of art and that a work of art may also amuse one or stir him up magically. Furthermore, art and magic and amusement are not nearly as different as Collingwood's manner of presentation suggests. Experiencing genuine art is not merely the awareness, the recognition, of a certain feeling; it is also the asserting of that feeling as one's own experience. Now when one experiences a work of magic or oratory, one also has a feeling which is raised to the level of consciousness. That this feeling is always raised even further in magic, having been placed in a certain class like that of fear, or snobbishness, or bullying, need not distinguish it from the feeling of art proper, for much of the time Collingwood admits that art also includes intellectual emotions. The only thing which distinguishes magic from art is that, in the sham form, only the artist experiences the emotions as part of an intellectual act and his audience receives the product of this activity passively, merely as emotion; whereas the true artist and his audience share not just an emotion, but also all the conscious and intellectual activity which is part of the aesthetic experience. The audience can distinguish art from magic not by the presence or absence of intellectual emotion, but only by the presence or absence in themselves of conscious activity and awareness.

If art and magical art are mixed, as they surely are in actual experience, then an audience would, I should think, often be tempted to view a magical work artistically, that is, joining the magician concreatively instead of remaining merely passive and aroused. At least, they would have to overcome their passivity at times, since the magician is most likely going to slip into a moment of artistry now and again. Having done so, they would not speak so absolutely of "Mr. Bernard Shaw" and "Mr. Galsworthy" as mere entertainers. They would show enough discrimination to distinguish artistic passages from magical ones and thus would present final judgments with considerable qualifications.

The most obvious reason for Collingwood's failure to advance even to this point is that he did almost no practical criticism. Setting aside some commentaries on late Roman and La Tène art, commentaries largely of a general and informative nature, we find that he never pushes himself in precision or detail beyond the level of polite conversation or that of newspaper book-reviewing.[31] He lacks the one thing which makes recent Italian aesthetics outstanding, experience in practical criticism as the basis and testing ground of all one's theories. Collingwood is acquainted with much English criticism contemporary with himself, as English aestheticians just prior to him seem not to have been. But acquaintance is apparently not enough. The aesthetician must practice criticism himself.

Had Collingwood done so, it is difficult to believe that he could have left his theory of criticism in so rudimentary a form. Furthermore, it seems unlikely that he would have left *The Principles of Art* so full of contradictions. Previously, I suggested that we can hardly be certain that an aesthetician has in truth grasped a concept, we cannot be sure that he means what we think he means, unless we can observe him putting that concept into critical practice. The surest evidence, we noted, that the heart of Gentile's *La filosofia dell' arte* is the concept of art as self-translation is Gentile's own late criticism of the poetry of Leopardi. And the weakest part of that masterpiece, Gentile's brief comments on inferior or pseudo art, is paralleled by the utter neglect in his practical criticism of inferior art. In a like fashion, Croce's delicate hold of the actualistic concept of art as cosmic might well appear incredible, if it were not for his superb practical development of the concept in his monograph on Ariosto.

If we are forced to say that, in *The Principles of Art*, Collingwood has failed to grasp fully and securely any one of his important ideas, we are not thereby compelled to conclude our study of his thought in a merely negative way. The absence of a De Sanctis in the culture of an aesthetician is no excuse for his failure to practice original criticism. *The Principles of Art* is full of contradictions just because Collingwood had no experience as a practicing critic. If aesthetics is to become a vital form of thought in our countries, it will not be enough for us simply to base our aesthetics upon the analysis of art criticism, as Morris Weitz recently suggested.[32] We must go beyond Weitz's advice and follow his own recent practice of basing his aesthetics upon his own practice of criticism. As the action of art is incomplete without its knowledge, as critical judgments are empty unless synthesized with artistic action, so the concepts of aesthetics will be vital and coherent only if grounded in the action and knowledge of practical criticism. The philosophy of art is inseparable from its philological activity. Even the failures of neo-idealistic aesthetics force this conclusion upon us.

Conclusion

*I*t is my belief that neo-idealistic aesthetics has not progressed beyond the form Giovanni Gentile gave it in his *La filosofia dell' arte*. I do not mean that it has not been an active force in contemporary Italian thought. Its influence, unquestionably, has been pervasive. To select, on the one hand, a small group of recent aestheticians, to the neglect of others, as those truly within the tradition could not but be arbitrary; for not one Italian thinker I know of is truly free from the influence of the movement. To consider all those under this influence, on the other hand, would require a study no shorter than the one just completed. If one seeks, however, for an advance, at the theoretical level, beyond the position of Gentile, I fear that he will be disappointed. Because of this, it is not inexact to say that neo-idealistic aesthetics has reached a conclusion.

It would, however, be an error to conclude this study with a neat definition of Gentile's position, as though it were the choice fruit justifying the entire intellectual movement. For everything in this study forces us to affirm that no product of thought, however ample it may be, is worth a moment's consideration, once it is released from the process of thinking which gave rise to it. To turn an act into a fact, to reduce a process to a product, is the death of the spirit. The life of the spirit requires that we turn whatever appears to be a thought into an act of thinking; and that has been the ruling principle of this entire study. One cannot, in conscience, violate that principle here with a brief summary.

If, however, we would hope to extend this movement into our own literary and art theory and practice, it is important for us to recognize some of the basic choices which were made during the development of the movement. These may be limited, for our purposes, to three.

Probably the most elemental choice was that between treating a work of art as something immediate and treating it as something mediate. The whole movement, it seems to me, was directed away from the first and towards the second. Even though Croce strove to retain some form of intuition as essential to art, in his mature theory of art as cosmic, he is thinking of intuition as something mediate, as a dialectical activity. He does not, it is true, succeed in establishing the dialectical nature of a work of art, for he never stops insisting that the elements of the artistic activity are indistinguishable from one another. Whether one speaks of the feeling or the image or the intuition of a work of art, he will be forced to speak of all three at once. As a result, even when he is closest to analyzing a work of art as mediate, Croce reduces it to something which is, for practical purposes, indistinguishable from immediacy. Gentile overcame the wavering of Croce by distinguishing between the essence of art and its existence. For him, the essence of art is feeling; but, for that feeling to exist, it has to be expressed in an objective world or vision; and that expression of feeling is synthesized by the artist's self-conscious act of thinking. Art, according to his position, is pure feeling; but the work of art is a dialectical synthesis. Even Gentile, however, finds that there is something immediate about the dialectical activity of art which distinguishes it from all other kinds of activity. For in art, as in no other activity, objectivity and dialectical thinking are dominated by the moment of immediacy, by the moment of feeling. Thus, when analyzing a poem, one is obligated to show just how the artist's critical and evaluative thinking and his artistic world are dominated and given form by feeling, by the essential principle of art.

The failure of both of Collingwood's theories of art may be attributed to the fact that he did not choose between immediacy and mediacy. In the *Speculum Mentis* he finds art to be a contradiction between pure imagination (pure immediacy) and artistic expression. The expression of art as he envisages it is not, however, a mediate act; it is simply the wildly unfulfilling and contradictory movement between a theory of relevance and pure images. The theory and the images are both abstract, and they are not brought together and reconciled. In *The Principles of Art,* however, it is not the art, but Collingwood himself who is contradictory. He presents two contradictory theories: according to one, art is immediate; according to the other, it is mediate. The choice is simply not made, in this his maturest work, any more than it was in the earlier work.

A second crucial choice made in neo-idealistic aesthetics has to do with the aesthetician's own method of thinking. That one could take over an aesthetics without also considering or adopting its philosophical method is a fond and futile hope. In any case, this study of neo-idealistic aesthetics is based upon the belief that one's aesthetics and his method of thought are inseparable. Now the choice forced upon neo-idealistic aesthetics was the choice between thought as distinction and thought as dialectical. Gentile chose, wholeheartedly, the dialectical. For him, the concept of the concept is the dialectical act of thinking; and he identifies this act of thinking with ultimate reality. No existent activity can be fully understood unless one studies it as the realization of the full act of thinking itself. No activity realizes only a part of that act, say, the particular concept of art or the particular concept of philosophy. As a result, all activities are ultimately at one. Because of this, it might seem that Gentile has thus reduced all experience to "the basic slate, the universal hue." But this is not the case. Each experience is differentiated according to which of the moments of the dialectic is predominant. Furthermore, because of the presence of the objective moment in every experience, one finds, in his analysis of an experience, that, if he pushes far enough, its full individuality will distinguish it from every other experience. According to Gentile, then, experience is ultimately at one; but it is also endlessly various; and, furthermore, it is to be distinguished according to the moment of the dialectic which gives it its dominant form.

A strong force is pulling both Croce and Collingwood toward a dialectic something like Gentile's. But neither allows himself to go the whole way. Croce may say that no experience is finally real except as the realization of the full *actus purus*. But he consistently identifies an individual experience with a part of that act, with a particular concept, a form of experience, and claims that we can best understand the experience as a manifestation of one of the particular concepts. He tends, to be sure, to introduce more and more elements from other particular concepts into the concept of art; but, at the same time, he continues to distinguish one particular concept from another and to treat each as a kind of picture the presence of which in an individual experience explains the reality of that experience. In other words, he tries to adopt the concept of thought as dialectical without giving up the concept of thought as the distinction of forms of experience. The result is confusion.

Collingwood seems bent upon a dialectical method of thought in his *Speculum Mentis*. But he does not choose between a dialectical series, which both Croce and Gentile transcended early in their careers, and an abortive, actualistic dialectic. In *The Principles of Art*, he appears to have adopted Croce's the-

ory of thought as the distinction between "levels of experience."
But much of the time he is thinking in a manner contradictory
to that theory; and, in the end, the levels of experience collapse, confusedly, into each other. His third method of thought,
the movement from imprecise common sense to precise and
uncommon thought the value of which depends upon its being
a refinement of the original common sense, simply does not
work, at least as Collingwood applies it. The thought at which
his movement arrives is almost as imprecise as the common
sense with which he began; and the main difference between
his point of origin and point of arrival is that, in the end, the
contradictions of this thought are more openly destructive
than they were in the beginning.

A third choice made by neo-idealistic aestheticians, and
probably the one which most clearly distinguishes their thought
from other aesthetics, has to do with whether aesthetics can
develop independent of genuine art and literary criticism. This,
of course, has nothing to do with whether an aesthetician
illustrates his theories by reference to particular works of art.
Everyone does that, in one way or another. It is rather a question of whether one must actually practice criticism along with
his study of aesthetics. Although Croce separated aesthetics
and criticism in his most clearly juvenile work, from a quite
early stage his entire career is a most emphatic affirmation of
the need to keep the two together. To my knowledge, no other
aesthetician of stature has produced a quantity of practical
criticism comparable to Croce's. His greatness, and for that
matter the significance of neo-idealistic aesthetics itself, depends largely upon the intimate and intricate dependence of
criticism and aesthetics on each other. Even Gentile, whose
mind was of a highly theoretical order, devoted a number of
volumes to practical literary criticism. And, in my estimation,
his essays on Leopardi are a major contribution to the study of
that great poet. Collingwood alone, of the aestheticians con-

sidered in this study, disappoints us by failing to link his aesthetics with practical criticism. It would be difficult, however, to show that he chose not to link them. In a comparable area, he linked most intimately his studies in archaeology and history with his theory of historiography. The pressures of time and illness may alone explain his failure to practice criticism and to connect it with his studies in aesthetics. One must, nevertheless, regret this failure; for surely it accounts for much of the ambiguity in his aesthetics.

If, in conclusion, we were to attempt an extension of neo-idealistic aesthetics beyond its present confines, we would need to consider these three choices seriously. We would be obligated to articulate the relationship between the immediacy and the mediacy of art and finally to choose one or the other. We would need to establish clearly the method of thought by which we would work out our aesthetics; and it seems that some form of dialectical thought must be preferred to any more analytical form of thought as distinction. Finally, it seems to me that we must integrate our aesthetics with full-fledged art- and literary criticism. More than anything else, such an integration is the spur which will set neo-idealistic aesthetics in motion again. A number of Italian critics are, I believe, working on this principle. It may be possible, however, that a more fruitful thing to be done now is to integrate this aesthetics with the criticism of a literature other than Italian. That, in any case, leaves open for us an immediate course of action.

Notes

Chapter One

1 All dates for Croce correspond with those in Fausto Nicolini's *"L'editio ne varietur" delle opere di Benedetto Croce* (Napoli, 1960).
2 *La critica letteraria: questioni teoriche,* 2d ed. (Roma, 1896), p. 178, and in Croce's *Primi saggi* (Bari, 1951), p. 165. All translations are mine.
3 I omit any consideration in this chapter of Croce's "La storia ridotta sotto il concetto generale dell' arte," an article written in 1893 and collected in the *Primi saggi.* This article is most important in the development of Croce's theory of historiography; but, in my opinion, Croce's comments in it on the nature of art are derivative and represent no independent thought.
4 I am translating "sentimento" as "feeling" rather than "emotion," following Douglas Ainslie instead of G. N. G. Orsini. Like "sentimento" the word "feeling" suggests not just something internal, but also the five senses (to feel something may mean to touch it); and neo-idealistic aestheticians, Giovanni Gentile even more than Croce, depend upon that implication.
5 *Estetica come scienza dell' espressione e linguistica generale,* 1st ed. (Milano, 1902), p. 80.
6 *Problemi di estetica,* 4th ed. (Bari, 1949), p. 23.
7 *Ibid.,* p. 18.
8 *Ibid.,* pp. 113-114.
9 *Nuovi saggi di estetica,* 3d ed. (Bari, 1948), pp. 27, 33.
10 *La critica letteraria,* pp. 39, 131.
11 *Problemi,* p. 343.
12 *Tesi fondamentali di un' Estetica come scienza dell' espressione e linguistica generale,* read before the Accademia Pontaniana di Napoli in 1900 and published in Vol. XXX of the *Atti* of the Accademia.
13 *Ibid.,* p. 48.
14 *Ibid.,* p. 36.
15 *Estetica,* 1st ed., p. 24.
16 *Nuovi saggi,* p. 34.
17 *La critica letteraria,* p. 37.
18 *Tesi,* p. 11.
19 *Ibid.,* p. 18.
20 *Speculum Mentis: or the Map of Knowledge* (Oxford, 1924), p. 87.
21 *Estetica,* 1st ed., p. 8.
22 *Ibid.,* p. 11.

23 *Ibid.*, p. 24.
24 *Ibid.*, p. 51.
25 Compare *Estetica*, 8th ed., p. 154 (editions after the third are unchanged) with *Estetica*, 1st ed., pp. 54 and 53, respectively.
26 *Problemi*, p. 14.
27 *Ibid.*, p. 25.
28 Gian N. G. Orsini, *Benedetto Croce: Philosopher of Art and Literary Critic* (Carbondale, Ill., 1961), pp. 142-144.
29 *Nuovi saggi*, pp. 33-34.
30 *Ibid.*, p. 34.
31 *Ibid.*, p. 20.
32 *Ibid.*, p. 59.
33 *Ibid.*, p. 68.
34 *Estetica*, 1st ed., p. 112.
35 *Ibid.*, p. 117.
36 *Problemi*, pp. 61 and 68; *Nuovi saggi*, p. 14.
37 *Tesi*, p. 26.
38 *Problemi*, p. 15.
39 *Ibid.*, p. 89.
40 *Ibid.*, pp. 119 and 481; *Nuovi saggi*, p. 16.
41 *Tesi*, p. 15.
42 *Problemi*, p. 113.
43 *Nuovi saggi*, p. 61.
44 *Ibid.*, pp. 64, 65.
45 *Ibid.*, pp. 61-62.
46 *Ibid.*, p. 68.
47 *La critica letteraria*, pp. 23-24.
48 *Tesi*, p. 44.
49 *Ibid.*, pp. 70-71.
50 *Problemi*, p. 137.
51 *Estetica*, 1st ed., pp. 95-96.
52 *Problemi*, p. 27.
53 *La critica letteraria*, p. 24.
54 *Ibid.*, p. 39.
55 *Ibid.*, p. 140.
56 *Ibid.*, p. 137.
57 *Estetica*, 8th ed., p. 143.
58 *Ibid.*, p. 144.
59 *Problemi*, pp. 39, 254.

Chapter Two

1 *Lineamenti di una Logica come scienza del concetto puro*, read before the Accademia Pontaniana di Napoli in 1904 and 1905 (Napoli, 1905), p. 26.

2 *Ibid.*, p. 31.
3 *Ibid.*, p. 89.
4 *Ibid.*, p. 26.
5 *Ibid.*, p. 9.
6 *Ibid.*, p. 33.
7 *Ibid.*, p. 16.
8 *Ibid.*, p. 19.
9 *Ibid.*, p. 26.
10 *Ibid.*, p. 11.
11 Raffaello Franchini, "Benedetto Croce filosofo," extracted from the *Atti* dell'Accademia Pontaniana, n.s., IV, 5.
12 Carlo Antoni, "Studi sulla teoria e la storia della storiografia," *Cinquant'anni di vita intellectuale italiana: 1896-1946*, Carlo Antoni e Raffaele Mattioli (Napoli, 1950), p. 70; and Raffaelo Franchini, "Intorno al nesso dei distinti e alla sua fondazione logica," extracted from the *Atti* dell' Accademia Pontaniana, n.s., III, 2.
13 "Ciò che è vivo e ciò che è morto della filosofia di Hegel," *Saggio sullo Hegel, seguito da altri scritti di storia della filosofia*, 4th ed. (Bari, 1948), p. 60.
14 *Ibid.*, p. 61.
15 "Benedetto Croce filosofo," *op. cit.*, p. 5.
16 *Cinquant' anni*, pp. 69-70.
17 *Logica come scienza del concetto puro*, 3d ed. (Bari, 1917), p. 35.
18 *Ibid.*, p. 4.
19 *Ibid.*, p. 31, and p. 28 of the 7th ed.
20 *Ibid.*, p. 160.
21 *Ibid.*, p. 346.
22 *Ibid.*, p. 227.
23 *Ibid.*, pp. 52-53. The italics are mine.
24 *Ibid.*, p. 54, and p. 49 of the 7th ed.
25 *Logica*, 7th ed., p. 48.
26 *Logica*, 3d ed., p. 146.
27 *Ibid.*, p. 147.
28 *Ibid.*, p. 150.
29 *Ibid.*, p. 157.
30 *Ibid.*, p. 103.
31 *Ibid.*, pp. 141-142.
32 *Ibid.*, pp. 145-147.
33 *Ibid.*, p. 273.
34 *Ibid.*, pp. 128-129.
35 *Ibid.*, p. 57.

Chapter Three

1 Quoted in Eugenio Garin's *Cronache di filosofia italiana* (1900-1943) (Bari, 1955), p. 401

2 Giovanni Gentile, *La riforma della dialettica hegeliana*, Vol. I of *Studi filosofici*, ed. Giuseppe Principato (Messina, 1913), p. 249.

3 In his review of Manlio Ciardo's *Natura e storia nell' idealism attuale*, *Quaderni della critica*, VI (1950), 95.

4 Garin, *op. cit.*, p. 415.

5 Roger W. Holmes, *The Idealism of Giovanni Gentile* (New York, 1937), p. 129.

6 See his "Il concetto della storia della filosofia," read in 1907 in the R. Univ. di Palermo and published in *La riforma della dialettica hegeliana.*

7 *La riforma*, pp. 147-148.

8 *Ibid.*, p. 118.

9 "La teoria dell' errore come momento dialettico e il rapporto tra arte e filosofia," *Frammenti di estetica e letteratura* (Luciano, 1921).

10 *La riforma*, p. 13.

11 "Una discussione tra filosofi amici," *Conversazioni critiche*, s. 2 (Bari, 1950), p. 70. Croce's articles from *La Voce* are published here.

12 *Ibid.*, pp. 76-77.

13 "*La Voce*" (*1908-1914*), Vol. II of *La cultura italiana del '900 attraverso le reviste*, ed. Angelo Romanò (Giulio Einaudi, 1960), p. 609.

14 *Carteggio Croce—Vossler 1899-1949* (Bari, 1951), p. 178.

15 "*La Voce*" (*1908-1914*), p. 607.

16 *Annuario della Biblioteca filosofica di Palermo*, III (Bari, 1913).

17 *Atti* dell' Accademia Pontaniana di Napoli (Napoli, 1912).

18 See Vito Fazio-Allmayer, "Tempo e progresso," *L'Arduo*, a.1, s.2 (March, 1921), 70.

19 "Res gestae e historia rerum," *op. cit.*, p. 25.

20 *Ibid.*, p. 24.

21 Croce himself saw support for his theory of the pseudo-concept in the thought of Avenarius and in that of Mach.

22 "La scienza come esperienza assoluta," *Annuario della Biblioteca filosofica di Palermo*, II (1913), 247.

23 *La critica*, XX (1922), 236.

24 *Giornale critico di filosofia italiana*, V (1924), 129.

25 Garin, *op. cit.*, p. 395.

26 See *Fascismo e cultura* (Milano, 1928), pp. 12-13, 163-164.

27 Garin, *op. cit.*, p. 412.

28 "Croce e Gentile," *L'Arduo*, a.1, s.2 (January, 1921), 8.

29 *La filosofia contemporanea*, II (Bari, 1929), 160.

30 *La critica*, XXII (1924), 50.

31 "Considerazioni su la logica del concreto di G. Gentile," *Giorn. crit. di filos. ital.*, V (1924), 61.

32 "Intorno alla logica del concreto," *Giorn. crit. di filos. ital.*, V (1924), 269-279.

33 *Ibid.*, 277.

34 See Chapter 5.

35 "Per una nuova critica militante," *Rivista di cultura classica e medióevale*, II (October, 1929), 9.

36 "Arte e filosofia," *Annuario della Biblioteca filosofica di Palermo*, III (1913), 141.
37 "Arte e critica," *L'Arduo*, a.1, s.2 (November, 1921), 6.
38 "Arte e religione," *Dante e Manzoni* (Firenze, 1923), pp. 152-153.
39 G. Gentile, "Il torto e il diretto delle traduzioni," *Rivista di cultura*, II (November, 1920).
40 "Arte e critica," *L'Arduo*, a.1, s.2 (November, 1921), 12.
41 *Ibid.*, 9-10.
42 *La critica*, XX (1922), 61.
43 *Ibid.*, 57.

Chapter Four

1 This is not true of his pre-actualistic criticism, which is largely Crocean.
2 "Il carattere di totalità dell' espressione artistica" (1917), pp. 117-134; "L'arte come creazione e la creazione come fare" (1918), pp. 147-156; "La riforma della storia artistica e letteraria" (1917), pp. 157-180, in the *Nuovi saggi di estetica*, 3d ed. (Bari, 1948).
3 (Oxford, 1959).
4 *Ariosto, Shakespeare e Corneille*, 4th ed. (Bari, 1950), p. 27.
5 *Nuovi saggi*, p. 150.
6 *Ibid.*, p. 123.
7 *Ibid.*, p. 122.
8 *Ibid.*, p. 125.
9 *Ibid.*, p. 127.
10 See Alfredo Parente, "La terza scoperta dell' estetica crociana: dialettica delle passioni e suo superamento nell' arte," *Benedetto Croce*, ed. Francesco Flora (Milano, 1953), pp. 27-105; and Vittorio Sainati, *L'estetica di Benedetto Croce: dall' intuizione visiva all' intuizione catartica* (Firenze, 1953), pp. 215-249.
11 *Nuovi saggi*, p. 167.
12 *Ibid.*, p. 177.
13 *Ibid.*, p. 153.
14 Gian N. G. Orsini, *Benedetto Croce: Philosopher of Art and Literary Critic* (Carbondale, Ill., 1961), p. 32.
15 *Nuovi saggi*, p. 125.
16 *Ibid.*, p. 125.
17 *Ibid.*, p. 150.
18 *Ibid.*, p. 167.
19 *Ariosto*, p. 4.
20 *Ibid.*, p. 26.
21 *Ibid.*, pp. 23-24.
22 *Ibid.*, p. 27.
23 *Ibid.*, p. 31.
24 *Ibid.*, pp. 43ff.

25 *Ibid.*, p. 43.
26 *Ibid.*, p. 46.
27 "Nota per una migliore critica delle arti figurative," pp. 281-285; "Ritorno su vecchi pensieri" (1922), pp. 299-313; "Per una poetica moderna," (1922), pp. 317-328 in the *Nuovi saggi.*
28 *Nuovi saggi,* p. 324.
29 *Ibid.*, p. 294.
30 *La poesia: Introduzione alla critica e storia della poesia e della letteratura,* 5th ed. (Bari, 1953), p. 83.
31 *La poesia,* p. 103. Here his arguments against translation seem equally applicable to re-evocation.
32 *Cultura e vita morale,* 2d ed. (Bari, 1926), pp. 239-243.
33 *Poesia e non poesia,* 6th ed. (Bari, 1955), p. 112.
34 "Leopardi: *Amore e morte," Poesia antica e moderna,* 3d ed. (Bari, 1950), pp. 373-378.

Chapter Five

1 Guido Calogero, *Estetica-semantica-istorica* (Torino, 1947), p. 10.
2 Adelchi Attisani, "Gli studi di estetica," *Cinquant' anni di vita intellettuale 1896-1946,* ed. Carlo Antoni and Raffaele Mattioli (Napoli, 1950), p. 308.
3 Armando Carlini, "Gentile '44," *Giovanni Gentile,* ed. Vittorio Vettori (Firenze, 1954), p. 74.
4 Giovanni Gentile, *Genesis and Structure of Society,* trans. H. S. Harris (Urbana, 1960), p. 54.
5 Giovanni Gentile, *La filosofia dell' arte,* 2d ed. (Firenze, 1950), p. 45.
6 *Ibid.*, p. 163.
7 Eugenio Garin, *Cronache di filosofia italiana* (1900-1943) (Bari, 1955), p. 490.
8 Giovanni Gentile, "Il torto e il diritto della traduzione," *Rivista di cultura,* II (April, 1920), 10.
9 Giovanni Gentile, *Sommario di pedagogia come scienza filosofia,* (5th ed.; Firenze, 1954), II, 157.
10 Guido De Ruggiero, "Arte e critica," *L'Arduo,* a.1, s.2 (November, 1921), 1.
11 See *Sommario,* I, 16-25.
12 *Ibid.*, p. 27.
13 *La filosofia dell' arte,* p. 110.
14 *Ibid.*, p. 156.
15 *Ibid.*, p. 120.
16 *Ibid.*, pp. 204ff.
17 *Ibid.*, pp. 242, 243.
18 *Genesis and Structure of Society,* p. 102.
19 *La filosofia dell' arte,* pp. 62-63.
20 *The Problem of Christianity,* II (New York, 1914).

21 Karl Vossler, *The Spirit of Language in Civilization*, trans. Oscar Oeser (London, 1931).
22 *La riforma dell' educazione*, 3d ed. (Milano, 1928), p. 72.
23 See H. S. Harris, *The Social Philosophy of Giovanni Gentile* (Urbana, 1960), chap. 8.
24 *La filosofia dell' arte*, pp. 245-246.
25 *Ibid.*, p. 246.
26 *Manzoni e Leopardi* (Milano, 1928), pp. 33-47.
27 *Ibid.*, p. 58.
28 Francesco De Sanctis, *Giacomo Leopardi*, ed. Walter Binni (Bari, 1953), pp. 34, 248.
29 *Manzoni e Leopardi*, p. 124.
30 *Ibid.*, p. 30.
31 *Ibid.*, p. 31.
32 In his introduction to De Sanctis, *Giacomo Leopardi*, p. xlii.
33 Walter Binni, *La nuova poetica Leopardiana* (Firenze, 1947).
34 (Firenze, 1957).
35 *La filosofia dell' arte*, pp. 228, 234-237.
36 *Ibid.*, p. 237.
37 "Giuseppe Pitrè 1841-1916," *Biblioteca del Leonardo*, XIV (Firenze, n.d.), 12.
38 *Ibid.*, p. 14.

Chapter Six

1 See H. S. Harris' introduction to his translation of Gentile's *Genesis and Structure of Society* (Urbana, 1960), pp. 14-20; Alan Donagan's *The Later Philosophy of R. G. Collingwood* (Oxford, 1962), appendices I & III, the latter of which contains excerpts from Collingwood's letters to Croce; and Croce's commemorative article on Collingwood in the *Quaderni della critica*, II (1946), 60-73.
2 The latter first appeared in the 14th edition of the *Encyclopedia Britannica*.
3 Carritt acknowledges Collingwood's assistance on p. v of his preface.
4 *The Hibbert Journal*, XIX (1920-21), 278.
5 *Quaderni della critica*, II (1946), 63-64.
6 Donagan, *op. cit.*, pp. 315-316.
7 *An Autobiography* (Oxford, 1939), p. 158.
8 *La critica* XX (1922), 57.
9 *Filosofi del novecento* (Bari, 1958), pp. 93-94.
10 *Outlines of a Philosophy of Art* (London, 1925), p. 43.
11 *Speculum Mentis: or the Map of Knowledge* (Oxford, 1924), p. 60.
12 *Ibid.*, p. 96.
13 *Ibid.*, p. 63.
14 *Ibid.*, p. 95.
15 *Ibid.*, p. 89.

16 *Outlines*, p. 50.
17 *Speculum Mentis*, p. 80.
18 *Ibid.*, p. 98.
19 *Ibid.*, p. 206n.
20 *Ibid.*, p. 87.
21 *Ibid.*, p. 81.
22 *An Autobiography*, p. 16.
23 See his *Three Lectures on Aesthetic* (London, 1931), pp. 65-75.
24 *Appearance and Reality: A Metaphysical Essay* (London, 1893), p. 464.
25 *Speculum Mentis*, pp. 293-294.
26 *Ibid.*, pp. 50, 55.
27 De Ruggiero, *Filosofi del novecento*, p. 94.
28 *Speculum Mentis*, p. 280.
29 *Ibid.*, pp. 68-71.
30 *Outlines*, p. 98.
31 *Speculum Mentis*, p. 223.
32 "Mr. Collingwood on Philosophical Method," *The Journal of Philosophy* XXXIII (1936), 98.
33 *An Essay on Philosophical Method* (Oxford, 1933), p. 73.
34 *Ibid.*, p. 75.
35 *Ibid.*, pp. 108, 171.
36 See, for example, *ibid.*, p. 62.
37 *Ibid.*, p. 163.

Chapter Seven

1 *The Principles of Art* (Oxford, 1938), p. 295.
2 *An Autobiography* (Oxford, 1939), pp. 152-153.
3 Alan Donagan, *The Later Philosophy of R. G. Collingwood* (Oxford, 1962), p. 315.
4 *The Principles of Art*, p. 205.
5 *Ibid.*, p. 164.
6 *Ibid.*, p. 215.
7 *Ibid.*, p. 223.
8 *Ibid.*, p. 209.
9 *Ibid.*, p. 206.
10 *Ibid.*, pp. 290, 291.
11 *Ibid.*, pp. 283-284.
12 *Ibid.*, p. 151.
13 *Ibid.*, p. 194.
14 *Ibid.*, p. 247.
15 *Ibid.*, pp. 249-250.
16 *Ibid.*, p. 269.
17 *Ibid.*, p. 317.
18 *Ibid.*, p. 321.

19 Compare *ibid.*, p. 327, with p. 82.
20 *Ibid.*, p. 82.
21 *Ibid.*, p. 323.
22 *Ibid.*, p. 316.
23 *Ibid.*, pp. 248, 317.
24 *Ibid.*, p. 288.
25 *Ibid.*, p. 294.
26 *Ibid.*, p. 295.
27 *Ibid.*, p. 297.
28 *Ibid.*, pp. 297-298.
29 *Ibid.*, pp. 88-89.
30 *Ibid.*, pp. 82, 83.
31 His comments on Pope and Browning in an address entitled "Ruskin's Philosophy," given in 1919, and now included by Alan Donagan in a collection of *Essays in the Philosophy of Art by R. G. Collingwood* (Bloomington, Ind., 1964) are so general or so tenuously related to art that they fall within this description.
32 "Aesthetics in English-Speaking Countries," *Philosophy in the Mid-Century*, III (Firenze, 1958), 81.

Index